# Time Is Money

## Also by Frances Leonard

*Women and Money*
*Money and the Mature Woman*

# Time Is Money

*A Million-Dollar Investment Plan for Today's*

*Twenty- and Thirty-somethings*

**Frances Leonard**

**Addison-Wesley Publishing Company**

Reading, Massachusetts   Menlo Park, California   New York

Don Mills, Ontario   Wokingham, England   Amsterdam   Bonn

Sydney   Singapore   Tokyo   Madrid   San Juan

Paris   Seoul   Milan   Mexico City   Taipei

Many of the designations used by manufacturers and sellers to distinguish their products are claimed as trademarks. Where those designations appear in this book and Addison-Wesley was aware of a trademark claim, the designations have been printed in initial capital letters.

This book is intended to provide accurate information about its subject matter, but it is sold with the understanding that the publisher is not engaged in rendering any financial, investment or other professional advice. If specific advice is required, a competent professional should be consulted. The author, editors, and publisher cannot accept any responsibility for errors or omissions or for the consequences of the application of the information in this book, and make no warranties, express or implied, with respect to its contents.

*Library of Congress Cataloging-in-Publication Data*

Leonard, Frances
    Time is money : a million-dollar investment plan for today's twenty- and thirty-somethings / Frances Leonard.
       p.  cm.
    Includes bibliographical references and index.
    ISBN 0-201-40962-3
    1. Investments.   2. Speculation.   I. Title.
HG4521.L37   1996
332.6—dc20                                        95-17911
                                                               CIP

Cover design by Suzanne Heiser
Text design by Janis Owens
Set in 10½ point Berkeley by Weimer Graphics, Inc.
Cover and text illustrations by Chris Reed
Charts by David Kelley

2 3 4 5 6 7 8-DOH-0099989796
Second printing, March 1996

For Sam, Zak, and Gabe
Stick with the program.

# Contents

**$**

# Acknowledgments

This mathphobe needed a lot of help learning the ins and outs of financial calculators and other essentials, so for his generous and always good-humored assistance, I am indebted to Francis J. Conlan, Ph.D., professor of mathematics extraordinaire.

As always, my agent, Sandra Dijkstra, was ever encouraging, and without her enthusiasm this book wouldn't be. I'm especially grateful to Ri Fournier, Sandy's one-time associate agent, who, if her arduous efforts on my behalf are any guide, will soon be a formidable lawyer.

Of course, in the end, editors make the book, and Sharon Broll's patience, kindness, and tact through the toils of two books are the reason you're reading this now.

# $

# Introduction

**W**ould you pay $48,000 for $1 million? That's not just double your money, or even ten times. It's more than twenty times your investment, and the best part of it is that nearly *95 percent of that million is free money for you.* All those nice extra zeros are yours for the asking. Just put up $87 every month for forty-six years and voilà! Your $48,000 has made you a millionaire. That's if you're 22. Everyone else between twenty and thirty-five will find their magic million numbers in Chapter Two.

The neatest part of the deal is what it will do for you decades before you get that million. After all, you've got better things to do than prepare for the old and gray. You've got dream houses to build, Harleys to buy, scuba trips to Fiji to take, and, perhaps, kids to school. Who wants to think about retirement when you're only twenty-eight?

Not you, I'm sure, and that is the purpose of this book.

Here's the deal: If you start soon enough, your dinky little monthly investment will take care of your golden years. *You won't have to worry about retirement for the rest of your life.* The hundreds of dollars per month that late starters need to save for retirement will be all yours—yours to do all the things you're dreaming about, instead of having to deny yourself all the good things just because you missed your best chance to amass a fortune mostly made of money you'll get for free.

Those who don't get with the program will sadly learn that just when they get the bucks together to take those trips abroad or buy that terrific vacation home, that's when retirement looms on

## Chart A

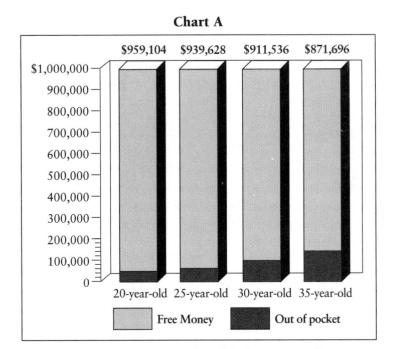

*Use your youth to make a million. Look at all the free money you'll get using the Four Step program, just for being young. The out-of-pocket cost for the 20-year-old is $40,896, for the 25-year-old is $60,372, for the 30-year-old is $88,464, and for the 35-year-old is $128,304.*

the horizon. They'll have to give up their dreams just to save humongous bucks every month in service of their old age.

But followers of the Four Step program won't have that problem. They'll enjoy all that their earnings can afford them, because retirement savings will be low, and under control. Join the Four Step program, and your youth and prime will be for you to enjoy—not to sacrifice to that improbable you with the cane and the wispy hair.

**Here's how the program works:** In Chapter Two you'll find your magic millionaire number—the dollar amount, based on your age, that you will invest monthly—the key to Step One. For

Step Two, you'll invest it in a stock mutual fund with the goal of earning an average of 10 to 12 percent yearly until you're sixty-seven, as explained in Chapter Four. Step Three commits your Four Step fund to a tax-deferred account like an IRA or 401(k), and Chapter Six brings you up to speed on all of that. Step Four gives you an easy way to protect your fund against inflation, so that your million will be worth a million when you need it, as described in Chapter Seven.

Of course, putting aside any amount of money in your twenties and thirties for the sake of your sixties is an unpleasant proposition. That's why the Four Step program is designed to reward you (well) in your thirties, forties, and on to retirement. While you're still young, the Four Steps will make you richer—by hundreds of dollars each month—than your buddies who squander their early years.

Start the program at age twenty-three, for example, invest $96 per month in an account averaging 10 percent per year, and you'll make your million by age sixty-seven. Let's say your twin brother also needs a million to retire comfortably, but he begins his program at age forty-two. He'll have to come up with $677 every month to reach the same million at the same age. You, of course, are still investing only $96 per month, so you have $581 more than your brother every month to spend on whatever you like. In fact, you are going to have over $159,000 more in goodies and luxuries than your foolish twin—to spend in your thirties, forties, and fifties—even though you'll both retire millionaires. The cost to you of your million will be $51,840; your brother will have to pay $211,224 for his. He will have $788,776 in "free" money—a fabulous deal, it's true—but you, because you got started thirteen years earlier, will have a free $948,160! For ease of illustration here, these numbers are not adjusted for inflation, but the proportions remain true even when adjusted. More on this in Chapter Seven. Don't despair if you are in your thirties or forties. Chapter Two will show you ways to "buy back" your youth if you've let a few impecunious years slip by.

That $159,000 more you'll have in hand than your brother?

This is what that kind of money looks like in your life, decades before retirement:

- A trip to Paris
- One Harley-Davidson big-twin
- A week in Tahiti
- The down payment on a $300,000 house
- A trip to the Greek islands
- One BMW
- A dive trip to Belize
- The down payment on a condo in Hawaii
- Five ski weeks in the Alps

And when you do retire, of course, you'll have your fortune. It will be a real one, too, because it is protected from inflation.

These goodies are your reward for starting early and getting into the program on the cheap. On the Four Step plans you're not just securing a great retirement; you're freeing up your dollars to be spent on fun things while you're still young enough to enjoy them.

Remember, *from 87 to 95 percent of your million will be free money,* depending on your age when you start the program. Meditate on that for a minute to let your mind grab hold of the enormity of the opportunity. Study Chart A. You won't sweat for this money, inherit it, marry it, or steal it. Free money like this isn't available to everyone. There is a window of opportunity that gets pretty costly after age forty. If you want it, you have a once-in-a-lifetime chance. It won't come around again.

**Introducing Suds 'n Suds, et al.:** You're going to be a capitalist, the part owner of companies from all over the world. To be a responsible owner, you need to know a little about how businesses work, how they are bought and sold to the public, and how your capital (the money you invest) can make (and lose) money for you. To this end, you will follow the fortunes and failures of three fictional companies. Through Suds 'n Suds's triumphs and travails, you'll learn about this beer parlor–laundromat combo's start-up, initial public offering, take-over offer, and the minefield of insider trading, plus a lot more that a rich capitalist needs to know. Loves-to-Tank is a hot-tub manufacturer, and it has much to teach you, too. And the rise and demise of Super-Testosteroney mutual fund will inform future financiers about the workings of this most popular type of ordinary investment.

**A word about assumptions:** With an eye to keeping order in our universe of numbers, throughout this book, unless stated otherwise, I'll be operating from these assumptions:

• Retirement age means sixty-seven. This is because for everyone born after 1960, full Social Security retirement benefits begin no sooner than age sixty-seven (instead of sixty-five, as at present, or even later than sixty-seven, if Congress so decrees), so it is likely that many pensions and retirement plans will adjust their own schedules accordingly. Result? Most people in your generation will work at least until age sixty-seven.

• Since the value of time and compounding plays such an important part in the Four Step plans, discussions will be generally limited to the three liquid financial-asset categories, i.e., stocks, bonds, and cash, and the mutual funds that hold them.

• All calculations use monthly compounding, unless otherwise stated. This is because in order to compare apples to apples, a uniform compounding period is necessary.

• All the Four Step plans begin with the first payment on the selected birthday, and the last payment on the sixty-seventh birthday. This results in compounding periods of forty-eight years for twenty-year-olds, and thirty-three years for thirty-five-year-olds. For the ages in between, see Table 1 in Appendix II.

• Tax codes and other laws, as well as securities regulations, in effect at the time of this writing *will* change. That's what Congress and state legislatures do to keep themselves busy. *It is the reader's responsibility to update all pertinent information* before acting on anything discussed in this book.

- *And throughout this book, you should be alert to this critical point:* It is one thing to predict the value in forty years of $10,000 placed in a bank savings account guaranteed to pay 5 percent interest compounded monthly. It will be $73,584, because you have a contract guaranteeing a future return. Even if the bank collapses, your account most likely will be insured by the federal government, up to $100,000, including principal and interest (although the future interest rate, in the event of such a calamity, could be adjusted downward to the market rate). But place your $10,000 in a stock mutual fund whose average return over the past forty years is the same 5 percent, and your balance at the end of the next forty years could be more or less than your savings balance. In stocks, bonds, and mutual funds, past performance is *never* a guarantee of future returns, and *no one insures your hopes*. At the same time, risk-management strategies are readily available to keep risk within acceptable bounds, and these will be explored in Chapter Five.

I'll begin the Four Step program by dazzling your mind with the staggering power of compounding, and how its most awesome miracles are reserved for the young. Then, I'll unveil the program itself, so that you can get started on your future right away. Time is money in the millionaire game. Beyond the Four Steps, I'll cover other things that make life good—getting that hot car, the dream house, the fine job, or Harvard for little Suzie— and the things that make life secure—paying your debts and saving for emergencies. In addition, see Appendix I for worksheets, Appendix II for additional tables to help you organize your program, and Appendix III for resources you might find helpful. Finally, there's a self-test at the end of each chapter just for fun.

To get yourself started, you might want to work on Worksheets 1 and 2 in Appendix I. These will help you analyze your cash flow and your net worth. Learning to recognize the pieces that make up your financial whole is an important first step. You're going to be very rich if you follow the Four Step program, and knowing where you are now is the best way to get where you're going.

# Money Makes Money

## And the money that money makes, makes

### more money

I t's not for nothing that the great Albert Einstein is credited with observing that compounding is the greatest mathematical discovery of all time. And as a young investor, you are in a position to take full advantage of its awesome powers. That's because compounding is the most powerful discriminator against age since arthritis.

Take, for example, a modest plan to retire as a millionaire. By investing at 10 percent annually, compounded monthly, and beginning at age:

- **twenty-five, you need only invest $117 per month**
- **forty, you need $547 per month**
- **fifty, you need $1,665 per month**

At twenty-five, you become a millionaire on a lifetime investment of only $60,372, thanks to the magic of compounding. Compounding does the heavy lifting here—$939,628 worth—while you're sleeping, playing, and walking on the beach. So when you set aside your $117 each and every month, think of the $1,821 pouring into your account free—a gift of time and compounding available only to the young. Age, with all its assets, cannot buy time, given so freely to the young. Compounding is the surest route to wealth without work ever devised, and all it needs is time to pull it off.

**Money makes money:** Before going any further, let's get down to the basics. Remember, interest can be paid in either of two ways: simple or compound. Simple interest is a simple concept. Put $100 into an account paying 5 percent annual simple interest, and forget about it for forty years. At the end of one year you'll have $105; at the end of ten years, $150; and after forty years, $300. Each year you are paid $5 only—never a penny more. That's because the $5 interest paid is not added to the original $100 when figuring the next year's return. Five dollars times forty years equals $200, plus the original $100 equals $300. Simple interest can never do anything more than that.

But put that $100 in an account paying 5 percent compounded monthly, and after forty years you'll have $736, or more than seven times your original deposit, and more than double what simple interest can do for you. Compound interest pays interest on the interest, and therein lies all the difference.

**A ten-year plan to a million:** Take, for example, Sophie. On her seventeenth birthday, she began putting her $2,000 annual part-time earnings into an IRA earning 10 percent (IRAs and 401(k)s are discussed in depth in Chapter Six). She did this every year until she was twenty-seven, at which time she married and stopped saving—never another dime. Her twin brother, Oscar, sowed his wild oats, then began his savings program at age twenty-eight. Oscar faithfully put $2,000 away each and every year until he was sixty-seven. He retired, boasted to Sophie he had more than $800,000, and chided her for her sloth. Sophie was pleased to tell him that her ten-year savings program from age seventeen to twenty-seven was now worth well more than $1 million! Sophie's program cost her $20,000 out of pocket; Oscar's cost him $78,000, and didn't take him as far, either. Oscar started ten years too late for Sophie's particular magic, but he didn't do badly either.

**A little makes a lot:** Take a look at how compounding magnifies yields. If, to celebrate your graduation from college, you put $100 in a stock index mutual fund, $100 in a long-term government bond mutual fund, and $100 in a money-market mutual fund, when you retire in forty-five years (assuming, for the sake of illustration, that historical averages continue throughout the period), your $100 will be worth $10,101 in the stock fund, only $863 in the bonds, and a mere $527 in your money fund. We'll explain all about mutual funds in Chapter Four, but for now note that although the historical average annual return on stocks is 10.3 percent—about twice that of bonds at 4.8 percent—in the end, compounding magnified your stock fund return not *twice*, but nearly *twelve times* over the bond fund, and more than *nineteen times* over the money-market fund.

Assume you inherit $10,000 from your uncle when you're twenty-six. You decide to do the right thing, and invest it immediately into a growth mutual fund. You like two similar funds. One has an average annual return over ten years of 12 percent, and the other of 13 percent. You split your inheritance between them, and forget about them until you retire. Assuming their historical returns hold, your 12 percent fund is worth well over $600,000—not bad at all. But your 13 percent fund is worth more than $1 million. Both funds started with only $5,000, so in either fund compounding made you a colossal winner. But that little 1 percent difference bought you over $300,000 more (and higher risk, too). Had the whole $10,000 been in the 13 percent fund, you'd have more than $2 million upon retirement in forty-one years—and more sleepless nights as well. Still, these illustrations make the point that over time, small differences are magnified by compounding. A little bit, then a little bit more, then a bit more equal an awesome return on your investment.

**Free money for the young:** Remember all the cars, trips, and houses you get for eliminating your retirement problem early on? Remember how you'll enjoy these goodies throughout your life, not just when you finally get your million? Another way to put that is to note that $1 saved at age twenty-five (compounded at 10 percent) is the same as $16 saved at fifty-three. In other words, it's sixteen times more expensive to launch your retirement program at age fifty-three than it is at twenty-five (although you'll only be about twice as old). A thirty-year-old, faced with the decision of whether to beef up his 401(k) with his small raise now, or wait until he earns a lot more later, should realize the true cost of delay. To get the same result at the end, for every $1 invested now (at 9 percent compounded), he'd need $2 if he waited until age thirty-eight, $4 at forty-six, $8 at fifty-four, and $16 at sixty-two. The Four Step program is not just an easy way to get rich, but it's an all-time bargain, to boot—thanks to compounding, the world's only perpetual money-making machine!

**The Rule of 72:** Since compounding is just a matter of rate of return over time, you can quickly make ballpark estimates of your future net worth by using the Rule of 72. Divide the rate of return on your investment (say, 9 percent) into seventy-two, and you've got a rough idea of how long it will take your investment to double (eight years). A 7 percent investment will double in about ten years; a 12 percent investment doubles in only six years. The Rule of 72 won't matter to your Four Step fund, since you know the end sum will be around a million, assuming your persistence and investment skills do their part. But for your shorter-term goals, it will be handy for you to know if your 7 percent account will double in time to provide your house down payment in six years, or if you'll have to go to 8 percent to get there.

**Time, compounding's partner:** Compounding needs time to work its miracles—the more, the better. You could turn $1 into $1 billion if you invested at 5 percent compounded over 500 years! Now, that's real money, but it also takes real time.

You don't have 500 years, of course, but you do have more than most people alive. In its early years, your Four Step fund will look pretty boring. It'll mostly be what you put in, and since those amounts are small, so will be your account. Compounding won't start thrilling you for a decade or so, giving you plenty of time to get up to speed as an investor. Then, when your fund is worth real money, you'll be right on top of where to put it. The chapters that follow show you how.

Have I got your attention? Get out your checkbook, and let's get started. Your Four Steps to a fortune are next.

 *Self-Test*
**Chapter 1**

1. If you are in your 20s or 30s, and make $1 million on the Four Step program, how much will be free money?
   **a.** 10–15%

    **b.** 20–30%
    **c.** 80–95%
    **d.** 99%

**2.** If you put $100 in an account paying 8% simple interest annually, at the end of 50 years the account will be worth:
    **a.** $500
    **b.** $5,388
    **c.** $864
    **d.** $480

**3.** If you put $100 in an account paying 8% compound interest annually, at the end of 50 years the account will be worth:
    **a.** $164
    **b.** $5,388
    **c.** $180
    **d.** $140

**4.** Over the past 70 years, in which of these asset classes would you have made the most money?
    **a.** gold
    **b.** stocks
    **c.** cash
    **d.** bonds

**5.** If you begin an investment program in your 50s rather than in your 20s, it will cost you this much more:
    **a.** 2 times
    **b.** 5 times
    **c.** 10 times
    **d.** 15 times

**6.** It is said that these two emotions drive investors:
    **a.** reason/logic
    **b.** love/joy
    **c.** hope/expectation
    **d.** fear/greed

**7.** An investment earning 7% annually will double in about how long?
    **a.** 5 years
    **b.** 7 years

    **c.** 10 years
    **d.** 12 years

**8.** Who said compounding is the greatest mathematical discovery of all time?
    **a.** Einstein
    **b.** Curie
    **c.** Pauling
    **d.** Hawkings

**9.** The miracle of compounding discriminates against:
    **a.** women
    **b.** age
    **c.** the poor
    **d.** youth

**10.** Delaying the start of your program by 10 years will cost you:
    **a.** a fortune in free dollars
    **b.** tens of thousands of dollars over a lifetime
    **c.** hundreds of dollars per month
    **d.** a, b, and c

*Answers on Worksheet 15 in Appendix I*

# Four Steps to a Fortune

*A modest little program*
*to make a million*

|  |  |
| --- | --- |
| **Step 1** | Find Your Number |
| **Step 2** | Invest at 10 to 12 Percent |
| **Step 3** | In a Tax-Deferred Account |
| **Step 4** | Protected from Inflation |

O ne, two, three, four, and when you retire at sixty-seven, you'll be a millionaire. A real one, too—not a cheesy, inflation-shriveled one—with many times more than $1 million in raw numbers.

Consider this chapter a jump start on your fortune. I'll sketch in the Four Steps so you can start now, but no cheating; you'll need the information in the chapters that follow to maintain your program over time.

## Step One
## Find Your Number

Your first step to your fortune is to pick a number you feel you can live with through life's ups and downs. The numbers below will make you a millionaire by retirement, but they won't be the only numbers identified along the way. You'll need to pay off debts and save for an emergency; you'll want a house, college for your kids; and there will be other short-term goals that catch your fancy. So pick a number from the plans outlined below, but try not to put all your eggs in the Four Step basket. Making your fortune is not about sacrificing your youth to your old age.

**The Four Steps know no borders:** You don't need to be a U.S. investor to use any of our plans, except the Golden IRA plan, since it is based on an American tax program. These numbers will all work, whether you're investing dollars, pounds, marks, yen or

## Modest Millionaire 10 Percent Plan

| If you make your last payment on your 67th birthday, and the first when you turn: | then your monthly investment should be: |
|---|---|
| 20 | $71 |
| 21 | $79 |
| 22 | $87 |
| 23 | $96 |
| 24 | $106 |
| 25 | $117 |
| 26 | $130 |
| 27 | $143 |
| 28 | $159 |
| 29 | $176 |
| 30 | $194 |
| 31 | $215 |
| 32 | $238 |
| 33 | $264 |
| 34 | $292 |
| 35 | $324 |

lire. A twenty-five-year-old Parisian will get to a million francs by investing Fr117 monthly for forty-three years at an average annual return of 10 percent, but depending on the currency exchange rate, Fr1 million may be worth only US$150,000, and £1 million about US$1.5 million. You'll need to adjust the numbers if the million won't be in U.S. dollars, but the Four Steps will work for Canadians and Australians, Spanish and Danish just the same. Time and compounding know no borders.

**The Modest Millionaire 10 Percent Plan:** I'll start with the Modest Millionaire 10 Percent Plan. It's the most sensible and the easiest, since it approximates the stock market's historical return. But if you don't like the numbers, keep reading. Maybe your future is in the more aggressive (and risky) Roller Coaster 12 Percent Plan, or the Golden IRA 10 Percent Plan. I'll even show you how to make the monthly numbers easier with a jump start, in the Hot Start $50 Plan. If even these numbers don't work for you, there are plenty more in the tables in Appendix II. If you can afford the payments on the 10 percent program, go for it. The lower the expected return, the surer you are to maintain it over time.

If you're not young enough to claim the lowest numbers, and yours seem a little steep, you have some choices. First, you can pick a number you can live with, knowing you will have plenty by retirement, but it won't be a million. See Tables 2, 3, and 4 in Appendix II if you're interested in this approach. Or second, you can cough up a mere $50 per month, whatever your age, with the Hot Start plan described below. And third, you can jack up your rate of return (and your risk) in the Roller Coaster plan.

**The Roller Coaster 12 Percent Plan:** If you're over twenty-five, maybe the Modest Millionaire numbers make you gulp. Let's bring them down by ratcheting up our investment return to 12 percent, a riskier but still feasible goal in a well-managed stock mutual fund, given your very long time-horizon, as described in Step Two, which follows. We'll call this the Roller Coaster 12 Percent Plan, to make the point that with the increase in return, you are accepting more risk and volatility. Since your investment horizon is somewhere between forty-eight years (for a twenty-year-old) and thirty-three years (if you're thirty-five), you are the ultimate long-term investor, which means you'll have time to recover your (inevitable) losses along the way. A 12 percent target will mean your fund will definitely fluctuate more than the 10 percent plan, and *you must accept this* if you select the Roller Coaster program.

See how an additional two percentage points over a long-term investment's lifetime comes to the rescue? Still, compounding's unrelenting bias against age is clear at a glance. One-year difference in age in the lowest age group brings a penalty of only about $5 per month. But at the upper end, the penalty is five times larger, or about $25 per month. The lesson here is clear: If you have to procrastinate, do it early in your life. Later years are ex-

## Roller Coaster 12 Percent Plan

| If you make your last payment on your 67th birthday, and your first when you turn: | then your monthly investment should be: |
|---|---|
| 20 | $33 |
| 21 | $37 |
| 22 | $42 |
| 23 | $47 |
| 24 | $53 |
| 25 | $60 |
| 26 | $67 |
| 27 | $76 |
| 28 | $85 |
| 29 | $96 |
| 30 | $109 |
| 31 | $123 |
| 32 | $138 |
| 33 | $156 |
| 34 | $176 |
| 35 | $199 |

pensive ones. Table 5 in Appendix II gives you the figures for a compromise 11 percent plan.

Look at the dilemma faced by mid-lifers: On the Roller Coaster 12 Percent Plan, a forty-five-year-old needs $780 per month to make that million, and at fifty-five, $3,135! On the other hand, if parents were to begin a program for their child on the fifth birthday, just $7 per month until age sixty-seven would do the trick; for a ten-year-old, it's $12; for a fifteen-year-old, just $21. If you have young children, siblings, nieces, or nephews, consider launching a Four Step account just for them. See the Afterword at the end of this book for more on this. A hint to your own parents to get you started, perhaps?

**The Hot Start $50 Plan:** Doggone, you say. You're only twenty-five, and it seems you've already missed the boat. Your Roller

## Hot Start $50 Plan

To have a million dollars by age 67, if you are 20 through 25, select a 10 percent (annual average) tax-deferred investment, pay only $50 per month into it, and launch your program with this lump sum:

| | |
|---|---|
| At 20: | $2,446 |
| 21 | $3,330 |
| 22 | $4,307 |
| 23 | $5,386 |
| 24 | $6,579 |
| 25 | $7,896 |

If you are 26 through 29, pay $50 per month into an account earning an average of 11 percent, with a beginning balance of:

| | |
|---|---|
| 26 | $4,663 |
| 27 | $5,834 |
| 28 | $7,140 |
| 29 | $8,598 |

If you are 30 through 35, pay $50 per month into an account earning an average of 12 percent, with a beginning balance of:

| | |
|---|---|
| 30 | $5,756 |
| 31 | $7,120 |
| 32 | $8,657 |
| 33 | $10,389 |
| 34 | $12,340 |
| 35 | $14,539 |

Coaster number is nearly ten times higher than the five-year-old's, and your Modest Millionaire payment is nearly seventeen times larger. Compared to $7, your $67 or $117 look enormous!

Don't worry, as there's a way to turn back the clock. Let's assume you like $50 per month as your number, no matter your age. You can jump start your program with the lump sum from the tables above, and make your million happen without going out on the limb to the tune of hundreds a month.

Age is still part of the picture, even though the payments are the same however old you are. Your beginning balance balloons as the years mount. To keep the program realistic, the older you are, the more risk you will have to assume. Therefore, the Hot Start $50 Plan is built on a 10 percent tax-deferred investment for ages twenty through twenty-five, 11 percent for ages twenty-six through twenty-nine, and 12 percent for ages thirty through thirty-five.

In the older age groups, these numbers look a little steep. But unlike many people under twenty-five, you have a work record. Some of you have IRAs or 401(k)s that will give you that jump start. If you're thirty-five, have worked since you were twenty-five, and took advantage of Uncle Sam's IRA opportunity to the tune of $2,000 per year, your nest egg is now more than $20,000. You can invest $151 per month under the Modest Millionaire 10 Percent Plan, slightly less than a twenty-eight-year-old, and still make your million by retirement age. Money can't roll back your real years, but it sure can erase years off your financial age. Table 6 in Appendix II illustrates the Hot Start $100 Plan.

Finally, recognize that $1 million is, after all, just a nice amount to aim for. You can retire well on less than that, especially if you'll have a pension in your future. Tailor a plan that's comfortable for you, then stick with it, observing all Four Steps faithfully, and you'll be fine. I don't, however, recommend a goal of less than $300,000 for those of you expecting a sound pension to supplement your Social Security. No pension in your future? Better shoot for at least $500,000 in today's dollars.

**The Golden IRA 10 Percent Plan:** If you have earnings from employment or self-employment, Uncle Sam has a gift for you. The individual retirement account (known to all as the IRA) allows you to put up to $2,000 per year of your earnings into a tax-deferred, and (sometimes) tax-deductible, account. Step Three is about tax-deferred accounts such as IRAs and 401(k)s. For now, whatever your age, milk Uncle Sam's gift for all it's worth—by putting $166.66 per month in the Golden IRA plan earning an annual average of 10 percent. When you retire you will have a

## Golden IRA 10 Percent Plan

| If you max out your IRA, beginning on the day you turn: | then at 67 your IRA will be worth: |
|---|---|
| 20 | $2,362,256 |
| 21 | $2,136,447 |
| 22 | $1,932,043 |
| 23 | $1,747,014 |
| 24 | $1,579,523 |
| 25 | $1,427,908 |
| 26 | $1,290,664 |
| 27 | $1,166,429 |
| 28 | $1,053,971 |
| 29 | $952,172 |
| 30 | $860,022 |
| 31 | $776,607 |
| 32 | $701,099 |
| 33 | $632,748 |
| 34 | $570,875 |
| 35 | $514,868 |

nice chunk of change. All totals above are rounded to the nearest dollar.

If you're twenty-nine or older, you won't make a million by age sixty-seven on the Golden IRA 10 Percent Plan. But even at thirty-five, half a million dollars is adequate to cushion most folks' retirement. If you protect it against inflation, as we'll show you how to do in Step Four, it will earn nearly $31,000 per year at a conservative rate of 6 percent (in today's solid dollars, not inflated ones). Along with your Social Security, you won't be rich, but you'll be $31,000 more comfortable than with Social Security alone. If that's not enough, accept the risk of investing for a higher return. Here are some modified Golden IRA numbers for ages twenty-nine through thirty-five, assuming $166.66 per month in an IRA or 401(k) (page 17).

Notice how in the later years, investment return has to jump substantially to keep the totals over a million. You can shoot for

## Golden IRA Roller Coaster Plan

**If you begin on your birthday at:**

| | | |
|---|---|---|
| 29 | and invest at 11%, at 67 you'll have | $1,282,754 |
| 30 | and invest at 11%, at 67 you'll have | $1,147,826 |
| 31 | and invest at 11%, at 67 you'll have | $1,026,891 |
| 32 | and invest at 11.5%, at 67 you'll have | $1,053,471 |
| 33 | and invest at 12%, at 67 you'll have | $1,071,784 |
| 34 | and invest at 12.5%, at 67 you'll have | $1,081,254 |
| 35 | and invest at 13%, at 67 you'll have | $1,081,531 |

more than 12 percent if you like—after all, you have a long time to recover your losses along the way—but I can't recommend it, because it's more likely than not that you won't make it enough of the time to average out over the full period. You're better off sticking with a lower, more stable return. Maybe the numbers won't work out to a million in the end, but you'll like the looks of them anyway. You will have a lot of money. Of course, if you already have a few thousand in your IRA, or 401(k), you may have the jump start you need to make your million with a very reasonable investment return.

Since, under 1995 law, you can invest up to $2,000 (or 100 percent of your earned income or alimony, whichever is *less*) in an IRA, you may be tempted to dump $2,000 in as a lump sum at the end of the year. Fine, but you won't make the most of your investment, unless you put it in on the first of the tax year, not the end. A $2,000 IRA contribution made at the beginning of each tax year (January 1) for thirty years, earning 10 percent, will be worth $361,886 over the period. Contributed at the end of each year, on December 31, the total is just $328,988, or nearly $33,000 less! Still, if an end-of-the-year lump sum works best for you, go for it.

**The price of procrastination:** You've seen how compounding's greatest miracles are reserved for the young. Of course, it's never

## 10 Percent Pricey Program for Procrastinators

| Age | Monthly Pmts |
|-----|--------------|
| 36 | $360 |
| 40 | $547 |
| 45 | $939 |
| 50 | $1,666 |
| 55 | $3,146 |
| 60 | $6,841 |

too late to take advantage of whatever time you've got left. It's *always* cheaper to build your investments today than tomorrow, no matter what your age. To give you an idea of compounding's relentless age discrimination, though, take a look at our 10 Percent Pricey Program for Procrastinators, that is, folks over age thirty-five. As usual, monthly contributions begin on the listed birthday, end on the sixty-seventh birthday, and are compounded monthly at an average annual rate of 10 percent.

The sixty-year-old has to put up $656,736 of his or her own money to make that $1 million—nearly $600,000 more than you do if you're under thirty. Still, in a mere eight years, that retiree picks up $343,264 of free money. You'll each have $1 million at the end, but *you* have hundreds of thousands more to enjoy— long before retirement!

Your $574,368 saved by not delaying your program until you're sixty could buy you all of this:

- The down payment on a $200,000 house
- Ten trips to Europe
- Ten new Cadillacs, fully paid
- Ten trips to Asia
- Stanford, full tuition paid, for little Jane
- One swimming pool
- A condo in Maui, fully paid

And that, as they say, ain't chopped liver.

Even the forty-five-year-old, with $939 to cough up monthly to reach that million, is miles ahead of the sixty-year-old. He or she puts up $259,164 to the sixty-year-old's $656,736, a difference of $397,572. The forty-five-year-old can put both his or her kids through Vassar, buy a cabin on a lake, rent a villa in the south of France every summer for ten years, and ski Switzerland during Christmas week every year until he or she retires a millionaire, all courtesy of compounding.

**A note to the married:** Obviously, if a million dollars (yielding an annual income of about $60,000 in today's dollars), plus your combined Social Security and pensions, won't be enough for the two of you, you'll have to increase your Four Step payments. If you are dead certain you will be together when you're sixty-seven, you probably won't have to double your Four Step payments; increasing it one-and-a-half times or so will probably do it for you.

The problem is, you can't be dead certain. One of you indeed may be dead. Be sure you each have a will leaving everything to the other, or at least the full Four Step fund. Even young people die, often in accidents.

With respect to divorce, all states will consider your Four Step fund the same as any other investment earned during the marriage, and divide it according to some formula used by the state. A handful of states would divide it equally; more will divide it "equitably," meaning according to what the court sees as just. Often this means a tilt toward the party whose name is on the fund, or whose salary earned it. To be safe—and fair—be sure it's in both your names. Even if the payments come from the salary of only one of you, it's both of you who forego present goodies in the service of a future reward.

If marriage is ahead of you, all states will consider the assets accumulated before the wedding to be your own separate property. At divorce, separate property is generally not divided between the parties. It goes with its owner. If you want to keep assets you bring to your marriage separate, be sure you keep them in segregated accounts, in your name only, and keep the investment records in a safe place, in order to substantiate your claim. With respect to an ongoing program, such as our Four Steps, most courts would consider that portion contributed after your marriage to be marital property, and thus subject to division upon divorce. If you want to keep your program going, but your before-marriage payments separate, see to it that your pre- and postmarital payments are in separate accounts. As the foregoing was written by this California lawyer, be sure to check with local lawyers if you're serious about protecting separate assets once you marry.

## Step Two
## Invest at 10 to 12 Percent

Your Four Step plan requires decades of patient investing, and if past history is any guide, only one class of financial assets will do the job for you over time, and that's stocks. Remember, over the last seven decades, U.S. stocks have returned an average of 10.3 percent annually; bonds, 4.8 percent; and cash equivalents (such as 90-day treasury bills or bank certificates of deposit), just 3.7 percent. You'll learn more about these things in the next chapter; for now, just understand that although historical performance is not a predictor of future performance, there is enough history now to be confident that over the decades of your investment period, stocks are the best bet for reaching your goal.

Stocks, yes, but not *individual* stocks. For beginning investors, buying individual stocks is just too risky. Fortunately, there are mutual funds. Thousands, even millions, of people send money to an investment company, which, in turn, invests those millions (or billions) of dollars, returning profits (and losses) to the customers from time to time. Some funds invest in bonds, some buy gold bullion, some buy international stocks and bonds, some stick to U.S. stocks, and some offer a mixture of securities. The investments are made by a professional manager (or management team), who is paid a fee, usually from 0.2 percent to 2.5 percent of the assets managed annually.

Since the Four Step plans will probably do best (over time) in the stock market, the first task is to find a stock mutual fund that has a good chance of returning 10 or 12 percent a year. There are many types of stock mutual funds, and they will all be covered in Chapter Four. For now, it's enough for you to know that one particular type, called an *index fund*, is set up to match the performance of the stock market generally. One particular index, the Standard & Poor's 500 (S&P 500), is the measure that resulted in the 10.3 percent stock market average return since 1926, so it makes sense to start out the Modest Millionaire 10 Percent Plan in an S&P 500 stock index mutual fund. Out of more than five thousand mutual funds, a mere handful consistently beat the S&P 500—only two did so every year for the six years ending in 1994—so a fund that mimics the S&P 500 makes good sense for a beginner's portfolio.

**You're on your way:** If you're new to investing, you might want to read Chapter Four on mutual funds before you continue. If you already have a handle on the mutual fund concept, this section will launch you on Step Two.

Listed below, in no particular order, are the telephone numbers for ten large mutual fund families:

* Fidelity          (800) 544-8888
* Vanguard          (800) 662-7447
* T. Rowe Price     (800) 638-5660
* Dreyfus           (800) 645-6561
* Scudder           (800) 225-2470
* Janus             (800) 525-8983
* Invesco           (800) 525-8085
* Franklin          (800) 632-2180
* Alliance          (800) 221-5672
* Dean Witter       (800) 869-3863

**Implementing Step Two:** Worksheets 3 and 4 in Appendix I contain a script and a chart to compare stock index funds from three large fund families. Those in the 10 percent programs will ask about S&P 500 index funds; those going for 11 or 12 percent will need to find a small-cap index fund. The worksheets suggest calling Fidelity, Vanguard, and T. Rowe Price because these large families include index funds, but feel free to call more funds if you like.

When the material comes from the funds, carefully compare costs. All S&P 500 index funds will strive to match the S&P itself, so you aren't looking for superior performance; they'll all be about the same. But even tiny cost differences loom large over time. For example, let's say Fund A charges 0.19 percent of your assets as an annual fee for its index 500 fund, which beats Fund B's 0.45 percent fee for its index fund. Fund C also charges 0.45 percent annually. Since all three funds track the S&P 500, any differences in performance should be negligible over time. Remember, they all strive to do no better, nor any worse, than the stock market generally. Funds A, B, and C do not charge an upfront sales commission (called a load), but Fund C charges a redemption fee of 0.5 percent of the assets withdrawn (sometimes called a back-end load, or exit load). Although 0.5 percent sounds minor, consider the bite if it were to be applied to your million—$50,000—ouch! Funds A and B require a $500 initial investment for an IRA; Fund C's entry level is $1,000. Neither A nor B sets a minimum for contributions thereafter; but C requires a minimum of $100 per contribution. A twenty-seven-year-old on the Modest Millionaire Plan of $157 per month over forty-one years would realize $89,019 more in Fund A than in Fund B, and $141,440 more in A than in Fund C, assuming the S&P delivers its historical average of 10.3 percent. In the world of compounding, small differences translate large.

As you can see, you must do your homework. Things such as fees and loads change rapidly in the mutual fund world. It's your job to call various funds to learn their current fees and load structures. The worksheets referred to will help you sort this out.

The Roller Coaster 12 Percent Plan almost surely won't make your goal in an index fund that tracks the S&P 500. There are index funds that track more than the 500 stocks in the S&P, and because they include the smaller, faster-growing stocks, historically they've earned higher yields (at higher volatility). The Roller Coasters should investigate mutual funds that track smaller companies, since historically smaller companies have returned over 12 percent annually. A fund that follows the Russell 2000 stock index would be a good start for you Roller Coasters. Call various fund families and learn if they provide such an index fund. Remember to compare costs and loads. When you've made your selection, you'll find the IRA application form will be a snap to fill out—easier than opening a bank account. Then simply attach your check, and you're on your way! To get together your initial contribution of, perhaps, $500 to $1,000, you may have to park your monthly payments in a savings account for a while so they can accumulate, but after the initial contribution, some funds will accept whatever monthly contribution you make, which in an IRA can be up to $2,000 per year.

After about five years, or $5,000, whichever comes first, you may want to branch out into other types of stock mutual funds, particularly if your index fund isn't delivering the yields you need to make your goal. You have plenty of time to get smart while you get started in the plain vanilla index fund. A well-managed *growth* mutual fund will probably be your next step, and you can read about that in Chapter Four.

 *Step Three*
## Invest in a Tax-Deferred Account

The Four Step programs rely on an average annual return of 10 or 12 percent, compounded monthly, in a tax-deferred account such as an IRA or 401(k). If you feel a little shaky on the concept, you might want to read Chapter Six, which covers tax-deferred accounts in depth, before going further.

In order to get you to save for your retirement, Uncle Sam offers a little inducement: If you will save your money until you are at least age 59 1/2, Uncle Sam will delay taxing it until you withdraw it, and even, in many cases, lower your current income taxes as well. In other words, Uncle Sugar will pay you to save. Sammy's no fool, though, and to keep you from sneaking a little out of your account here and there ahead of time, Congress has made some rules:

- First, anyone with earned income or alimony can set up an individual retirement account (IRA) up to $2,000 per year per worker, so that a married couple can squirrel away a total of $4,000 per year, assuming both work. If only one spouse works, the limit for the couple is $2,250. If you earn less than $2,000 per year, your maximum contribution is 100 percent of your earnings (and alimony). These 1995 rules can change anytime.

- Second, almost any kind of account can be in your IRA—mutual funds, bank savings, certificates of deposit, brokerage accounts. It's up to you. Just instruct the financial institution to set up an IRA for you, and voilà! Nothing is easier. They are dying to hear from you, and will make it very simple indeed. An IRA is not a type of account per se; rather, it is like a magic wand that you wave over your account to make its earnings nontaxable until they are withdrawn (and often tax deductible as well).

- Finally, some tax-deferred programs have to be set up at your workplace, chief among them 401(k)s. Unlike IRAs, these rely on payroll deductions, and often include a matching contribution from your employer. Because 401(k)s and their like (hereafter when I refer to 401(k)s, I also mean their siblings, such as 403(b)s, TSAs, SEPs, and Keoghs) are always tax deductible, it is usually better to fund them to their maximum before you fund your IRA. The exception would be if your employer offers nothing but lousy investment vehicles. Like IRAs, 401(k)s are not normally available to you without penalty before age 59 1/2, and accumulate on a tax-deferred basis until withdrawn.

I know, I know. You're thinking you don't want to tie anything up until you're so old. Why not just keep your options open by keeping your Four Step fund in a taxable, non-IRA account?

The problem really isn't now, it's later. When your fund hits $50,000, and you are earning enough to be in a higher tax bracket, it may cost you thousands per year in taxes. And when you are halfway to your million, taxes on your fund's earnings will be thousands and thousands more than your miserly monthly Four Step payment—and that's stupid! If you pay the taxes out of the fund, rather than out of your pocket, it will devastate your compounded return down the line. And because there is an annual limit on IRA contributions, you can't just move a $10,000 taxable account into an IRA at the point you think the taxes are bothersome. Best to bite the bullet from the start, and sock your Four Step money away in a tax-deferred account.

If you are ineligible for a tax-deferred account because you are not employed, you probably aren't paying taxes anyway, so put your Four Step payments in a taxable account until you have taxable earnings, then switch your savings into an IRA. Remember, if this summary confuses you, read Chapter Six, then reread Step Three.

## Step Four
## Protect Your Fortune from Inflation

A million dollars sounds like a lot of money, but as a generator for retirement income, it is not out of line. At a reasonable 6 percent investment return, a million dollars earns $60,000 per year. In addition, you'll have a few thousand dollars of Social Security per year, and perhaps a pension. Of course, you'll have to protect your Four Step fund from inflation along the way; otherwise, your $60,000 won't cut it when you retire.

**Here's what you do to keep your fortune worth a fortune:**
On the first of every year, find the consumer price index (CPI) for
the year just ended (it will be in your newspaper's financial pages
or the *Wall Street Journal*, or call your library's reference librarian).
Then adjust your Four Step payments upward by that percentage.
A thirty-year-old on the Roller Coaster plan, for example, would
increase the $123 payment by 4 percent, say, to $128. Next year,
the $128 becomes $134. A twenty-one-year-old Modest Millionaire would go from $79 to $83 to $87 over three years, assuming
an inflation rate of 4 percent. See Table 15 in Appendix II, showing inflation adjusted contributions.

Make this simple adjustment every year, using the correct
inflation figures for the year preceding, and your million will be
worth a million when you retire. *This won't be as painful as you
might think*, because your wages will generally keep pace with
inflation through cost-of-living increases, and since you are in
the early stages of your career, you will probably have real
raises along the way as well. Inflation is a very real threat, but
easily handled. It's important enough that Chapter Seven is devoted to it.

**What can go wrong with the Four Steps?** The Four Step formulas are mathematical. If all elements of the equation are in
place, the result will not vary. If you faithfully follow the program, you'll reach your goal by age sixty-seven. Are there any
variables? Of course. Any variation in any of the elements of the
equation will throw off the result.

*You* have control over Step One—the amount you put in, and
how faithfully you do it. You *do not* have complete control, however, over Step Two—the return you select. The 10 or 12 percent
return you aim for can never be more than a target. You can increase your chances greatly by investing intelligently—*but you
must understand going in that your final result utterly depends on all
parts of the equation holding true.* I've used monthly compounding
in these calculations, but your investment may compound daily,
or continuously; if so, your result will be a little higher. Annual

compounding will reduce the total somewhat. I have assumed monthly deposits. If you accelerate your savings rate by depositing the annual total on the first day of the year, you will have more in the end. If you deposit it all on the last day of the year, you will have less. If your investment achieves an average of 7 percent over four or so decades, you won't have your million, but you won't be a loser, either. You'll have hundreds of thousands of dollars more than you would have with no investment program at all. Steps Three and Four, like Step One, are completely under your control.

The most important thing is to study the Four Step plans and notice how things change rapidly for the worse as you age, whether you are looking at deposit amounts, final results, or the yield required. Your number today is the lowest it will be for the rest of your life, and the only way you can keep it is to stick with the program without fail. If you backslide, you'll have to jump in again at a higher number to make it all work.

That's it. There's the program. Four easy steps to a fortune. You can get started this very minute: First, find your number in the tables above or in the additional tables in Appendix II. Then, call the mutual fund you've selected for an S&P 500 index fund application (for an IRA). If your numbers are higher than $166.66 per month (the 1995 annual limit for an IRA), open a second, taxable index fund account or, better yet, put the balance into your 401(k). Complete Worksheet 5 in Appendix I to organize your program.

In a week or so when the application comes, return it the same day. At the end of the year, adjust your payment for inflation. Keep at it until your sixty-seventh birthday. Enjoy all the money you won't have to save for retirement. And then enjoy your riches.

That's all there is to it. Except . . . you really do need to know more to keep your fund up to date, and invested wisely and safely. And that's the business of the rest of this book.

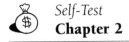

*Self-Test*
## Chapter 2

1. The Modest Millionaire program uses 10% as a target, because:
   a. banks pay 10%
   b. it's a round figure
   c. it approximates the historical return of the stock market
   d. none of these

2. Compared to the 10% programs, reaching a million on the 12% plans will be:
   a. easier
   b. harder
   c. chancier
   d. impossible

3. You can lower your Four Step numbers by:
   a. starting with a lump sum
   b. cheating on your age
   c. accepting a lower goal
   d. a and c

4. One of these does not affect compounding's magic results:
   a. frequency of compounding
   b. currency
   c. yield
   d. time

5. The Golden IRA plan uses $166.66 per month for all ages because:
   a. there is a $2,000-per-year limit under 1995 law
   b. it's affordable
   c. it's tax sheltered
   d. it's inflationproof

6. A compounded investment made at the beginning of every year will be worth the same as one made at the end of every year over time:

   ☐  True    ☐  False

7. Delaying the launching of your Four Step program until age 60 will cost you about:
   a. $100,000
   b. $200,000
   c. $400,000
   d. $600,000

8. The Standard & Poor's 500 is:
   a. a stock car event
   b. a stock market index
   c. the Dow Jones
   d. none of these

9. Which of the following threaten(s) your investments?
   a. inflation
   b. taxes
   c. fees and costs
   d. a, b, and c

10. Which of the Four Steps is not entirely within your control?
    a. Step 2: yield
    b. Step 3: taxes
    c. Step 1: contribution
    d. Step 4: inflation protection

*Answers on Worksheet 15 in Appendix I*

# Stocks and Bonds

*Finance 101 for the pre-rich*

On a fine, foggy day, Mary and Mike, graduate students at Berkeley, met in a laundromat near campus. Over a period of weeks, they fell into the habit of going there together, and stepping next door to have a beer while their clothes cycled. The bar did a good business because of the laundromat, so Mary and Mike had a brainstorm. Why not set laundromats in beer-and-pizza parlors?

After researching the idea, they went to the bank for a loan to cover the $100,000 cost. The bank was intrigued by the idea, but was only willing to loan them $10,000, since Mary and Mike had no track record as business operators, and nothing to pledge as backing for the loan (no collateral). Mary's and Mike's parents each loaned them $20,000. Now the young entrepreneurs had their good idea, and $50,000 in loans (debt).

They talked three friends into buying into the venture for $10,000 each, Mike and Mary each put in $10,000, and they were in business. The Suds 'n Suds beer parlor–laundromat was a smash hit. The owners were able to pay back their parents and the bank on schedule, and even made $50,000 profit by their third year.

Suds 'n Suds now had five owners—Mary, Mike, and their three friends (Steve, Sue, and Joe)—each with an equal stake in the venture (or share). Mike, Joe, and Sue became the board of directors of Suds 'n Suds. As such, they were, by law, where the buck stopped. The board, chaired by Mike, was ultimately answerable to the owners for the fate of Suds 'n Suds. The board hired Mary as chief executive officer (CEO) to run the company. As CEO, Mary was staff. She was hired by, and answered to, the board even though she was a 20 percent owner like the others. Steve, despite his 20 percent share, wanted nothing to do with the business, other than to receive (he hoped) a share of the profits from time to time. The simple role of shareholder was plenty for him. The board decided to put half the profit back into the business by establishing another site, and distributed the remaining $25,000 profit to the five owners in equal shares, or $5,000 each (dividends). Suds 'n Suds's owners are called shareholders, stockholders, or equity owners.

Suds 'n Suds decided it had an idea whose time had come. It wanted to be the McDonald's of laundromats, but it didn't want to wait for the business to earn enough to expand in dozens of cities across the country. So Suds 'n Suds went public. The board of directors hired an investment banker to sell the new shares. It offered 100,000 shares of common stock to the general public at $15 per share, thus raising $1.5 million for expansion (common stock is the name for ordinary shares of ownership; it is the usual way to buy shares in companies). Mostly institutional investors, such as pension funds, insurance companies, and mutual funds, bought Suds 'n Suds's stock on its initial public offering (IPO). Just like Mike, Mary, Steve, Sue, and Joe, these new investor-owners are entitled to a share of the profits (if any), and a capital gain if they sell their shares for more than they bought them for. As a publicly traded company, Suds 'n Suds was listed on a major stock exchange, meaning people could buy and sell shares through their stockbroker.

Upon going public, the five original owners' single shares were multiplied to 20,000 shares each. In addition, each received options to buy 50,000 additional shares of Suds 'n Suds at 25¢ each. This meant that after the IPO, the five original owners each owned $15 × 20,000 shares, or $300,000—*plus* the right to buy 50,000 more at 25¢ each. When Suds 'n Suds was selling for $45 per share, Steve exercised his options. He paid 25¢ per share, or $12,500 for 50,000 shares, and then sold them all, plus his original 20,000 shares, two days later at $47 per share.

Steve, who had never worked for Suds 'n Suds, nor served on the board, grossed $3,290,000 (plus dividends) on his original $10,000 investment, because he chose to be an owner rather than a lender, like Mary's and Mike's parents. Steve risked losing everything, and was rewarded magnificently for assuming that risk.

Early in their planning, Mike and Mary decided to make Suds 'n Suds a corporation. They could have run the business as a simple partnership, but there were drawbacks to this idea. In general, partners are personally liable for any judgment against their enterprise. In other words, if the janitor left soap on the floor, and someone slipped and was paralyzed for life, the million-dollar judgment would be satisfied not just from the liquidation (sale) value of Suds 'n Suds and all its assets, but also from the personal holdings of Mary and Mike. They preferred not to take that risk, so they hired a lawyer to incorporate Suds 'n Suds before they opened their doors. Generally, the owners of a corporation are not personally liable for negligence judgments against the corporation—although the full value of the business generally is.

Mavis, in Chicago, bought 300 shares of Suds 'n Suds common stock at $21 per share through her broker, who recommended the stock as having the potential for big capital gains. Mavis, being a careful investor, ordered a free copy of Suds 'n Suds's annual report from the company's shareholder relations department before she plunked her money down, although she could have received a copy free by calling the Public Register's Annual Report Service (see Resources, in Appendix III). Her $6,300 stake in the company entitles her to 300 votes for members of the board of directors annually, plus the right to vote for certain other corporate matters, and an annual report from the president or chairman of the board. She is entitled to go to the annual meeting in Berkeley, but like most stockholders, chooses not to. Mavis, and thousands of others like her, owns Suds 'n Suds.

Suds 'n Suds, by now a howling success, sees its stock soar to $90 per share. Because many people buy stock in 100-share lots (the stockbroker's sales commission may be cheaper with 100-share *round lots* than with smaller *odd lots*), the board felt that the high price was inhibiting sales of the stock, since a 100-share purchase would require $9,000—more than most small investors care to come up with all at once. To bring the price down, the board of directors declared a two-for-one stock split. The stock split was a marketing move, nothing more.

Because of the split, Mavis now owns twice as many shares of Suds 'n Suds (600), each worth half as much as before the split.

Before, her 300 shares were worth $90 each, or $27,000. After the split, her 600 shares were worth $45 each, for the same $27,000. Remember, she paid $6,300 ($21 per share × 300) originally, so split or no split, Mavis is looking at a fat $20,700 capital gain. In addition, every three months (quarter) Suds 'n Suds pays her cash dividends, her share of the profits.

Now the board of directors decides it's time to expand into smaller towns. They have a choice as to how to raise the needed $5 million. They can take it from Suds 'n Suds's own cash reserves; they can issue more stock; or they can borrow it from a bank or the public. The board decides not to draw down reserves, because it will be a few years before the new sites will make money, so they want to have their reserves on hand to dip into, if need be. Neither do they want to issue more shares of stock at this time, because the stock market is in one of its periodic dives, and Suds 'n Suds's stock isn't selling for enough to make a new offering worthwhile. Plus, the board doesn't want to pay an investment banker up to 6 percent of the offering price to sell the new shares. The board decides to borrow the money from the public, by issuing bonds.

Alex, through his broker, buys $5,000 worth of Suds 'n Suds corporate bonds, which will pay him 8 percent interest per year, in semiannual installments, for twenty years, after which Alex's $5,000 will be returned to him. The Suds 'n Suds bond is an *uninsured* IOU, but the companies that rate corporate bonds according to their creditworthiness gave this Suds 'n Suds bond issue an A rating, which makes it "investment quality" (Standard & Poor's ratings of AAA, AA, A, and BBB are considered investment-quality bonds; bonds rated BB and lower are called junk bonds). Neither Alex's semiannual interest payments (coupon) nor his principal is guaranteed. If Suds 'n Suds doesn't make good on the loan (defaults), Alex may be out of luck.

Alas, poor Suds 'n Suds. In Seattle, a group of people interested in investing in promising start-ups (venture capitalists), bankrolled a coffeehouse–laundromat combo, which took off like a rocket, expanded nationwide, and cut deeply into Suds 'n

Suds's business. Profits turned into losses, the reserve was drawn down. The board of directors cut the dividend to the shareholders, then eliminated it. Suds 'n Suds began closing outlets, laying off staff, and selling assets to raise cash. The stock price plummeted to $10, as investors deserted the sinking ship.

Soon Suds 'n Suds couldn't make the payments due its bondholders. It was in default. Bad went to worse when Suds 'n Suds was hit with a $10 million judgment for sexual harassment, because the bartender at one large outlet couldn't keep his hands off the beer servers. Suds 'n Suds owed more than it owned. It was bankrupt. The bankruptcy receiver (someone appointed by the bankruptcy court to oversee the orderly sale of assets and payment of creditors) sold all the remaining assets—the pizza ovens, the washing machines and dryers, the kegs—and came up with $3 million. A $10 million harassment judgment, plus $8 million in outstanding bonds, spelled big trouble for Suds 'n Suds. Back taxes and the receiver were paid off the top, and what was left was divided among the creditors.

*Sayonara*, Suds 'n Suds.

Alex, the bondholder, received three cents on the dollar of his $5,000 investment, or $150. But Mavis, the stockowner, got nothing. In a bankruptcy, the common stockholders come in last. They stand behind the tax collector, the receiver, the secured and unsecured creditors (Alex and the beer server plaintiffs), and the employees. If there isn't enough to pay off the debts, the owners (Mavis—and Mary, Mike, Sue, and Joe, et al.) take nothing. Steve, who sold out at $47, faxed them his best wishes from his private island near Fiji. Mavis's original $6,300 investment, once worth $27,000 on paper (known as a paper gain, because she did not *realize* her profit by selling her stock when it was worth that), goes down the drain.

Every share of common stock carries the same risk as Suds 'n Suds. Even mighty businesses like IBM, Bank of America, and Chrysler once fell upon woeful times, and took their investor-owners down the big dip on the roller coaster. It is this risk of a specific company—even a good one like these (or Suds 'n Suds)—taking a dive, or even going bankrupt, that makes *individual* stock ownership inappropriate for our Four Step programs.

As we've said, the stock market averaged a little more than 10 percent per year over the past seven decades. In any one decade, however, the range was from 0.9 percent (the depression decade of 1928–38), to 20.1 percent (1948–58). In nine decades during this period, the stock market returned less than 5 percent; in sixteen it returned more than 15 percent. This is why you want a long time-horizon when you're investing in stocks. Chapter Five will go into risk in some detail, including strategies for reducing it, but for now, learn about stocks and bonds generally to help you pick the right mutual fund—*not* to invest in individually.

Here's why stocks (held in mutual funds) are really the only responsible way for young investors to make their money grow. Suppose your grandfather began investing $50 per month in each of the three financial categories in 1926, for the benefit of his three children. He dedicated the stock fund to his firstborn, his bond fund to the second, and the cash to the baby. At the beginning of 1993 he would have:

- $5,612,294 (stocks)
- $297,110 (bonds)
- $176,496 (cash)

Don't you hope you are the heir of his firstborn! Due to time and compounding, the final result over sixty-six years is *nearly twenty times in favor of the stock market over bonds, and nearly thirty-two times stocks over cash.*

Never forget inflation. Your grandpa's stash lost an average of 3.1 percent annually over the years since 1926. Subtracting that from the yields means a real gain for stocks of 7.4 percent (or $1,047,495 over the period), 1.7 percent for bonds ($73,008),

## Chart B

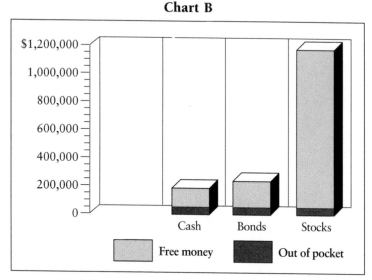

*Judy contributed $48,024 over the lifetime of her Modest Millionaire program, which she began on her 22nd birthday. Since she netted the historical 10.3% return in her stock mutual fund, more than $1 million was free money. Had she invested in cash or bonds, she'd have barely kept ahead of inflation.*

and a scant 0.6 percent for cash ($48,572). If Gramps had practiced Step Four of the program, he'd have beaten the inflation dragon.

Let's bring these figures home. Assume Judy begins her investment program on her twenty-second birthday, helped along by her graduation gifts. She puts $87 per month in each financial category, with her final payment on her sixty-seventh birthday, when she retires. Assuming historical averages hold, Judy has:

- **$1,124,274 in stocks**
- **$175,251 in bonds**
- **$126,142 in cash**

Judy invested out-of-pocket only $48,024 in each category. In the case of stocks, *$1,161,106 was free money*, compared to only

$127,227 in bonds, and $78,118 in cash. More than $1 million for Judy with no more effort on her part than consistent contributions each and every month, and an average investment in the stock market over forty-six years. Remember, Judy will be adjusting her monthly contributions annually to keep up with inflation (a painless procedure, since her income will be climbing as well), so her total at age sixty-seven will be much more than $1 million—although worth $1 million in today's money.

Although U.S. financial history since 1926 (when the averaging period in the examples began) includes the Great Depression, World War II, Korea, Vietnam, and the postwar booms, nothing says that historical averages will be duplicated in the future (nor does anything say they won't—no one knows). Surely, over the short term (fewer than ten years, say) they will not. But the longer your investment time-horizon, the more likely your returns will look something like these numbers in the end. No guarantees, of course, but one thing is probable: stocks will outpace bonds, and bonds will outpace cash over the long term.

You already know that a stock mutual fund is the first place for your Four Step account. Still, you need to know something about stocks and bonds generally. When you're sorting through the mutual funds that are candidates for your Four Step fund, you'll want to understand the basics in order to make an intelligent choice among the several thousand funds gently (or raucously) waving their flags for your attention—and bucks.

**Income and growth:** As you saw, Suds 'n Suds's owners (some of them, anyway) made money two ways: by buying the stock low and selling high, and through distributed dividends. Stocks can be losing value on paper, and still be making money for their investors because of the dividends. When evaluating the amount of money a stock can make for you, always look at the *total return*: the combination of capital gain and dividends paid. A stock that gained in value from $10 to $12 over the period of one year had a 20 percent capital gain. If it also paid dividends worth 3 percent per share, the total return would be 23 percent.

Some investments earn no income at all; instead, their investors hope the asset will increase in value over time, so they can sell it for more than they bought it for. Gold bullion and coins are such an asset. You buy gold for, say, $385 per ounce and hope to sell it at $425, thus realizing a capital gain of more than 10 percent. If gold prices plunge, you'll lose money if you realize your loss by selling at the lower price. Your gold earns no income, so your capital loss is unmitigated by earnings.

**Indexes:** The Standard & Poor's Composite Stock Price Index is a measure devised by a private company, Standard & Poor's, Inc. S&P follows the stock prices of 500 large American companies on a daily basis, and reports them on an index, which varies daily, according to the rise and fall in price of those 500 stocks. Dow Jones is another company that compiles several indexes, the most oft-quoted being the thirty companies listed as the Dow Jones Industrial Average (DJIA). The thirty include such familiar names as AT&T, Boeing, Coca-Cola, Disney, General Motors, and McDonald's. Although the media trumpets the Dow Jones average ("the Dow jumped twenty-five points today, after a plunge of sixty-two yesterday," or "the market was off five points in heavy trading today"), the S&P, because it comprises 500 companies instead of only thirty, is the better measure of stock market performance generally.

I use the S&P 500 as my measure whenever I say the stock market returned "10 percent in 1993," for example. And when I say "10 percent," I mean a combination of dividends and capital gain. Stock market averages can be quoted without the dividends, and would therefore show a lower number, but the Four Step programs depend on reinvested dividends and gains for the all-important purpose of compounding, so the inclusive figure is more relevant for your purposes.

There are other indexes as well, offered by S&P and Dow Jones, as well as other companies that measure only certain sectors of the market, such as utilities, foreign markets, and small-company stocks.

**Bonds are IOUs:** If not individual stocks for the Four Step plan, why not individual bonds? As we saw with Suds 'n Suds, the bondholders are in a better position than the equity owners when it comes to a bankruptcy. The bond world is divided into corporate and government bonds. Corporate bonds are issued by companies like Suds 'n Suds. If it's an American company, we call it a domestic bond. Government bonds range from the absolutely safe U.S. treasury securities to the sometimes more risky bonds issued by state and local governments or their agencies (collectively called municipal bonds whether or not it's a municipality that issued them). Uncle Sam's short-term issues, up to one year, are called bills; the intermediate-term issues, to ten years, are called notes; and the long-term instruments are called bonds. There are also foreign bonds, both corporate and government.

A bond is an IOU, otherwise known as a debt instrument. The bondholder is the creditor, and the issuer is the debtor. You loan your money to the debtor, who holds it for a stated term (perhaps five, ten, twenty years), at the end of which your principal is repaid. In the meantime, generally twice a year, sometimes quarterly, you are paid the agreed percentage (the coupon rate). Most bonds, both corporate and government, are *unsecured*, meaning that if the company or agency gets in trouble, you do not have a lien against any of its property that you can repossess. You know about liens—your car loan is secured by a lien against your fine car. If you default, the creditor repossesses. A mortgage is another kind of lien. If the homeowner defaults, the lender can force the sale of (foreclose on) the house in order to get its money out.

Bonds are repaid at the end of their term, which can be as long as 30 years for U.S. treasury bonds (or more rarely, 100 years for corporate issues) or as short as 90 days in the case of U.S. treasury bills. Short-term bonds are usually those with terms that end (maturities) in 2 or 3 years, and certainly no more than 5 years; intermediates mature between 5 and 10 years; and long-term bonds go out longer. The U.S. 30-year bond is referred to as the long bond, and is usually cited as the benchmark for long-term securities.

Corporations use bond money to build their business; governments use it to pay for (finance) projects such as building schools, prisons, or highways. Uncle Sam finances the deficit with your bond money. In other words, when Congress spends more money on the FBI, the military, the national parks, and Medicaid than we taxpayers hand over to the IRS, the government operates at a deficit. Uncle Sam borrows from us—and international investors, too—by issuing treasury bills, notes, and bonds to pay for the difference. The interest on this massive debt is now a large part of the federal budget.

The first problem with bonds for the Four Step program is that they simply don't grow enough over time to achieve the 10 to 12 percent that is the heart of our plans. An average return of 4 percent is simply not enough for a young investor with decades in his or her time-horizon.

In addition, a prudent bond portfolio needs diversity, just as a well-designed stock portfolio does. Bonds are subject to several risks. The most obvious is credit risk. If the debtor can't make the coupon payments, the creditor (that's you) has very little recourse. Obviously, a diverse portfolio, made up of bonds from many different companies, or government agencies, in several different economic sectors, lowers credit risk. Bond-rating services also help you determine the creditworthiness of a particular issue, but unfortunately, you can hold a bond that was rated A when you bought it, and then falls to B (below investment grade) somewhere along the line. A good rating is a guide, but no guarantee.

Then, there is interest-rate risk. You may feel your principal is safe when you buy a $5,000 twenty-year U.S. treasury bond, paying 8 percent. And sure enough, over twenty years, you'll get a check from Uncle Sam every six months for $200 ($400 per year). In twenty years you can count on getting your $5,000 back—unless the United States is flattened by nuclear warfare, or the government falls to a genuine revolution that reneges on its debt, such as happened after the communist revolution in China. In the investment world, the risk of those calamities occurring in the United States are considered to be so negligible as to be not worthy of consideration.

But let's suppose that ten years into your twenty-year term, prevailing interest rates have zoomed to 12 percent. Your 8 percent looks pretty puny, so you decide to sell your bond, and buy a brand new $5,000 bond paying 12 percent. You can't give your 8 percent bond back to Uncle Sam (or Disney) before it matures, but you can sell it on the secondary market—the bond market— where bonds already issued, but not yet matured, are bought and sold.

But you have a problem. Who is going to pay you $5,000 for an 8 percent bond when he or she can buy a brand new one paying 12 percent? No one, that's who. So you have to sell your bond for less than you paid for it, that is, at a discount. You *hate* that, because the very reason you got into treasury bonds in the first place was to protect your principal, since corporate bonds generally pay more interest than U.S. treasuries to compensate you for a higher credit risk. Of course, if you hold your treasury bond to maturity, you will get your full $5,000 back, but you would be losing the annual 4 percent interest you could be making, with equal safety, in the prevailing 12 percent market.

The closer you are to the bond's maturity, the lower the interest-rate risk. For that reason, short-term bonds are much more stable than long-term bonds, since they are always within a couple of years or so of maturity, but they may pay considerably less interest, as well. Interest-rate risk is the reason bond prices on the secondary market *fall* when interest rates *rise*. Older, lower paying bonds just aren't as attractive as the new highfliers.

*Call risk* is present when you own a callable bond. With such a bond, the issuing company or agency reserves the right to call in the bond (retire it) after a period of years, but before maturity. This means they pay you off early, which is the same as your retiring the debt on your car when you pay it off early. Why is this a problem? You've got your money back, after all. But you bought the bond because you expected to lock in 8 percent interest over twenty years. After ten years, the bond is called. Now you no longer have your 8 percent stream of income; instead, you have your $10,000 back, but nowhere to invest it above 6 percent. The issuer called it because it didn't want to be paying you 8 percent on your old bond when it can issue brand new bonds, and get away with only paying 6 percent. When buying bonds with a nice, fat interest rate, you have to know whether they're callable (yes, often, if corporate or municipal, but not generally if U.S. treasury issues), or if the high interest rate is because of low credit ratings.

The risks of foreign bonds include the above, and are complicated by currency risk. When you buy your British bond, for example, the pound sterling might be worth $1.50, but that will vary as the interest is paid to you over time, sometimes giving you more, sometimes less, as the dollar rises and falls against the pound. Of course, currency swings also affect the value of your principal, since it is denominated in pounds, not dollars.

**Buying (or selling) stocks or bonds:** When Mavis bought her 300 shares of Suds 'n Suds, she went to her stockbroker, who put the order through for her and charged her a commission. She found her broker through the yellow pages, where she saw familiar names such as Dean Witter, Merrill Lynch, and Smith Barney. She also saw brokerages advertising themselves as discount brokers. While full-service brokerages employ researchers to analyze and recommend securities to their customers, discount brokers generally only execute their client's order to buy or sell.

Since all brokers charge commissions on both buy and sell orders, Mavis, because she did her own stock picking, decided to save a lot of money by going with a discount broker, such as Charles Schwab, Jack White, or Fidelity Investments. She called the brokers and asked their commission on a theoretical set of trades ("buy 100 shares of stock at $50; sell 50 shares at $12; is there a charge for inactive accounts?"). There are discount brokers, and there are deep discount brokers. The latter are bare bones in the service department, but charge the lowest commissions. Mavis was able to open her account by phone and mail.

When Mavis instructed her broker to buy Suds 'n Suds, the broker executed the order by communicating it to the particular stock exchange that listed the company. The big ones in the United States are the New York Stock Exchange, the American Stock Exchange, and NASDAQ, and there are many more exchanges around the world as well—London, Toronto, Hong Kong, Paris, Tokyo, Frankfurt, Johannesburg. The purchase was handled almost instantaneously; the broker was able to confirm it and tell Mavis her price while she was still on the phone.

Mavis never received an actual stock certificate of ownership, because her shares were held by the broker in its name (street name). She received a periodic statement from her broker, informing her of the ups and downs of her portfolio. When Suds 'n Suds paid dividends, Mavis's broker held them in her cash account until she instructed it to buy more stock, or send her a check. On her statement, her securities were listed as long (meaning she owned the stock), or short (meaning she borrowed the stock). Brokerage services such as short trading, margin buying, options, and commodities futures are discussed in Chapter Eight.

The broker didn't guarantee or ensure Mavis's investment, but as a member of the Securities Investor Protection Corporation (SIPC), Mavis's account was protected up to $500,000 for losses due to the malfeasance or insolvency of the brokerage itself. Most large brokers buy private insurance to supplement SIPC, usually up to several million dollars' worth.

**The three Ds of stock investing:** The secret to successful stock investment over the long term can be stated in three rules:

- First, *diversify*. If you own shares in lots of different companies, when IBM plunges, maybe Apple soars. And McDonald's and Coca-Cola drift up, while Disney and Wal-Mart don't move much at all.
- Second, *diversify*. Maybe you own lots of different companies, but they're all in the same or related industry. Ford, General

Motors, and Chrysler will have their own individual fortunes, of course, but they will also move in tandem when the American auto industry as a whole slumps because of competition, say, from Japan, or from a big jump in steel prices.

- Third, *diversify*. Perhaps you've scattered your stock holdings among several different industries: autos, pharmaceuticals, consumer goods, electronics. But they are all American companies, and when the American stock market falls (turns bearish), they will likely fall with it. Mixing some international companies into your holdings (your portfolio) makes sense, because international markets don't always rise and fall in concert.

For an investor with less than $50,000 to put into individual stocks, diversify-diversify-diversify is difficult to achieve. You'd probably want at least twelve to twenty different companies, spread across industries, and internationally as well, before you could protect yourself against unacceptable losses due to the fortunes or misfortunes of individual companies, industrial sectors, or national markets. Fortunately, there's a solution for the individual investor: mutual funds, which are the subject of the next chapter.

**Introducing the Fantasy Forty:** Here's a good way to test your stock-picking skills without risking a dime of real money. Put together a fantasy portfolio of stocks, taking one month to assemble it and keeping in mind diversity and brokers' commissions. "Buy" your stock in 100-share lots, and pay $30 plus 2 percent of the investment to your discount broker on each purchase and sale. When you've assembled forty stocks, stop buying and value your portfolio. Keep track of the price movements on a weekly basis. Plot your progress on a graph, if you like. Continue to keep an eye out for likely candidates for your holdings, but here's the rule: Your portfolio cannot hold more than forty stocks, so if you come across one you just have to buy, you'll have to pick one to dump, too.

Do this for one year. Along the way you'll be terribly tempted to put real money into one hot security or another. Unless you have money to burn, resist this urge! You can afford to miss this great opportunity—consider it tuition—because all your life, when you begin investing real money in individual stocks (if you ever do, and in the Four Step programs you don't really need to), there will always be hot deals popping up. You can list your Fantasy Forty on Worksheet 6 in Appendix I.

The Fantasy Forty are for your play money. Now it's time to commit your real money to a Four Step plan. The next chapter, on mutual funds, will get you started.

 *Self-Test*
**Chapter 3**

1. Since 1926, there were nine 10-year periods when the stock market returned about:
   **a.** 10.3%
   **b.** 5%
   **c.** 15%
   **d.** 0.9%

2. Since 1926, there were sixteen 10-year periods when the stock market returned about:
   **a.** 15%
   **b.** 10.3%
   **c.** 3%
   **d.** minus 1%

3. The CEO answers to the company's:
   **a.** president
   **b.** workforce
   **c.** board of directors
   **d.** union

4. An IPO is:
   **a.** the first time a company's stock is offered to the public

    **b.** an Individual Profit Opportunity
    **c.** generally unavailable to ordinary investors
    **d.** a and c

5. Someone who owns 300 shares of a company:
    **a.** owns 30% of the company
    **b.** controls 300 votes for the board
    **c.** owns 3% of the company
    **d.** has no say in the board election

6. John owns 100 shares of Suds 'n Suds. After a 3-for-1 split, John owns:
    **a.** 33 shares
    **b.** 150 shares
    **c.** 300 shares
    **d.** 200 shares

7. Before the split, John's shares were worth a total of $1,500. After the split, they were worth a total of:
    **a.** $1,000
    **b.** $1,500
    **c.** $4,500
    **d.** $6,000

8. A junk bond is:
    **a.** often called a high-yield bond
    **b.** issued by a company after it goes bankrupt
    **c.** not available to investors
    **d.** good for the Four Step program

9. In a bankruptcy, the bondholders are paid before the shareholders:

    ☐ True    ☐ False

10. When interest rates rise, the prices of already issued bonds:
    **a.** rise
    **b.** are unaffected
    **c.** fluctuate
    **d.** fall

*Answers on Worksheet 15 in Appendix I*

# Mutual Funds

*The 10 to 12 percent solution*

Whit Mavis loaded her portfolio with Suds 'n Suds stock *only*, she goaded the diversity god into a rage. In its wrath, it invoked the dreaded single-company risk, and hurled Mavis down the tubes with Suds 'n Suds. Gene liked the looks of Suds 'n Suds, too, in the months following its IPO, but he knew better than to assume the risk of owning just one company. Instead, Gene invested in a stock mutual fund that included Suds 'n Suds among its holdings. When Suds 'n Suds stock went south, the mutual fund dropped in value 0.5 percent, which was a disappointment, for sure, but not nearly the disaster suffered by Mavis.

What follows will help you get up to speed in the mutual fund universe. But don't delay your start. *Time is money.* Get into your plain-vanilla index fund now, educate yourself over the next few years while that fund builds, then diversify your funds according to your best judgment, and finally, *enjoy yourself.*

**Why mutual funds?** Mutual funds offer diversity to the small investor, good customer service, low-cost investing in stocks and bonds, and the opportunity to make small, steady investments that, over time, should compound to your goal of a fortune. Over the last two decades, investments in a growth stock fund substantially outpaced funds in real estate, gold, and bank certificates of deposit, and was the only asset class to achieve average annual returns in the double digits.

We're shooting for 10 to 12 percent average per year in the Four Step plans, so it's obvious that a stock mutual fund is where we start.

**What is a mutual fund?** A mutual fund, in concept anyway, is very simple. Thousands—or millions—of people pool their funds, hire a manager to invest the funds for them, and divide the profits or losses among them. The manager charges an annual fee for this service, usually based on a percentage of your investment. Virtually all funds require a minimum initial investment, generally $1,000 to $3,000, but some leading funds are as low as $50, and others are as high as $20,000 or even more. If your fund is going to be in an IRA, your minimum initial contribution will usually be much lower, perhaps $50 to $500.

The fund manager makes investment decisions according to the objective announced by the fund. These range from money-market funds (very short-term government and corporate IOUs—low risk and low payback) through short-term government bond funds, long-term bonds, junk bonds, stock and bond (balanced) funds, blue-chip stock funds, small-company funds, growth stock funds, aggressive growth funds (volatile, with potential for higher return), gold funds, and international stock and bond funds. We'll talk more about these later.

Structurally, there are two kinds of mutual funds: closed-end funds and open-end funds. Closed-end funds issue a set number of shares to the public, like a stock IPO (remember Suds 'n Suds). After that, the demand for this limited issue determines the price of the share, just as with shares of common stock. The closed-end fund is traded on the stock market, meaning you have to buy into it through a stockbroker, and its price will range up and down according to the demand for the fund. You'll pay the broker a commission for buying the closed-end fund for you, which lowers your yield.

You want to confine your Four Step money, at least for the early years, to *open-end* funds, since they are much more commonly rated and discussed in popular financial literature, and are therefore easier for the beginning investor to evaluate. Hereafter, when I refer to mutual funds, I mean open-end funds.

An open-end fund is sold at its net asset value (NAV) on the day you buy. The NAV is simply the value of all the assets held by the fund (the securities it owns for its investors), less its liabilities, divided by the number of shares outstanding. It is refigured at the close of every trading day (a trading day is any day the stock markets are open, which are weekdays, except for some holidays). As the assets rise in value, up goes the NAV; as they fall, it sinks. As more people buy into the fund, the manager buys more assets. The number of outstanding shares are ever increasing, or shrinking, depending on the popularity of the fund, as opposed to the closed-end fund with its settled number of shares.

Do not compare NAVs among funds, because they are meaningless for that purpose. A fund with a NAV of $20 is not twice as valuable as one with a NAV of $10. Open-end funds are sold through brokers and financial planners and, quite easily, directly from the fund itself.

Let's take a whimsical look at how mutual funds work through the fortunes of a fictional mutual fund—one fraught with literary license.

**Super-Testosteroney:** Slim, Jake, and Hoss were rounding up cattle in the wilds of Chicago when Jake had an epiphany: "Boys," he said, "these cattle futures just aren't our thing. We're losing more than we brought to the party—and worse, we're looking like fools. There's got to be a better way." Slim said, "Jake, I never had the guts to tell you this, but I was a stockbroker once. I lost money then, all right—plenty of it, too—but here's the thing, *none of it was mine.* I used OPM (other people's money) and they paid me when they made money, *and they paid me, too, when I lost it for them.*" "No way, dude," said Hoss. "No one's that dumb." "I like it," said Jake. "I *love* it."

The three urban cowboys decided that a mutual fund seemed like just the right thing. They hired a lawyer to do the paperwork and an ad agency to flood the country with the good news, and the Super-Testosteroney fund was in business. In the prospectus, the boys gave themselves permission to invest 100 percent of the fund in anything legal. Since the first purpose of the fund was to make Slim, Jake, and Hoss superrich, they charged a high 2.5 percent annual management fee on all the assets they could attract, and then waited for the bucks to flow in.

Things were great at first. Lots of people wanted to jump on the bandwagon. But Super-Test's high fee, when deducted from its gross returns of 13 percent, meant investors were getting 10.5 percent return on their investment—not enough for an aggressive growth fund when its peers were making 12 percent. The inflow dried up. Super-Test stalled. To meet the demand for redemptions, the fund had to sell millions of dollars of its holdings.

The worried threesome pondered the problem. To get super-rich, they needed hundreds of millions, if not billions, of OPM to invest. The bigger the fund, the more their 2.5 percent was worth. Even erstwhile cattle speculators could figure that one out. To make their yield competitive, they could do either of two things: cut or waive their management fee, or jack up the risk. Loathe to cut their fees, the cowboys opted to load Super-Test with derivatives, gold, third-world debt, new office buildings and shopping malls, Japanese companies, Mexican debt, junk bonds, and IPOs. It was a galloping bull market, and the rising tide was floating all ships. Super-Testosteroney soared, returning 93 percent in a year when the average aggressive stock fund returned 23 percent.

And the believers bought it. And bought, *and bought it*. Until they bought the farm. Super-Test's assets grew from $100 million to $1 billion, then $2 billion. And Hoss, Slim, and Jake were the happiest cowboys east of the Mississippi. Then the bear struck, and the average stock fund fell 20 percent. But not Super-Test. No, Super-Testosteroney conspired to lose 75 percent of its investors' money, before its fickle participants deserted the ship, and hapless Super-Test closed its doors.

Mutual funds are *not insured or guaranteed*. Your investment can be worth more or less when you redeem it than when you invested it. You can do much to mitigate risk, however, not the least of which is a lengthy holding period (at least ten years). The fund's manager is not the custodian of the funds. They are held by a separate institution, usually a bank, so that even if the fund's sponsor goes broke, the assets should be safe. If the sponsor goes bankrupt, the fund's assets are not subject to creditors' claims. So with mutual funds, don't waste your time worrying about the safety of your funds with respect to anything other than the investment skills of the manager—or lack thereof. Super-Test's customers lost their shirts not because management was dishonest, but because it was stupid.

Fortunately, there are at least hundreds, if not thousands of funds whose managers are neither stupid nor sleazy, and finding the right one for you is the (very doable) challenge of Step Two.

**Self-educate:** You can get up to speed on mutual funds very easily—and for free, too. You've already started by reading this book.

Next, set aside three hours a week for library time. Find *Kiplinger's Personal Finance* magazine and *Money* magazine, and read every issue published in the last twelve months. Read every word, especially the boring ones. Read every word in all the ads, especially the fine print. Read the performance charts. You are not doing this with an eye to buy. You are just familiarizing yourself with the field, the jargon, the way information is presented, and certain concepts. Twelve issues of each magazine should get you started.

You can track your fund's performance in the financial pages of your daily newspaper. More on this in Chapter Eleven, where there is an explanation of how to read these pages and a complete self-education program in four steps. For now, though, remember that day-to-day swings are of no concern to the long-term investor, so daily or weekly monitoring of your fund(s) is not necessary; it's just for fun.

**Loads and no-loads:** Mutual funds are easy to buy into. Some banks, any stockbroker, or a financial planner will be delighted to sell you a fund, generally for a sales commission. The commission can be quite high, but averages around 5 percent of your investment. It is commonly called a load.

Nearly half of all funds, however, do not charge a sales commission; you buy them directly from the fund itself. Some fund families are all no-load, others are all load, some are mixed.

Let's see how a load will affect your return over time: Jenny bought a growth stock fund with a 5 percent load from a financial planner. Her initial investment totaled $1,000. She added $100 per month to her fund until retirement. Al did the same thing, but with a no-load fund. Both funds performed identically over forty-four years, earning an average 10 percent per year, at which time Jenny and Al retired.

Jenny had $976,344—a nice sum, certainly. But Al had over $50,000 more. That's because he wisely chose to invest in a no-load fund, rather than pay a 5 percent sales commission on the initial investment and on each subsequent contribution! Jenny's initial $1,000 fell to $950 after the planner took the commission, and each $100 Jenny contributed monthly thereafter was worth only $95, for the same reason.

Here is a mantra: A sales charge does not improve fund performance, a sales charge does not improve fund performance, *a sales charge does not improve fund performance!* It just buys a salesperson.

All funds, load and no-load, make their money off the annual management fees; some also charge something called a 12(b)-1 fee, which management is supposed to use to promote the fund. There can be custodial and transaction fees as well. Some, in an effort to appear to be no-load, charge nothing up front, but impose a redemption, or exit fee, when you redeem your shares (back-end load). Sometimes a redemption fee declines over time, disappearing after five years or so. This is to encourage you to stick with the fund. A *pure* no-load fund should be free of front- and back-end loads and 12(b)-1 charges. Some financial planners or other salespeople may imply that load funds outperform no-loads. No. Remember the mantra. You may hear that no-load funds charge higher annual fees than load funds. No, again. In fact, the opposite has been demonstrated to be true. There are studies to suggest that load-payers do better over time because, as customers of brokers or planners, they are encouraged to stick with the fund during bad times.

One major problem with evaluating the performance of mutual funds is that most performance charts do not adjust for sales loads, although they do adjust for annual fees. The argument is that it's too hard to account for a front-end or back-end load when you don't know how long the fund will be held. In other words, should the $110 load chopped out of your $2,000 investment be deducted over one year, three years, five? Some charts adjust for the load on their five-year and ten-year ratings, but you should be careful when you compare the performance of various funds to analyze the effects of a load, particularly on programs like the Four Step plans, which use monthly contributions over much of a lifetime. Each and every one of those contributions will be worth less in a load fund.

This is not to say you'll never, ever want to purchase shares in a load fund. There are superstar load funds, and superstar no-load funds. If you have satisfied yourself that a particular load fund's performance justifies the cost of its load over time (and don't forget, every contribution you make to it will be loaded as well), then go for it. You can buy load funds directly from the fund, rather than from a broker or planner if you like, but the fund will charge you the load anyway. You may also prefer professional guidance in your investment selections as described in Chapter Eleven, in which case, you pay for the advice through the sales loads. Be mindful, though, of the conflict inherent in buying products recommended by someone who will profit by the sale.

**The prospectus:** Every fund is required by the Securities and Exchange Commission to provide certain information to its applicants. This is contained in a prospectus, a pamphlet clearly labeled as such that will come with your application, and perhaps periodically throughout your ownership of the fund. Take the prospectus seriously. If you are investigating several funds, line their prospectuses up and compare. Are they all written in plain English, or is there an obvious attempt to obfuscate? Is the bad news right up front with the good? How do the costs compare (easy to do, since the SEC decrees the format)?

**The annual report:** Every fund is required to report to its shareholders at least annually. Many also report semiannually, and some issue quarterly reports. Look for a letter from the chairperson boasting about the fund's performance (or explaining it away as just one of those things beyond anyone's control). The more forthcoming and candid the letter, the better. The annual and periodic reports are not a repeat of the prospectus. For one thing, they list all the investments held by the fund. This gives you a much better picture of what the fund is involved in than the prospectus, which tells you what the fund *can* invest in, not what it *is* investing in. To ensure that the fund's managers will have wide discretion, the prospectus will frequently list risky devices that the fund never (or hardly ever) gets around to using. If you are really interested in a fund, ask for the prospectus and the annual report.

**Costs:** All funds charge a management fee, usually annually. They range from below 0.2 percent to over 10 percent in a handful of funds. Although this varies, index funds are usually the cheapest, because they are simply tracking the market and can be managed by computer. Bond funds are next, with stock funds generally the most expensive. Recently, stock funds' fees hovered around 1 percent of assets, and bond funds' fees at less than 0.7 percent. A 1 percent fee means that if your fund earned 8 percent, you'll put 7 percent in your pocket. It's deducted from your return. In the first two or three pages, the prospectus will list the fund's costs, including loads, if any.

The annual management fee removes the manager from the temptation to churn the fund in order to boost his or her pay. Stockbrokers, because they earn a commission on both the buy and sell sides of a transaction, can be tempted to trade an account excessively in order to generate commissions. Churning is illegal, but in the gray area, difficult to prove. Annual fees, tied to asset value, remove this temptation from the mutual fund manager.

You must deduct the annual fees from your stated yield to get your true yield—and that's before you adjust for inflation (and taxes, for taxable accounts).

In the Modest Millionaire plan, for example, we're aiming at an average annual total return of 10 percent, net of fund costs. We've already seen how, historically anyway, this will be easiest to achieve in stock funds. Let's say we find three funds that interest us:

- **An S&P 500 index fund, with an annual cost of 0.19 percent.**
- **A domestic growth fund, with an annual cost of 1.2 percent.**
- **An international fund, with an annual cost of 2.2 percent.**

Over five years, the index fund returns an average of 13 percent annually; the growth fund, 14 percent; and the international fund, 15 percent. After costs, each fund returns 12.8 percent, but the growth fund and international fund did so with higher risk. You expect to be compensated for a higher risk with a higher return (over time), but over these five years, you weren't paid anything for your risk. So the most cost-effective investor was in the more conservative index fund, as it worked out. Of course, at the beginning of the five-year period, the three investors couldn't know how it would turn out; perhaps the growth or international fund would have justified their costs. But this illustration makes the point that it's essential, when you're comparing funds, that costs be a big part of the equation. Relying on performance figures only is a fool's illusion.

It's been documented that especially among money-market and bond funds, costs are inversely correlated with performance. In other words, the better the performance, usually the lower the costs. That's because bonds are a limited universe, and active management does not produce the performance differentials in the range that stock fund managers sometimes achieve. There's another reason, too. To keep their numbers competitive with low-cost bond funds, the managers of higher-cost funds have been known to stuff their portfolios with risky securities. Why should you incur a higher risk for the same return as a low-cost fund? That's just stupid. So when you are well along in your Four Step program, and begin bringing bond funds into the picture, be a stickler about costs. Go for cheap.

There is a lower correlation between expenses and performance among stock funds, although the funds charging the highest fees generally show only an average performance. A stock-fund investor should probably avoid those charging more than do 80 percent of their peers.

We've already seen how small differences write large when given enough time. Here's how twenty- and thirty-year-old Golden IRA participants would make out in identically performing funds, earning an average of 10 percent per year until each retires at sixty-seven, with these varying cost ratios:

| Twenty-year-olds | Thirty-year-olds |
| --- | --- |
| • $2,197,993 (0.19%) | • $814,687 (0.19%) |
| • $1,992,482 (0.45%) | • $756,782 (0.45%) |
| • $1,230,285 (1.75%) | • $527,090 (1.75%) |

One wise twenty-year-old nearly doubled his money by shopping for a fund with the lowest cost ratio commensurate with performance. The frugal thirty-year-old did splendidly as well, earning over $250,000 more than her careless colleagues, which tells us that even when the compounding period shortens, *cost matters*.

Because the better reporting services, and the funds' ads themselves, generally take management fees (but usually not loads) into consideration when reporting performance, some funds artificially boost their performance figures temporarily by reducing or waiving management fees. There will be an asterisk or footnote explaining this in the fine print—always the most interesting part of any ad, prospectus, annual report, or performance chart. Although the waiver may be explained away as a bona fide effort to boost participation in a new fund, it seems sneaky enough to me that I'd look hard at any fund that boosts its performance figures this way before I'd opt in.

Loads are left out of the equation in most performance charts because of the difficulty of factoring in costs that are not charged

## Chart C

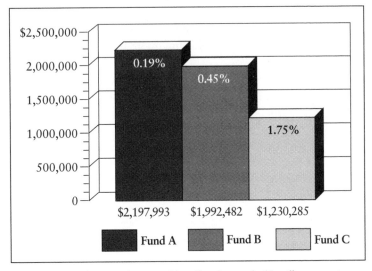

*Golden IRA member Jonathan, age 20, will make nearly $1 million more in Fund A, costing 0.19% annually, than in Fund C, costing 1.75%, although both funds will earn an identical annual average of 10%.*

annually. The fine print at the bottom of ads and charts is where you'll find this information.

Get in the habit of always deducting the costs of the fund, including loads and hidden loads like redemption fees or 12(b)-1 charges, from performance. Don't consider management fees only, because they don't represent all the costs. Some funds separate operating costs from management fees, which can make the management fees look misleadingly small. The full story is found in the prospectus in the expense (or cost) ratio, which is all costs and fees expressed as a percentage of assets. Worksheet 4 in Appendix I is meant to help you calculate the costs of any mutual fund you may be considering.

**Fund families:** Here and there you'll find a lone ranger among the five thousand or so funds, one that operates solo and attracts business due to reputation, solid performance, or the high load it pays salespeople to push the fund. The vast majority, however, are sponsored by fund groups, or families. Fidelity Investments is the largest mutual fund family in the world, with load and no-load funds numbering over two hundred; the Vanguard Group is the largest no-load family. Dreyfus, Scudder, Janus, Strong, Twentieth Century, Invesco, and T. Rowe Price are just a few of the dozens of other families that sponsor the thousands of funds.

Think of a fund family as a brand name. You might respect Kellogg's, for example, but that doesn't mean you like all its individual cereals. You might like Kraft's mayonnaise, but hate its cheese. Big Mac is for you; Egg McMuffin is not. Same thing with funds. You needn't marry a particular family, although as a beginning investor, you should be doing business with just one until your account reaches at least $5,000 or so—more, if it's meeting your needs.

The large families do pride themselves on an overriding reputation that is not necessarily linked to performance, per se. Some families, for example, are the low-cost specialists; look to these first for index and bond funds (the Vanguard Group comes to mind). Others excel in aggressive growth funds; some are known for their breadth of offerings and customer service; still others for their international experience. This does not mean that any of these families always has the best fund for you in their particular niche, or that they will always outdo the others in that respect either. They won't.

A large family can probably satisfy your needs for decades. When your Four Step account heads into the six digits, you may want to branch out. There is no cost reason to confine yourself to one family, except some families waive custodial fees for IRA accounts totaling over a certain amount, say $5,000 or $10,000. The management fee, of course, would continue.

Most mutual fund families have their winner funds and losers. But there are a handful that consistently beat the pack, and a few with an extra helping of duds. It may have to do with the way the family recruits, nurtures, and trains its managers. Still, it all comes down to the performance of the particular fund you're in, rather than the record of the family as a whole.

I am not being coy by not naming names. It would be futile in such a rapidly changing field as this. Furthermore, your own research program, as sketched earlier and spelled out in Chapter Eleven, is something a future millionaire just has to do. You are beginning a serious program, one that can make you seriously rich. So you have to bring your brains to the table, as well as your informed judgment.

**Managers:** We live in a starstruck society, and the sober world of finance is not immune. Some fund managers have achieved superstar status because of their fund's superior performance over time. It's an unfair system (no surprise) because the diligent manager of a balanced fund, whose 11 percent return precisely matches his investor's expectations, will never shine in the charts the way the aggressive growth manager's 45 percent annualized return over the period of one quarter will (an 11.25 percent return for the quarter would be annualized to 45 percent—11.25 percent × 4—a fictional number, since no one knows if the other three quarters in the year will justify that hypothesis). In a down market, the balanced fund may lose 2 or 3 percent of its investor's money, while the aggressive fund torpedoes 15 percent, yet the sizzling fund's manager will be the hotshot to the balanced fund's Mr. or Ms. Anonymous.

Management history is important to you when evaluating a fund's historical performance. Even though history doesn't predict the future, especially in the financial world, it is nevertheless useful to know something about the track record of current management before investing in a fund. For this, you need to know how long a particular manager has been in place. If a fund's stellar performance was earned under different management, you have reason to question whether that performance will continue. Only a handful of stock funds in existence for the past ten years have the same manager. For this reason, the more useful performance charts list the manager and his or her tenure.

Some fund families have a stated aversion to the celebrity system, so they manage their funds by committee, or rotate their managers. Some managers handle several funds in one family, each with different objectives, and therefore different results.

**Minimum investments:** Most funds impose an initial purchase minimum, ranging from $50 to several thousand. Most are in the $1,000 to $3,000 range, with lower amounts required for IRAs. Often the performance charts appearing in the personal finance magazines will include minimum purchase amounts; certainly a call to the fund will get that information.

**Net Asset Value (NAV):** Remember, the NAV is the value of all the assets held by the fund, minus all liabilities. Your $1,000 purchase will buy you 61.728 shares at an NAV of $16.20 per share. When the NAV reaches $20.55, your 61.728 shares will be worth $1,268.51. If the NAV falls to $14.87, your investment will fall to $917.90. And don't forget, if you purchase a load fund, your original $1,000 will be diminished by the load. A 3 percent load will mean only $970 will go to work for you, since the other $30 will go to work for the salesperson. Instead of 61.728 shares in the above example, you will start with only 59.877 shares.

Most funds set a minimum amount for additions as well. Usually these are in the $100 to $250 range, although IRA contributions are set lower, usually around $50, or there is no minimum. Since a twenty-year-old on our Modest Millionaire program has a monthly contribution of $71 (and everyone else is higher), there should be no problem locating a fund that will accept your magic number in an IRA account. Many performance charts list the minimum amounts; a call to the fund will deliver that information.

And remember, the 3 percent load mentioned above will also come off each monthly addition. The twenty-two-year-old with an $87 monthly Modest Millionaire payment will really only get $84.39 worth because of the load. Over the years of the Four Step program, this cut, even without figuring in the initial load, will cost the investor more than $30,000 in a fund averaging 10 percent per year—and that's in a so-called low-load fund.

**Reinvesting dividends and gains:** Your fund's application will ask you whether you want dividends and gains reinvested.

The answer is *yes, yes, yes!* This catapults your fund into the mystical world of compounding. The answer is yes.

A stock fund, because it holds stocks, will usually earn dividends and (hopefully) capital gains on its holdings. At least annually, it will distribute these to its investors. Since you have instructed the fund to reinvest them for you, you will notice in the statements the fund sends you from time to time that your share balance has increased (although your dollar balance may not have, if the NAV has fallen). A bond fund will do the same, with reinvested interest and gains. If you plunked down the initial purchase price in a fund, and never added to it again, the number of shares you own will increase over time anyway, because of these reinvestments.

Beginning investors have a tendency to overlook these increments, concentrating instead on performance as measured by changes in the NAV. Remember, especially in the bond world, your investment can show a gain, even though the NAV has fallen, because of income distributions. These little distributions, often measured in just a fraction of a share, are what turn your $50,000 into a fortune.

**Objectives:** Even the superstar fund managers are not free souls. Every fund states an investment objective, so that investors will be able to match funds to their own goals. A flashy Southeast Asia stock fund would be a woeful choice for a widow living off her investment income (because it will be unstable over the short term); nor will her government bond fund get you to your goal. Different strokes for different folks, as they say, but never so true as in mutual funds.

Here are a few types of funds appropriate for your Four Step plan, and some that are better left for your Fantasy Forty:

**Growth funds:** Growth funds generally own stocks, but there the similarities end. For starters, many growth funds denominate themselves large cap, mid cap, or small cap. The term cap is jargon for market capitalization, which is simply the number of shares outstanding, multiplied by their price. Suds 'n Suds, for example, would be considered a small-cap stock by most experts if it had 5 million shares outstanding selling for $20 apiece, for a total market capitalization of $100 million. If you priced the stock market as a whole this way (all the shares of all the companies listed, times their price), large caps might come off the top one-fifth (quintile), small caps the bottom quintile, and mid caps the remainder. This definition is very loose, however; some small-cap funds go higher on the scale, some lower, and so forth.

Why do you care? Remember that 10.3 percent stock market average. The S&P 500 stocks are from the large and upper mid-cap quintiles. Small caps have averaged about 2 percent more in yield over the same seventy-year period. After you've given your S&P 500 index fund a chance to show you its stuff and educate you in the ways of stock-fund investing—a period of at least two years, but better, five—you want to assess its overall performance. If it is averaging 10 percent, no problem. Stick with it. If not, the 10 percenters among you—the Modest Millionaires, Hot Starters, and Golden IRAs—might aim for a solid growth fund with an objective of capital appreciation (*capital gain*) through investing in large-cap (blue chip) American stocks.

Historically, anyway, this type of investment would fall short of the expectations of the Roller Coaster riders among you who need to pick up that extra 2 percent in something a little riskier, say, small caps. Funds listed as aggressive growth generally include small caps in their mix, perhaps some international stocks, and maybe some risky maneuvers that are not investments per se, but rather tricks of the trade. Some performance charts separate small-cap funds into their own category, some don't.

**Growth and income funds:** These funds are for the investor nearing retirement who wants to begin dampening growth in favor of income, but is not yet ready for a pure-income portfolio (bonds). These funds invest (usually) in large companies that pay good dividends, but are still expected to grow in value to provide inflation protection and some capital gain.

**Index funds:** As we've discussed, since the S&P 500 is the generally recognized benchmark of American stock market performance, some funds aim to match it, not beat it. This is for the investor who looks at the historical averages, and feels comfortable with that. An S&P 500 index fund will seek to do no better, no worse than stocks generally. All nonindexed stock mutual fund managers hope to beat the S&P; some do, but most don't over time. A fund that underperforms the market is in the position of telling its investors that they paid more for the fund and got less than if they had stayed with an index fund (which, since they are managed by computers rather than humans, have the lowest annual cost). Underperformance is expected from time to time in any actively managed fund; by definition, you are adding risk when you try to beat the market. But a fund that underperforms for two or three years in a row would, in my portfolio anyway, be a candidate for the boot.

There are many indexes, including small stocks, international stocks, and various bond indexes. If you want to match the performance of small caps, you wouldn't go into the S&P 500. Instead, you'd find a small-cap indexed fund. How? Find the fund families in the mutual-fund listings in the financial pages of your newspaper, and start phoning. You can get their 800 numbers from the 800 information operator.

As you know by now, an index fund is the right way for you to start your Four Step fund. The Modest Millionaires, Golden IRAs, and Hot Starters should start with an S&P 500, and the Roller Coasters with a small-cap indexed fund. With index funds especially, since they all strive to deliver the same performance, cost should be a major factor in your decision. Paying a load would be ridiculous, in my opinion, since no-load funds are so easily located and set up; and the annual fees should be the lowest you can find.

**International funds:** In the international arena, there are terms of art: an international fund was originally understood to invest only in stocks of companies outside the United States; a worldwide (or global) fund could invest anywhere in the world, including the United States. But these lines have become somewhat fuzzy, so it's up to you to read each prospectus. Even ordinary domestic growth funds might have at least some international investments. If you intend to allocate 10 percent of your portfolio to international stocks, and the fund you select invests 50 percent in the United States, you've defeated your purpose. The larger funds have set up toll-free numbers to dozens of countries, so that investors outside the United States can invest in U.S. mutual funds of any kind. The larger fund families have offices all over the world, and some are managed outside the United States, in London or Hong Kong, for example.

International investors have two objectives: greater portfolio stability through geographical diversity, and increased return, since underdeveloped areas of the world have more distance to grow. Some funds concentrate on huge companies in developed countries, such as Volvo, Telecom Argentina, Hoffman-La Roche, Toyota, Philips Electronics, Nestle, Nokia, Credit Suisse, Grupo Televisa, British Air, Placer Dome, and Telmex.

Some funds operate in emerging markets (third world), some in "new" Europe (former communist countries), and some in single countries, such as Canada, Mexico, Turkey, Israel, Germany, or Japan. Many single-country funds appeal mainly to those with ancestral ties. Regions such as Latin America, Southeast Asia, Europe, or the Pacific rim are well represented as well. As you can see, the narrower the focus, the lower the diversity, and, therefore, the higher the risk. At a certain point you approach speculation, so these sexier funds are for your future, if ever, when you can play around with $5,000 or so because it represents no more than 2 to 3 percent of your portfolio. For now, put them in your Fantasy Forty portfolio and learn from the experience.

International investors take on extra risk, with the hope of extra reward. Overseas markets, especially those in third-world countries, may not be as well regulated as the U.S. exchanges, the governments may not be as stable, the skill level and natural resources may be lower, the workforce may be uneducated or rebellious, capitalism may be a new idea, and finally, even in highly developed areas like Canada, Japan, and Europe, the dollars you invest are converted into the local currency, which rises and falls against the dollar, adding an extra level of risk when you cash out (currency risk).

Currency risk is more than theoretical. A stock may perform well on the London exchange, but if the pound declines against the dollar, gains disappear when you convert your pounds back into dollars to spend or invest in the U.S. Currency fluctuations are more extreme than stock market fluctuations. While the stock market has declined more than 20 percent in only one year out of the past thirty, the dollar–pound–deutsch mark relationship has moved more than that on plenty of occasions. Like most other investment risks, currency risk is highest in the short term, and tends to diminish over time.

Many investors hope to hedge their domestic investments with their international holdings; if the American markets fall, perhaps the others won't. Sometimes this works over the short term; often it doesn't, over time. An investor with at least a ten-year time-horizon has a reasonable hope for reward, since in every ten-year period within the past thirty years, international stocks have outperformed the S&P 500.

For the Four Step plans, international funds shouldn't be considered until you've built your holdings beyond $10,000. Then, perhaps, you might invest 10 percent internationally until you've reached $50,000, and then another 10 percent; after $100,000 you might want a maximum of 30 percent of your holdings in international companies. But that's years from now, and the investment climate may be so different as to make these proportions quite irrelevant.

**Sector funds:** There are dozens of funds that concentrate on a particular segment of the economy: technology, electronics, health services, pharmaceuticals, utilities, leisure, natural gas, retail, food and agriculture, software. You name it, you can invest it. These funds, of course, defeat one of the main reasons you want a mutual fund, and that's diversity. They are for the trader who has confidence (bets?) that a certain sector of the economy is on an upswing, and wants to concentrate his or her holdings there. Market timing is the rule among sector traders, since "buy and hold" works best over broadly diversified holdings with a long time-horizon. The savvy investor who calls it right can make quite a lot of money in sector funds, certainly beating the S&P. But there are plenty of losers as well.

**Bond funds:** Bonds were discussed in the last chapter, including the differences between corporate and government bonds, maturity, coupon (interest) rate, and creditworthiness. Bond funds are often called "income" funds, as opposed to "growth" funds (stocks), but this can be misleading, since some equity funds emphasize high-dividend-paying stocks, such as utilities, and consider themselves to be income funds as well. Still, in the broadest of generalities, stocks are growth, while bonds are income.

You'll remember that bonds, as measured by the twenty-year U.S. treasury bond, have returned 4.8 percent annual average since 1926, meaning that bonds probably won't be the first place you'll look to fund your Four Step program. But bond-fund managers, unless their fund's objectives tie their hands, invest in a mix of bonds, hoping to beat the historical average. Many do, even over a period of years; however, achieving your goal through bonds will almost surely be a far greater challenge than through stocks. Keep your bond investing for shorter-term goals, as discussed in Chapter Ten. Money you need in fewer than five years should not be in stocks.

One point needs to be made about bond mutual funds, as opposed to bonds themselves. Remember, when you buy a $5,000 ten-year 8 percent bond from, say, Nike, you expect Nike to repay $5,000 in ten years, with $400 interest paid to you annually until then. If you want to sell your bond at any time before maturity, you can do so quite easily by going through a stockbroker, who will sell it on the secondary market, or the bond market. But you probably will not get precisely $5,000 for your "used" bond, because its 8 percent interest rate may be more or less than what newly issued bonds are paying. If someone can buy a new $5,000 bond paying 10 percent, they won't pay you $5,000 for your lousy 8 percent bond. The price you can get for your bond will fall. Of course, if a new $5,000 bond only carries a 6 percent coupon rate, buyers will bid up the price of your precious 8 percent bond, and you'll receive more than its face value, or a capital gain.

These interest rate fluctuations won't affect you at all if you hold your bond the full ten years. Nike will (probably) pay you the 8 percent interest on schedule, plus your $5,000 at maturity. The rise and fall of bond prices in the secondary market are of no concern at all to anyone holding bonds full term. And the closer you are to maturity if you wish to sell the bond, the lower the volatility in price. If you sold your Nike bond after eight years, your risk of losing principal would be less than if you sold it after a year or two. That's because the buyer of your eight-year-old ten-year bond is, in effect, buying a two-year bond, since it matures in two years. It's easier to predict interest rate swings over a two-year period than over a ten-year period, so the buyer is assuming a lower risk.

A bond *fund*, on the other hand, has no set maturity date. The manager is constantly buying and selling the bonds in the portfolio, so you can't eliminate interest rate risk by "holding to maturity" as you can with individual bonds. There are some bond funds with "target" dates, meaning they invest in securities that will all come due in a targeted year, but since they buy long-term securities, they can be *very* volatile.

**Tax-exempt bond funds:** People in the higher tax brackets can save tax dollars by investing in tax-exempt bond funds, often listed as tax-free, or municipal bond funds. These invest in municipal bonds, which are bonds issued by states and local governments. They are exempt from federal income tax, and in some states, from taxes in the issuing state. A Californian or New Yorker, for example, can buy into a "double tax-free" California or New York fund, which invests only in bonds issued in California or New York, and escape state and federal income taxes on the interest earned by the fund.

Even if you are in a high tax bracket, these funds are not for you if you are trying to amass your fortune in one of our programs. You need stocks, not bonds. Anyway, the Four Step programs should be in tax-deferred accounts such as 401(k)s or IRAs, so shielding them again from taxes is both useless and a sure money loser, since these funds pay lower returns than ordinary bond funds.

**Balanced funds:** Balanced funds invest in stocks and bonds, often in some stated ratio, such as 55 or 60 percent stocks and the remainder in bonds. This is the mix favored by huge pension-fund administrators, so it seems a reasonable approach for an investor just prior to or just beginning retirement. It's too bond heavy for someone under age thirty-five who's investing for the long term, however. Because of the ample mix of equities, balanced funds are probably not the best place for very short-term funds either. When you're within ten years of your goal, balanced funds will be an excellent way to begin toning down your investment strategies toward the more conservative (income-oriented) mix appropriate for retirees. But for now, think growth.

**Socially conscious funds:** Under pressure from their constituents, some institutions such as colleges, unions, dioceses, charities, convents, and state and local governments became aware of the things to which their pension, endowment, and investment dollars were contributing. Boycotts forced dollars out of South Africa, tobacco, gambling, nuclear power, oil, nonunion industries, and defense contractors, and into environmental cleanup, recycling, consumer protection, equal-opportunity employers, organic foods, and unionized industries. Activist capitalists hoped that enough pressure would force the share prices down (making it more expensive for the boycotted companies to raise funds), resulting in the company's abandonment of the disputed policy or product.

Mutual funds were quick to follow, with more than two dozen socially conscious funds now operating to please whatever your conscience dictates. Since your social conscience may not match mine, you can readily see that a close reading of the prospectus is a must. Perhaps you want a fund that shuns alcohol, and I want one that promotes the environment. We both need to match our principles to the fund, to avoid unhappy surprises.

How do the conscience funds do as investments? Poor to middling, for the most part. Since the Four Step programs are based on a net average annual return of at least 10 percent, you can see that investing in a fund that consistently *underperforms* the S&P's 10.3 percent seventy-year average won't make you a millionaire. It becomes a question of economic responsibility to yourself.

It's up to you to decide how important that million is to you. Many conscientious investors prefer to leave investment choices up to the fund manager they've selected in an ordinary fund, hoping for the maximum gain consistent with their risk tolerance, then use part of their profits to benefit directly the particular cause of their choice. Others, with an aversion to a particular industry, say tobacco or defense, do their own conscientious selection by scrutinizing the annual or semiannual reports of the ordinary funds they are interested in, to eliminate those that invest in such stocks. If Philip Morris or Northrop are on the list, that fund is out.

**Money-market funds:** Many mutual fund families include at least one money-market fund. At your age, money-market funds are best seen as parking places for windfalls or lump sums as you integrate them into your Four Step fund, or other account, such as taxable investments for your house down payment. A money-market fund invests in very short-term (often thirty days or less) IOUs that businesses trade among themselves (commercial paper).

They pay a little more than your bank savings account, allow check-writing privileges, *are not insured or guaranteed by anybody*, but to date have a remarkably safe track record. The longer the maturity of the IOUs held by the fund, the more risk you assume. Most money-market funds stay in the 30-day range, which is considered quite safe. Risk rises steeply with average maturities over 120 days.

Annual fees are critical to your money-market fund total return. Higher-yielding funds get there in either (or both) of two ways: longer maturities, which increase risk; or lower costs, which don't. Look for the latter when you select your fund.

You might consider a money-market account for your emergency funds, as we'll explain in Chapter Nine. Since the fund strives to maintain your principal intact, your funds are accessible, and it pays more than a bank savings account. When financiers speak of "cash," they often are referring to funds held in money-market accounts. You will barely beat inflation in one of these. They are no place for your Four Step money.

**Asset allocation funds:** As your funds build up (and you get older), you'll need to diversify your holdings among asset classes. The 100 percent stock allocation represented in the index funds I've recommended you begin with may not be appropriate over the long term. It's a start-up strategy. The next chapter addresses asset allocation for your portfolio, generally differing mixes of stocks, bonds, and cash. Before you get there, though, you should know that some mutual funds purport to make it easy for you: the fund manager invests in varying (or fixed) proportions of stocks, bonds, and cash.

The theory is that you need look no further than such a fund. No need for you to put together your own mix of stock funds, bond funds, international funds, and so forth. All your money can go into the one fund, and then you can forget about it. Some of these funds have more than met their investors' expectations over time. Others have not done much more than match the markets, which means you've paid too much for active management, since a mix of index funds would do the same thing at a much lower cost.

Asset allocation fund investors expect a less thrilling ride when the market dives, since their manager is supposed to have aligned the fund in anticipation of market swings. No one, not even the most skilled fund manager, can accurately predict the market all (or even most) of the time, however, so some asset funds occasionally disappoint in this regard—like all mutual funds.

**Precious metals funds:** Gold and other precious metal funds invest either in gold itself (bullion and coins) or in the stock of mining companies. Some funds do both. Like sector funds, gold and other precious metal funds are for those who think they know something the rest of us don't. When they're right, they're really right. When they're wrong, it's awful. A teensy bit of your Fantasy Forty might land here, just for the experience, but not your Four Step money until you're into six figures—if even then.

**Real-estate funds:** A few funds offer you the opportunity to invest in real estate, through the convenience of a mutual fund. Often this is commercial property, such as malls and office buildings; sometimes it is residential, such as apartments. The mutual fund does not own real estate directly; rather, it invests in real-estate investment trusts (REITs), a security packaged by real estate developers and owners. A real-estate fund certainly adds diversity to your portfolio, since the real-estate market acts independently from the stock and bond markets that drive most mutual funds. Still, real estate has its ups and downs. A large portfolio well diversified internationally, with a good representation of stock and bond mutual funds, might venture up to 10 percent of its assets in real-estate mutual funds. But for now, give one a whirl in your fantasy portfolio.

**Performance:** Performance, of course, is the bottom line. What do you care whether your fund holds Malaysian rubber, Thai silk, Canadian gold, or good old General Motors, so long as it earns what you need it to earn. For your Four Step program, the goal is clear: 10 or 12 percent (net of costs) per year, on average, over three or four decades. For the fifteen-year period preceding 1993, the average annual return for all general stock funds operating over the period was nearly 15 percent. If history is any guide, the Four Step goals should be quite feasible in any one of a number of mutual funds, with track records going back ten or twenty years.

The problem is history is not a guide. All the performance charts in the finance magazines, on-line databases, and professional tracking services cannot predict the future. It's been documented, in fact, that they don't, but you don't need statistics to corroborate the obvious: If past performance predicted future performance, there wouldn't be nearly five thousand mutual funds vying for your Four Step plan. There'd be only one—the historical top performer. Everybody would be in that fund, because its history would predict it will remain the top dog.

Still, it will take discipline not to be seduced by today's happening fund. When you see that your fund delivered 11 percent for the year, but one heavily invested in Hong Kong came up with 58 percent, of course you'll be tempted to jump ship. That's fine for your Fantasy Forty, or even your taxable short-term portfolios (if you can afford to lose them), but your fortune will be reached by your 10 or 12 percent fund. Keep your eye on that goal for that fund. That's all the performance you need to know to make your million.

History doesn't predict, but that doesn't make past performance irrelevant. Some funds (and fund families) have a pathetic track record. There's no reason in the world to select one of those for your Four Step plan. You want a fund with a sound record as measured against *like* funds; a fund under the same management over a long period. Ten thousand dollars in the average stock fund over the past thirty years would have grown to less than $250,000 by the end of the period; in the best performing fund, that same investment would yield nearly $4 million! That's a spectacular reward for the right pick, so it pays to pay attention.

**Use and misuse of performance charts:** Read the percentages returned over three, five, even twenty years. It is useful for you to know if the fund is a consistent performer, or if its reputation is riding on one blow-out year in the past. Understand that the market's performance in general accounts for most of those numbers over the period. For example, all the funds that returned 31 percent in 1991 can be said to owe 97 *percent* of their performance to the market, since the S&P returned 30 percent that year.

The more critical number, therefore, is the percentage by which the managed (non-index) fund outperformed (or underperformed) the S&P over a period of years. Plus 1 percent? Plus 2 percent? A managed fund consistently beating the market by 2 percent is doing very well indeed. So it's more important for you to know if the fund returned 8 percent in a 6-percent year, or 17 percent in a 15-percent year, than it is for you to dazzle yourself with 13 and 14 percent returns in years when the market did the same. You'd have been better off in an index fund, because of the lower management fees. The better performance charts list the S&P and other market indexes for comparison.

The successful investor reads the charts and other rating devices such as Morningstar's star system (Chapter Eleven) as just one piece of information, to be weighed together with a good reading of the prospectus, the annual or semiannual report, an evaluation of the manager's track record during his or her tenure, and current economic trends. A comparison of the annual costs of similar funds is imperative, and, of course, if it's a load fund, an adjustment in the return to reflect the load. If this sounds like a lot of work for a beginning investor, don't worry. You'll start out in an index fund for a couple of years at least, and can use that time to educate yourself.

**Buying a mutual fund:** Load funds are sold by financial planners, some banks, stockbrokers, and, in some cases, directly from the funds themselves. No-load funds are purchased directly from the fund, via an 800 number, which you can locate easily in the ads or performance charts in the personal finance magazines, or by calling the 800 information operator and asking for the number of the fund family that sponsors the fund. Most funds really have the application process down to its bare essentials. The one- or two-page form is easier to complete than opening a bank account. Study the prospectus, attach your check to the application, and you're in!

Most funds will gladly receive automatic transfers from your payroll or bank, a terrific idea for the Four Step programs, since you won't have to discipline yourself to be persistent each and every month. Otherwise, just write a check every month and send it in with the easy form the fund will provide, tucking both into the also-supplied handy return envelope.

Some investors never seem to have met a mutual fund they didn't like. Dozens of funds, sponsored by numerous different families, may grace the portfolio of such investors. As you can imagine, the flood of mail is awesome. Statements differ in style, making evaluating the total portfolio a hassle. Some fund families are better communicators than others.

Now there's a way around this for the well-diversified mutual fund investor. Several discount stockbrokers will open no-load mutual funds for you, often with no transaction fee to the broker. The discounter makes its money through a kickback from the funds. The advantage to the investor? One monthly statement from the broker listing all the disparate funds, as well as the great advantage of telephone switching among fund families with just one call to the discounter.

This service won't mean much for you capitalists just starting out. You'll probably be in one fund for a number of years, so it makes better sense for you to be dealing with the fund directly. Down the line, though, when you begin to branch out, keep the discount brokers in mind. They can make your life much simpler.

**Redemptions, switching:** You can get your money out of mutual funds quite easily. Most allow telephone redemptions, meaning all you have to do is call the fund, and they'll put a check in the mail (although in unusual circumstances, by law the fund can delay as long as seven days). In most cases, money can be wired to your bank for an extra fee. In all cases, a written request for redemption will be honored.

Later on, when you're happily living off your assets, you can instruct the fund(s) to send you a check every month, quarter, or whatever—for the interest, interest and dividends, or a set sum in any amount—until you die, or the fund runs out, whichever comes first.

If you have more than one fund with them, most families will let you switch money between the funds with just a phone call (teleswitching). Some funds charge for switching, others limit the numbers of free switches per year, and some allow unlimited switching at no charge. This feature will become important to you after a few years, when your money builds to the point that you want to move beyond your starter fund.

Now you understand mutual funds, and stock, bond, and money-market funds. But before you commit your Four Step money beyond your index fund, you need to understand the relationship of risk to reward, and how these will play out in your portfolio over the long term. The next chapter will talk about this, and show you ways to mitigate risk with time-proven strategies tailor-made for the Four Step programs.

 *Self-Test*
**Chapter 4**

1. Mutual funds offer:
   **a.** diversity
   **b.** convenience
   **c.** low cost
   **d.** a, b, and c

2. Mutual funds are also:
   **a.** risk free
   **b.** insured by the government
   **c.** as safe as a bank account
   **d.** none of these

3. Mutual fund managers are paid by the sales commission, or load:

   ☐ True    ☐ False

4. The NAV is:
   **a.** the total of the fund's assets less its liabilities
   **b.** a good way to compare the value of funds
   **c.** usually stable
   **d.** a, b, and c

5. No-load funds:
   **a.** do not perform as well as load funds
   **b.** cost more because of higher management fees
   **c.** are not recommended for beginners
   **d.** none of these

6. In general, index funds have the lowest costs:

   ☐ True    ☐ False

7. Money-market funds are protected by government insurance:

   ☐ True    ☐ False

8. Annual costs of mutual funds:
   **a.** are trivial
   **b.** don't matter over the long term
   **c.** can make or break the fund's performance
   **d.** are the single most important factor in fund selection

9. If the dollar drops in value, a U.S. shareholder's value in an international fund:
   **a.** falls
   **b.** rises
   **c.** is unaffected
   **d.** fluctuates

10. A bond fund is not the best place for your Four Step money because of:
    a. too much risk
    b. insufficient yield over time
    c. cost
    d. a, b, and c

*Answers on Worksheet 15 in Appendix I*

# Now You See It—Now You Don't

*Strategies for reducing risk*

Charles Ponzi was one sly dude. He promised investors that if they'd loan him their money for a mere eighty days, he'd return it, plus 40 percent! He did it, too—*and the suckers loved it.* It all worked for a while, but any dope could see it couldn't go on forever. They didn't have calculators back in 1919 Boston when Charlie was afoot, but the end point should have been pretty obvious: If you pay the first tier of investors off with the money brought in by the second tier (which has to be larger than the first tier in order to pay the exorbitant interest owed) and so on until the whole world comprises the final tier, the thing will collapse under its own weight, leaving the later tiers footing the bill. This happened, of course, and the Ponzi (or "pyramid" scheme, so-called because of its layers of ever-larger tiers) is illegal most places today.

I mention Ponzi in this chapter on risk because the financial markets have been likened by some distrustful souls to a giant pyramid scheme, with those on the inside forming the tip of the pyramid. They buy low, then sell high to the next layer, which sells higher to the next, and so on until the poor saps in the general public come into the market just in time for one of its famous swan dives to perdition.

There's just enough truth to the suspicion to keep it alive. When more people want concert tickets than there are seats, it's a scalper's market. Prices bid up to whatever the market will carry. The same is generally true in the financial markets. If lots and lots of people want Reebok stock, its price will soar. Those who buy in at the top are in the best position to scream on the ride down.

But the financial markets are not Ponzi schemes for a lot of good reasons. First—in the United States, anyway—they are regulated by the Securities and Exchange Commission in Washington, as well as by the states. Second, the markets are not operated in the dark. It's up to the investor or the broker to know the price history of the stock and whether its current price is tenable, and there are plenty of reporting services making this information accessible. Then, no promises are (properly, anyway) made to any investor, let alone guarantees; and finally, no one person stands behind the scheme, manipulating it to his or her sole advantage.

Yes, hanky-panky does occur from time to time. Wherever there are pots of money, it's inevitable. But the theory of the markets, and for the most part, the practices, too, are not out to get you.

This may be a little hard for you to believe. In conversations with scores of would-be investors in their twenties and thirties, I've noticed a marked tendency to exaggerate three potential financial calamities:

- **The collapse of the stock market**
- **The demise of Social Security**
- **The ravages of inflation**

People just starting out don't have much, and what they do have is hard come by. The thought of losing it is sickening. But risk comes in many flavors, including the risk of paranoia that keeps the investor from rewards that can be reasonably earned with acceptable risk. Social Security and inflation will be taken up in later chapters. This one will take an intelligent look at risk, and show you established ways to manage it. Of course, you won't sock every last penny into securities. Life itself is risky, and you'll need money close at hand for emergencies. Chapter Nine will go over your emergency fund.

Risk is a fact of life for any investor, including those in insured bank accounts, who, even if they manage to keep up with inflation, lose out to opportunity cost, the difference between what their funds *could* have earned with reasonable safety, and what they *do* earn in the bank account.

Fortunately, a large chunk of risk is avoidable through the various strategies outlined here. You can bring your investment risks down to a tolerable level through such simple techniques as using your head, dollar-cost averaging, diversifying, and long time-horizons. Each of these methods is a perfect fit with the Four Step programs. You might want to complete Worksheet 7 in Appendix I to assess your own risk comfort level.

Because the Four Step plans are tied to stock mutual funds, at least for the early decades, the following discussions mostly refer to the risks of stock investing. The risks particular to bonds were covered in Chapter Three, in the section on bonds.

Is risk tied to reward? Of course. The more risk, the more (potential) reward or loss. The less risk, the more stability. Bonds are generally considered less risky than stocks, cash (i.e., money-market funds and treasury bills) least risky of all. All investments have some risk, of course, if for no other reason than inflation. Even bonds unavoidably fluctuate with the rise and fall of interest rates.

**Lies, damned lies, and statistics:** Mark Twain said it—he knew figures don't lie, but liars can figure—so the first risk mitigator is your judgment. Learn to separate facts from opinions (or worse, wild hopes). It is your responsibility to recognize hype, especially when it's presented as sober statistical fact.

Take, for example, mutual fund ads. With thousands of funds competing for your dollar, it's depressing but not surprising to find that even responsible, successful funds have sometimes resorted to sleazy tactics to get your attention. The regulators have cracked down on the more egregious distortions, but you still need to keep your wits about you.

For example, some funds with nothing else to hang their hat on have been known to present cumulative return for their fund, rather than average annual return. Over a period of ten years, for example, the cumulative return might be expressed as 403 percent. Wow, you think. My money would have quadrupled in that fund. What they don't tell you is that the S&P 500's cumulative return over the same period was 500 percent, so their wonder fund underperformed the market by about 20 percent over a significant time period. Average annual return is the number you want to see, along with the S&P's annual performance over the same period, or some other appropriate benchmark, such as an international-stock or small-cap index. Cumulative return, because it includes all that neat compounding, is not a useful statistic for comparative purposes. It masks things you want to know. A fund with one spectacular year out of ten underperforming ones might show the same cumulative return as the steady performer that beat the market ten years out of ten.

Some funds, especially new ones, waive management fees for a year or so, in order to improve their numbers on the performance charts. A fund competing in the growth-fund sector might want to beat the (hypothetical) 15 percent average for such funds in order to attract new money, so without factoring in the 1.9 percent fee (since it's waived), their fund shows a fine return of 16.9 percent, and you're suckered in. Sooner or later, the management fees will kick in, lowering your yield accordingly. Somewhere, the ad will note the fee waiver, or if such a waiver was in effect for part of the period over which they are reporting such dazzling returns, but it won't be in the headline. *Always* read the fine print. That's where the good stuff is.

Another trick is to present your fund as one type, while investing more aggressively than investors expect for that kind of fund. Such a situation was uncovered by one of the personal finance magazines, which noted that the particular fund included "Growth & Income" in its name, but, in fact, was invested as a growth fund, with very little attention to income. Because growth and income funds deliver lower returns, in exchange for more stability, this growth fund always starred in the growth and income category. The magazine's editors decided that henceforth, despite its name, the fund would be carried in the growth-fund portion of the magazine's performance charts, where its investment style most suitably placed it. This magazine's editors read the annual reports to uncover a fund's actual investments— and so should you. Your job, as always, is to read the prospectus before you send money, so that the fund's objectives square with yours.

Some funds will ballyhoo their hot numbers at the top of the ad, then seriously narrow them in the fine print at the bottom. One such shouted its position in the "top 15 percent of all general equity funds.*" Follow the asterisk to the fine print, and you'll note that the period in question was May 6, 1982 through December 31, 1993, an odd reporting period, gerrymandered to fit the fund's needs. Farther down, the copy bellows: "The only small company fund to beat the S&P 500 six out of the last six calendar years.\*\*" Oops! The double asterisk whispers that "Returns would have been lower if the fund had not waived certain fees in the period covered." What fees? How much? How long? We aren't told.

One large fund, hot in the seventies, plunged terribly and never recovered its luster. Soon its very name came to be a code word for "loser." On the performance charts, it was hopeless, because even with improving numbers, its pathetic history dragged down its longer-term scores. What to do? Why, create a new identity, of course. The fund changed names, and emerged on the charts as a spanking new fund, with its dismal past consigned to the dustbins of history. New investors have yet to see their bright hopes realized, as the fund plods along, as it has in the past, disappointing all who yield to its false promise.

Here's an equivalent situation: A large, old fund family advertises its emerging markets fund with one-year, five-year, and ten-year average annualized returns of 63.37 percent, 18.21 percent, and 13.16 percent, with the latter two marked with the dreaded asterisk. We learn in the fine print that the fund "adopted its present name and investment objective" less than three years earlier, meaning the five- and ten-year returns are irrelevant to the present. We aren't told if the earlier objectives were international, domestic, balanced—what?

A successful fund, which shouldn't have to resort to such tricks, screams in huge letters across a full-page ad, "America's #1 Balanced Fund." Farther down, a table presents annualized returns over ten years, five years, and one year (most tables reverse the order, showing the most recent figures first). The reason for the reverse is evident when you see that the fund was number one over ten years and number one over five years, but number two in the preceding year. This is the number two fund, advertising itself as the number one fund.

Tax-exempt bond funds, because they have lower real returns than taxable bond funds, entice investors by showing the "taxable equivalent" yield, in other words, the yield you'd get in a taxable fund after paying the tax. Many ads use the highest tax bracket to present these figures, thus boosting their yields unrealistically high for most investors, whose lower tax brackets produce a much lower net return. Antics like these are unbecoming.

The National Association of Securities Dealers (NASD) and the SEC oversee mutual fund advertising. Under their rules, a fund that advertises its ranking must provide perspective by reporting one-, five-, and ten-year rankings. It also has to define the category it says it tops, and report how many other funds are in that category. Performance figures must be calculated through the most recent quarter, and except for money-market funds, performance reports for periods of less than one year are now prohibited.

**Measuring risk—beta:** Call the preceding parade of horribles judgment risk. It's largely avoidable through self-education and attention to the right materials.

Other risks are avoidable, too, although not all of them, as we shall see. One helpful device doesn't mitigate risk, but measures it, so you get a better shot at avoiding unacceptable risks. The indicator is the beta, and, because it measures past performance, it is no guarantor of the future of a particular security or fund. The beta indicates how widely the investment historically varied from the stock market generally, usually as measured by the market's proxy, the S&P 500.

With mutual funds, beta measures market risk (see the discussion that follows), the unavoidable risk of stock investing. The S&P 500 is defined to have a beta of 1.00. A fund with a beta of 1.33 has been one-third more volatile than the S&P, both on the up side and the down. One with a beta of .90, on the other hand, has been 10 percent more stable than the stock market generally. If the S&P 500 drops 10 percent, the .90 beta fund historically drops 9 percent, and the 1.10 beta fund drops 11 percent. Same deal going up. A riskless investment, such as a ninety-day U.S.

treasury bill, or an insured savings account or certificate of deposit, has a beta of 0.

An S&P 500 index mutual fund will aim for a beta of 1.00, and its investors will be content to swing up and down with the market generally, but they don't expect to experience the thrills of a beta 1.68 investor. An investor going for a low-beta portfolio will give up some return in exchange for the lower risk.

You'll see the betas for mutual funds listed on many charts, often including those in the popular financial magazines. Like all indicators that measure past performance, use the information the beta gives you carefully. It cannot predict the future, and, because it usually uses the S&P 500 as its benchmark, it is not very useful for funds that aren't invested in the market tracked by the S&P, such as international, sector, and gold funds. Specialty funds should properly be assigned betas correlated to benchmarks relevant to their peer group.

Although you'll commonly see the beta listed, many analysts prefer the standard deviation as a measure of volatility; therefore you'll sometimes see it listed as a risk measure, instead of the beta. The beta measures the volatility of the fund against the S&P 500; standard deviation measures how much the fund fluctuates from its own average. A high standard deviation means high volatility.

**Avoidable and unavoidable risk:** For both stocks and bonds (and real estate, collectibles, gold—anything bought and sold), the investor faces one unavoidable risk, known as market risk. When, for whatever reason, the stock or bond market as a whole falls, your investments therein probably will as well. The only way to avoid market risk is to stay out of the market, which carries risks of its own (see the discussions that follow on opportunity cost and market timing).

Market risk is said to account for about 30 percent of the risks of stock investing; the remaining 70 percent is related to the individual company, and is avoidable through the risk-reduction strategy of diversification.

Some experts speak of this 30 percent–70 percent division of unavoidable and avoidable risk, and note that an investor in love with Eskimo Pie, say, and holding only shares in that company, assumes 100 percent of the risk associated with stock investing (market plus company risk), while the diversified investor assumes only 30 percent of the risk—the unavoidable 30 percent represented by market risk. While the stock market does provide a higher reward for taking on higher risks, it only does so for unavoidable risk, that is, market risk. Avoidable risk, such as specific stock risk, is not rewarded. Since most mutual funds are well diversified, and index funds certainly are, the Four Step program is right on target with the great risk slayer: diversification.

**Opportunity cost:** Stan tried to be prudent by dividing his holdings equally among stocks, bonds, and cash, with the latter two for safety. He put $3,000 in each asset class, then forgot about them for forty years. At the end of that time, because historical averages held throughout the period, he had $181,459 in an S&P 500 stock index fund, $20,385 in a bond index fund, and $16,702 in a money-market fund. But Stan's investments in bonds and cash took on another risk over the long term, a hidden risk called opportunity cost. In those investments, Stan lost the opportunity to make $329,384 more than he did. Opportunity cost weighs heaviest on the young investor, since the longer the investment period, the more things (including mistakes) compound. Opportunity-cost avoidance is why the Four Step programs, tailored for folks thirty-five and under, start out in stock mutual funds.

**One-size risk does not fit all:** You can't risk your emergency fund. You want every bit of it there when you need it, so it should be very conservatively held. As explained in Chapter Nine, you want most of this in plain-vanilla bank accounts.

Your taxable investments—for things you need before you are 59 1/2, such as a house down payment, tuition for the kids, or early, early retirement—should be in accounts tailored for each need and time period. For example, a house in five years, tuition in fifteen, and early retirement in twenty each carry their own appropriate risk-reward ratio. This is discussed in depth in Chapter Ten on short-term goals, but for now just understand that intelligent risk-reduction strategies are not an all-or-nothing matter.

Your total net worth should comprise an array of investment choices, with a mix of risk appropriate to the objective. Your Four Step plan, as outlined in this book, is long-term money. Even the oldest of you, the thirty-five-year-olds, have thirty-three years to go; the twenty-year-olds have forty-eight. You have the longest time-horizons of any investors in the world (excluding kids, who don't make their own investments anyway). This means your riskiest investments will be placed in your Four Step account. How risky that will be depends on you and your psychology. If long-term bonds are as fancy as you want to get, then understand the opportunity risk, and live with that.

**Riding the bear:** A bear market is Wall Street slang for a prolonged market slump, generally agreed to be a 20 percent drop in value of the stock market as a whole. (Wall Street, by the way, a street in Manhattan's financial district, has come to refer to the U.S. financial community in general.) A bull market is a sustained rise. Fortunately for stock investors, historically the American markets have spent about 80 percent of their time going up and only 20 percent going down. Still, since World War II, the bear has growled at least nine times, with market dives of 20 percent or more. Since 1926, the fourteen bear markets have averaged 36.2 percent (S&P 500). On one single day in 1987, the market dropped a full 23 percent! Bears and bulls feed on both stocks and bonds, although stocks, with their greater volatility, are usually more dramatic when they roar. Long-term bonds did, however, drop more than 17 percent in 1987—and slumped lower than stocks in 1994—so you can't even consider bonds (especially long bonds with more than ten years to maturity) a completely safe haven. Since your Four Step plan is very long term, you must expect to ride both bears and bulls (again and again) during your investing career.

Riding the bull is fun. The trick is to avoid the temptation to "take your profits" by jumping off too soon. The perils of market timing are discussed below.

Riding the bear takes some doing. You don't want to get bucked off just as the ride smooths out. It may comfort you to know that over the past three decades, the recovery periods for various styles of mutual funds after each bear market have been calculated. The worst-case scenario was (predictably) in the aggressive growth funds, which took a bit more than three years to recover after the worst bear market. Government bond funds took as long as two years, and funds that held both stocks and bonds took a little more than one year. This reinforces the notion of diversification, since the balanced funds recovered faster than either stock *or* bond funds by themselves.

Three years (even one year) is a long time to watch yourself lose money. It takes nerves of steel to wait it out. Try to focus on your investment objectives. For the Four Step plans, we're talking about a very long time-horizon, so the day-to-day (even year-to-year) fluctuations in the markets should cause you no concern at all. Try to view market corrections (a bear cub, so to speak) and full bear markets as variations on a long-term, upward trend.

History teaches that there is more to lose by being out of the market when it begins its upswing than there is by hanging in during a decline. Historically, anyway, recoveries do their greatest work early, so by the time the market timer decides it's time to buy back in, the best is over. Every market swing can hit your portfolio twice: what you lose in a decline, and what you miss in a recovery by being on the sidelines. Although the future is not dictated by the past, it seems prudent to stay invested, even during the inevitable declines, which should be viewed as buying opportunities.

**Inflation:** Inflation poses the biggest risk to your million being worth a million down the line. All investments, savings, and cash holdings are equally exposed to this relentless gobbler of returns. Fighting inflation is Step Four of the program, so it's important enough for its own chapter. Chapter Seven describes an easy way to defeat inflation, so that your fortune will be worth a fortune when you need it.

Most risks, including specific company risk and inflation risk, are avoidable, at least in substantial part. In fact, there are a number of proven strategies that go a long way toward reining-in risk.

**Dollar-cost averaging:** Your Four Step plan automatically takes advantage of one long recognized tactic for minimizing risk. When you invest a fixed amount month after month, market fluctuations will guarantee that some months you will get more shares for your money, others less. Because your Four Step payment goes further (buys more shares) when the market is down (and shares are therefore cheaper), you inevitably lower the average cost of your holdings, thus increasing your profit when you finally cash out. This happy circumstance gives you reason to rejoice during market sell-offs (mini bears), because you are building your holdings faster than when the market is high. You defeat the very purpose of dollar-cost averaging if you pull your contributions whenever the market swoons.

Dollar-cost averaging works on a mathematical principle known as the harmonic mean, but you don't need to know the complexities of that to enjoy its benefits. It's easy to figure out, and it is just surprising that it works so well to make money for you, in both up markets and down!

Think of mutual fund shares for a minute. If you're a thirty-four-year-old on the Modest Millionaire program, investing $292 month in and month out, you will get more shares in your fund in some months than in others. When the NAV is high (say, $15), your $292 will buy 19.47 shares; when it is only $10, you'll get 29.2 shares. As your shares accumulate, more will be low-priced ones—inevitably—because low-priced shares are accumulating faster than the high-priced ones. In time, the average price (the cost basis) of your shares will get lower, as the cheaper shares overtake the more expensive ones. From an investor's point of view, this is ideal! At some point you may want to sell your shares, at which time you can sell them all at the high price, even though their average price was low.

See what happened to Chris and Ed. They each received $500 at Christmas. They each owned shares in the same growth (stock) fund. Ed put his entire $500 in on January 1, when the share price was $12.50 (he got 40 shares). Chris put $100 in on January 1 (8 shares), $100 on February 1 (9 shares), $100 on March 1 (10 shares), $100 on April 1 (9 shares), and $100 on May 1 (8 shares). Each has invested $500, yet Ed has 40 shares worth $12.50 per share, and Chris has 44 shares also worth $12.50 per share. Chris has a $50 profit, *plus* the interest earned on the portions of her $500 left in the money-market fund while she was dollar-cost averaging her gift into the stock fund. Ed has no profit and no interest, while Chris made money even when the stock price stayed the same during the period. This strategy works whether the market is rising or falling. Over time, by sheer mathematical necessity, a higher proportion of Chris's shares were bought "low" rather than "high." The goal for every investor!

Here's another look at the magic of dollar-cost averaging: Kim, a Golden IRA member, deploys her $166 per month into her stock index fund. During the first six months, the shares cost her $10 per share. In the second six months, they were $20 per share. At the end of the year, they are selling for $15 per share, so she's even, right? Wrong. Kim has a nice 12 percent profit. She bought 99.6 shares at $10 (16.6 × 6 months), and 49.8 shares at $20 (8.3 × 6 months). Kim has 149.4 shares, which at the current $15 price are worth $2,241—for a 12 percent gain over her $2,000 total investment! Kim is a winner, even in a flat market, because of the magic of dollar-cost averaging.

Since you've instructed your fund to reinvest all distributions, you get the benefit of dollar-cost averaging automatically. Rejoice when your statement reports your reinvestment bought you three shares against last time's two. The market is down—hooray! More shares for your portfolio. And of course, the Four Step programs automatically take full advantage of dollar-cost averaging by investing a set amount, monthly, over decades of time. Be delighted when your payment buys more shares because the market's down. That means all the more little shares are just lying in wait in your portfolio for the right moment to balloon to a bundle.

**Time, the risk slayer:** In the end, risk really has more to do with time than anything else. The 10.3 percent stock market average since 1926 embraced one year when stocks soared 54 percent, and another when they tanked 43 percent. As you can see, if you had invested one-year money (funds you needed in one year) on the first day of the minus 43 percent year, you would have been a very unhappy puppy indeed at the end of the year. A one-year investment in the stock market, even if diversified through a mutual fund, is a gamble, pure and simple. In one out of three years (statistically, anyway), you'll end the year with less than you began.

On the other hand, long-term money in a stock mutual fund with no more than an average performance over the period poses (historically) very acceptable risk for most investors. Since 1926, no investments held for at least twenty-five years reflecting the stock market average lost money. Since even the oldest investor addressed in this book (thirty-five) has a thirty-three-year time-horizon until age sixty-seven, history, although no guarantor of the future, is at least reassuring about the past.

In general, then, investment risk declines as the holding period lengthens. Something too risky for a five-year time-horizon might be quite acceptable for fifteen or twenty. This is why we separate your Four Step (very long-term) fund from your shorter-term accounts, most especially, your emergency fund. Time affects risk dramatically. As a young investor, you have more of this precious leveler than the rest of the world. Use it to your advantage.

**Diversify, diversify, diversify:** Diversity was discussed in Chapter Three, but since it is of singular importance to you as a long-term investor, consider this a brush up. If time is the first great risk leveler, then diversification is its twin. The Nobel Prize was awarded to the economists who first proved the notion that you both reduced risk and enhanced return with a diversified portfolio. A stock index fund is, by its very definition, highly diversified. Other types of funds are perhaps less so.

Remember Suds 'n Suds, the hapless beer hall–laundromat. Shareholder Mavis went down the tubes with Suds 'n Suds because she bet her entire holdings on its future. She did her homework, too: she analyzed the company according to public information; she visited a few Suds 'n Suds outlets to satisfy herself that customers were ten deep and the staff well-trained and happy; and she sought the advice of her well-informed stockbroker. But Mavis assumed 100 percent of the risk in owning stocks by having only one company in her portfolio. Despite all her conscientious research into Suds 'n Suds, Mavis couldn't know that a Seattle coffeehouse–laundromat company was about to burst on the scene, and that Suds 'n Suds's fickle clientele would forsake their pints of bitter for bitter coffee.

Had Mavis held a well-diversified mutual fund, which itself had 3 percent of its holdings in Suds 'n Suds, she would have enjoyed the benefits of the company's growth, and been insulated against its fall. At most, the value of her mutual fund shares would have fallen 3 percent, but it's much more likely that the fund's experienced manager, with all of his or her contacts, would have smelled trouble long before Suds 'n Suds's bankruptcy. The manager would have sold out the position rather than riding it down, so Mavis's hit would have been more in the area of a fraction of 1 percent rather than 100 percent.

As your holdings mount, you'll want to begin diversifying among types of funds. As has been pointed out, there's plenty of opportunity for all kinds of diversification: stocks and bonds, both domestic and international; precious-metal funds; real-estate funds; speculative funds; and ordinary money-market funds. When one of your funds goes up, perhaps another is going down. However, there is such a thing as over-diversification. For beginners on the program, your S&P 500 or small-cap index fund should provide diversification enough for your first $15,000 or so; some experts would say it holds enough for the trip all the way to your goal.

**Timing the market:** One discredited risk-reduction technique does deserve mention, since it remains popular among speculators, and even some investors. It's the tempting game called market timing. The market timer attempts to sell stocks (or bonds) when the market peaks, and buy them when the market is at its lowest.

Of course, "buy low, sell high" is the market's oldest adage—and too obvious to be belabored. But short-term timing as a tactic has been discredited statistically. Assume a hapless investor fed $200,000 into the market in $5,000 chunks for the forty years ending in 1993, plowing it in on the day in each year that the market hit its absolute high (generally considered the very worst day to invest). Her investment would have grown to $2.8 million at the end of the period, for a 10.7 percent annual gain. The chances of anyone being so unlucky as to buy always on the worst possible day is remote. But look how the world's greatest market timer would fare by putting the same $200,000 in, $5,000 per year, on the market's best possible day, its annual low: that lucky investor would have achieved 11.5 percent, a mere 0.8 percent more than the first poor soul.

This analysis suggests that it doesn't much matter when you buy in, but it doesn't speak to whether it pays to jerk your money out when you see the clouds gather. Both the lucky and unlucky investors just described were buy-and-hold investors. But could they have bettered their returns by pulling their funds when the going got tough? The data suggest not. Historically, it has proved more costly to dodge the bear than to live with it. Most market run-ups travel fastest in their earliest stages. By the time the bear dodger decides it's time to get back in, the best times are over. The numbers suggest you have more to lose by being on the sidelines at the beginning of a market advance than you do by enduring its slide.

You don't have to rely on your own gut instincts if you can't resist the discredited lure of timing: Lots of folks make their living peddling newsletters that purport to tell you "when." The *Hulbert Financial Digest* (which rates the performance of investment newsletters) researched twenty-nine market-timing newsletters and found only four that bested the S&P 500 over a period of five years. When taxes were taken into consideration, only one beat the S&P, and that newsletter required seventy-nine switches in sixty months just to beat the S&P by 0.1 percent!

So much for market timing. If the experts can't do it, don't you try. "Buy and hold" are the bywords for your Four Step funds. Market timing means pulling in and out of the market short term, as you play your hunches on where it's headed. It's a form of gambling. Leave market timing to others; you'll reach your goal without it.

**Asset allocation:** Discredited market timing refers to short-term moves designed to take advantage of market volatility. Over the long term, of course, you will adjust your portfolio from time to time, either because your own objectives or time-horizon changes, or in response to long-term market trends. At the beginning of the 1980s, for example, interest rates were at a cyclical peak. A period of falling rates was reasonable to foretell. Sure enough, rates fell to a low in early 1994. Investors getting in at the bottom of the interest rate cycle do well to remember that rising rates erode bond principal, and since higher rates cost companies more when they borrow, they also cut profits, which may be reflected in stock prices. This kind of long-term strategizing is reasonable (although for the very long-term investor, like you, not necessary), and it is not the frantic switching that characterizes the market timer. Buy and hold doesn't mean you lock yourself into a position forever. You needn't marry your investments, but you should do a good enough job selecting them so that they have your respect.

In the first years of your Four Step program, even record drops in the market will have little effect on your outcome over time. But when you're close to your goal, even an ordinary bear market

## Chart D

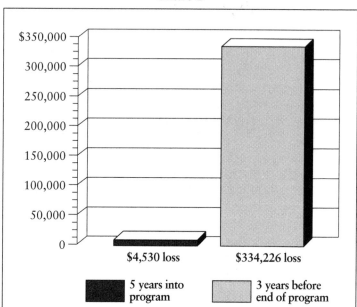

*If a 26-year-old Modest Millionaire's Four Step fund dropped 45% five years into the program, the loss would only be $4,530; but three years from the end of the program, the loss would be $334,226. Thus, risk strategies take on increasing importance as the program progresses.*

can hurt you badly. Chart D illustrates how a twenty-six-year-old's Modest Millionaire program would fare if a 45 percent drop in the stock market occurred both five years into the program and three years before the end (a 45 percent decline was suffered in 1973–74, the greatest postwar bear market to date).

Ten years into the program, you'll have some money to think about. Everybody except the Roller Coasters aged twenty-five and under will have at least $15,000 in their program, which is a sensible place to start thinking about asset allocation. Many respected experts call this decision the single most important judgment you'll make in your investing career. It has been established, in fact, that so long as you allocate your resources wisely,

## Chart E

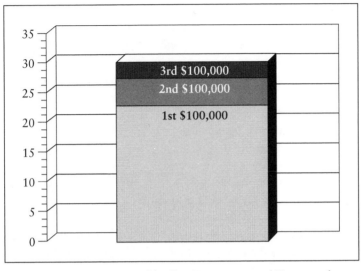

*Although it will take a 28-year-old Roller Coaster investing $85 per month at an average annual rate of 12% about 21 years to reach the first $100,000, the second $100,000 will take less than 5 1/2 years, and the third a little more than 3 years. That's the thrill of compounding as the years mount.*

the particular fund or investment you choose within each asset class is of secondary importance.

First, for a look at how much you can expect to have ten years after you start, refer to Tables 7 through 10 in Appendix II. Don't be surprised if the numbers are lower than you expected. Even though you'll be at least one-quarter of the way into the program by years, you won't be approaching $250,000. That's because compounding takes time to work its miracles, so although it will take a twenty-eight-year-old on the Roller Coaster plan more than twenty-one years to get to $100,000, it will take under six years to reach the next $100,000, and only a little more than three years for the next.

If the stock market matches its historical trends during the ten years after you begin the program, you will be on your way to your goal in either an S&P 500 stock index fund (Modest Millionaires, Golden IRAs, and Hot Starters), or a small-cap index fund (Roller Coaster riders), which means a no-load fund, with the lowest annual cost you can find.

If the S&P and small-cap markets *do not* maintain an annual average of at least 10.3 percent and 12.3 percent respectively over the first five years or so of your program, move your Four Step money into a managed growth fund that is consistently beating the relevant market by whatever percentage you need to make your program's required percentage (10 percent, 11 percent, or 12 percent, net of costs). If market conditions are such that these percentages cannot be met without undue risk, be prudent. You only need that average over four decades or so; you don't need to sustain 10 or 12 percent as an annual minimum.

After ten years, it will be time to begin diversifying your Four Step fund into different stock funds. Until around age forty-five, you'll want to be fully invested in stocks in order to take full advantage of your youth and the time-horizon to recover your (inevitable) losses.

Since you know your number for your Four Step plan, your task will be to build the stock segment of your portfolio toward that goal, commensurate with good sense. If, over a five-year period, the market is returning lower numbers than you'll need, then you might consider these more aggressive approaches to spark up your portfolio: small-cap funds, international stock funds, aggressive growth funds, and high-yield bond funds. You should not aim to outperform the S&P 500 by more than two percentage points. More than that really shoots up the risk curve. If the market has a sustained period (more than five years) of, say, 6 percent returns, your Four Step goal of 10 or 12 percent should be put on hold until those amounts are again within two percentage points of the S&P.

Fully investing in stocks (or stock funds) until age forty-five is a "hotter" approach than tradition dictates, but still within the parameters of good sense for your long, long time-horizons. The rule of thumb used by many financial planners states that the bond (or fixed-income) segment of your portfolio should equal your age as a percentage of your financial net worth. In other words, this formula would advise a thirty-two-year-old to have 32 percent of his or her portfolio in bonds or their equivalent; a forty-five-year-old, 45 percent.

In my opinion, this formula is too conservative for you. The Four Step programs don't mature until age sixty-seven, so a forty-five-year-old still has a time-horizon of more than twenty years. If the numbers play out, and you do your part, at age sixty-seven you're a millionaire! Since this book is not about retirement, we'll leave your investment challenges after age forty-five to other advisers.

Remember this: Your judgment on how to allocate your portfolio among the asset classes of cash, bonds, and stocks will very likely, in the end, be more important to your bottom line than the specific investments you select to build those segments. Nobel Prize-winning analysis, no less, has established this. Remember, too, that to make your goal you need an average of 10 or 12 percent net of costs. That's an average, not an annual goal, so don't be upset or take unnecessary risks if the market underperforms your expectations for as long as five years running. One million dollars is a fun number to pin your hopes on, but it isn't everything. You can have just as much fun with $900,000 as with $1 million—and even with a lot less, if need be.

As the years turn into decades, you'll begin to have an idea about where your program is going. You'll be much better off accepting some variation in the final number than you will be trying to maintain unrealistic yields in the face of a prolonged market slump. If the market overperforms, you'll be in fat city. Keep your good sense in good times and bad—since over the next three or four decades you're sure to experience both—and even if you don't amass a million, you'll have pots of money at the end.

**Adjusting your allocation:** Once you've begun a conscientious allocation program, you'll find that gradually your proportions will ease out of balance. Let's look at $10,000 deployed in a typical early retirement allocation of 60 percent stocks and 40 percent bonds (or stock and bond funds).

In year one, bonds do well and stocks lag, so that the portfolio value is still $10,000, but the allocation is $4,500 bonds and $5,500 stocks. What to do? If you sell bonds to buy stocks so that your portfolio is readjusted to a 60-40 allocation, aren't you screwing yourself by selling the strong part of your holdings in favor of the weak? Readjusting your mix every year in this way would seem to be a sure loser. The other option is to set your allocation once only, then let it run without further adjustment, allowing normal market conditions over the years to keep the proportions in flux. The first method utilizes a kind of dollar-cost averaging, in that you are selling your more costly holdings to increase the depressed (or cheaper) portion of your portfolio. Over time, this option should lower your cost basis. In fact, it's been established that the two methods, over time, result in very little difference to your bottom line in the end, with the first method holding a very slight advantage.

**You have only one net worth:** Although asset allocation will not be much of a consideration in the early years of your Four Step program, you should begin to think of your net worth as one figure. Calculate your emergency savings; the equity in your house; the sum of such major possessions as cars, art, antiques, jewelry, and collectibles; and your taxable and tax-deferred investments, less your debts, including student loans, credit cards, mortgages, and car loans. The resulting figure is your net worth. Worksheet 2 in Appendix I can help you get a handle on this.

Consider your Four Step fund, your IRA, 401(k), and other restricted funds as part of the same whole asset allocation. Don't allocate the asset classes within each fund. Instead, allocate them by taking into consideration all your holdings together. If you've determined a mix of 80 percent stock, and 20 percent fixed income is your goal, you don't have to maintain that division within your Four Step fund, or your other funds such as 401(k)s. It's enough that your holdings as a whole represent that proportion.

## Chart F

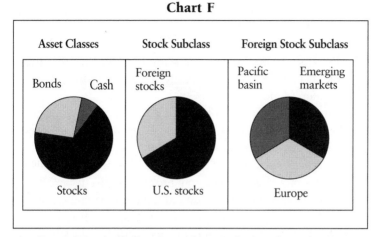

The allocator begins by dividing the portfolio into the three financial asset classes. In the second pie, he further diversifies by breaking each asset class into subclasses. The third pie is an example of an aggressive approach in the international subclass of the stock asset class.

Work out the percentages each asset class represents—real estate, stocks, bonds, cash—and hard assets such as collectibles, art, cars, and so on. Draw a pie chart; Worksheets 8 and 9 in Appendix I can help you do this. Form a judgment from the pie. Are your holdings dangerously overbalanced in one sector? Long-time homeowners might find they're overly exposed to fluctuations in the real-estate market. Stock investors might see that too much of their net worth is dedicated to that sector. And so forth. Redrawing the pie annually is a good habit, even if you don't have enough financial assets to allocate. It helps you see your financial profile as one picture, and keeps you from overcommitting your resources to one sector merely out of habit.

**Subdividing the sectors:** Chart F illustrates the way someone within ten years of retirement might want to allocate his or her financial assets, ignoring for this purpose hard assets such as real estate and antiques.

This is just step one. The investor now has to determine the allocation within each asset class. For example, the 60 percent of the portfolio devoted to stocks will be invested in what way? Growth? International? So another pie chart is devised to represent the stock sector; and perhaps another one after that if the portfolio is large enough, and the investor seeks further diversification among fund types.

By structuring the portfolio in this way, the investor gains a handle on his or her affairs. Since some experts attribute 90 percent of an investor's success to the right asset allocation rather than a particular selection of investments, this discipline deserves your attention, even though you probably won't have enough money for a while to allocate around. By the time you do, financial products and times will have changed, so use these charts as illustrations only; when it's time to begin actually allocating your assets, seek up-to-date information.

**Don't get stupid:** I want to emphasize that chasing highfliers should *never* be the core of your retirement fund. Appropriate risk does not mean reckless risk. The 10 percent program is designed to approximate the historical returns of American businesses as reflected by the S&P 500 over the past six decades. The 12 percent program moves up the risk ladder, in return for a lower present cost (monthly contribution). You'll spend less now in the 12 percent program, but the risk of not making your goal in the end is higher. Once again, your choice.

Look at any long-term return over 12 percent as luck. Over the last decade, stocks and bonds have soared. Double-digit returns in both categories were the norm. You, the longest of long-term investors, will be pleased at above-average returns, because you know you'll need them to average out the slumps when the market underperforms its average, as it will do many times over your investment lifetime. You won't be so stupid as to adopt a 15 or 20 percent return as your long-term goal, because you won't get it, over time.

**About chumps and monkeys:** P. T. Barnum said a sucker is born every minute, and never is it truer than in the financial world. That's because, as you've already guessed, even regulated financial markets offer a ripe opportunity for gamblers (who are politely called speculators) to do their thing. Every so often, just like in Las Vegas, someone gets lucky. Word gets around. More try their luck. Most flame out. There are just enough lucky strikes to keep the stupid interested.

All speculative theories occasionally bear fruit, or they'd die on the vine. Psychologists have established that to keep the suckers coming, you don't need a preponderance of reward; you don't even need the rewards to equal the losses. An occasional reward will do the trick—to the gambling personality. Research psychologists discovered this principle with lab animals. In order to keep the animal pressing the lever, a pellet of food was offered. Researchers sought to establish how few pellets they could get away with supplying, before the animal wised up and quit pushing the lever. They learned that after a consistent run of zero rewards, the animals, indeed, gave up. But if, at random and occasional intervals, a reward was provided, the animals continued to press the lever indefinitely. Walk into any casino and watch the monkeys pulling the levers, in the service of their occasional reward.

The same principle applies to investing. It's awfully easy to cross the line between investing and speculating. If you have buckets of money, and enjoy putting 1 or 2 percent at risk, I have no quarrel with you. But the Four Step programs have no place for these kinds of fun and games, so keep those funds, at least, on the straight and narrow. They have one job to do, and, if you keep the numbers at 10 or 12 percent, they'll do that job without the need for speculation. If market performances fall well below historical levels, and continue to do so throughout decades, you'll do better to lower your expectations of a million (you'll still have plenty), than you will to abandon investing and turn to speculation. You don't want to be the monkey.

The Four Step program is going to make you seriously rich. Long before retirement you will have hundreds of thousands of dollars in your IRA or 401(k). Certain other people will hope to get their hands on your money by offering you all sorts of dubious ways to get richer quicker. Lately, investment "opportunities" offered by phone have been popular, especially in the wireless communication field.

Remember, the government *never* approves an IRA investment. It merely certifies that the technicalities are met for tax purposes. Someone who says an "investment" is a "government-approved" IRA should not be trusted.

One threat to your growing wealth can hardly be classified as risk, since—like inflation—it's a virtual certainty. I'm talking about taxes here, and failing steps on your part, you'll never make your goal with Uncle Sam as your everyday partner. Step Three, as you know, slays the tax dragon through the use of tax-deferred programs, the subject of the next chapter.

 *Self-Test*
## Chapter 5

1. Which of these risks is accounted for in the Four Step plans?
   **a.** inflation
   **b.** stock-market cycles
   **c.** taxes
   **d.** a, b, and c

2. Cumulative, rather than annualized yield, is the better measure:

   ☐ True     ☐ False

3. The beta is one way to measure an investment's:
   **a.** historical risk
   **b.** performance
   **c.** yield
   **d.** cost

4. About how much of the risk of stock investing can be avoided through diversity?

    **a.** 30%
    **b.** 50%
    **c.** 70%
    **d.** 99%

5. A bear market is generally described as this much of a drop:
    **a.** 10%
    **b.** 15%
    **c.** 20%
    **d.** 50%

6. Historically, the U.S. stock markets have risen what percentage of the time:
    **a.** 80%
    **b.** 50%
    **c.** 95%
    **d.** 60%

7. Dollar-cost averaging is:
    **a.** a payroll deduction plan
    **b.** a way to reduce risk
    **c.** tailor-made for the Four Step plans
    **d.** b and c

8. The greatest risk slayer of all is:
    **a.** judgment
    **b.** time
    **c.** inside information
    **d.** low yields

9. The most successful investors are short-term market timers:

    ☐ True    ☐ False

10. Which of the following are zero-risk investments?
    **a.** bank CDs
    **b.** cash
    **c.** long-term bonds
    **d.** none of these

*Answers on Worksheet 15 in Appendix I*

# 6

# Falling in Love with Your 401(k)

*The alphabet soup of 401(k)s, IRAs, TSAs, SEPs, and Keoghs*

In the fabled land of Taxonia lived the good witch Glenda and her many delightful children. Glenda's oldest children were skinny and weak, because Glenda had no way to protect them from wicked old Uncle Sam, who crept in at midnight every April 15 and sucked their blood. Glenda tried hiding her children, but it was no good; thirsty Sam found them all and sucked their blood—and cut off their hands—just to teach Glenda a lesson.

Then Glenda discovered the power of her magic wand. As each new child was born, she waved her wand and blessed the child with a new name: IRA, 401(k), 403(b), SEP, and Keogh. Strange names, for sure, but Taxonia was a strange place. These children grew big and healthy, because they were surrounded by a magic shield—and even prowling Sam couldn't touch them.

But Glenda's magic wand protected her children only until they grew up. After years and years, when bloodthirsty Uncle Sam came for his due, Glenda couldn't shield her children anymore. Fortunately, by then, they were strong and muscular, and easily able to handle Sam. They even felt affection for some of Uncle Sam's many projects—roads, parks, schools, and the wilderness.

You live in a country like Taxonia, and since you're going to be very rich, your Uncle Sam sure does want to be your partner. Now, maybe you think he's kind of muscling in on you, and since your good uncle declines to support you in your old age, you think maybe you'd better keep those riches for yourself.

Good witch Glenda hears you, and agrees. Her magic wand will protect your investments, provided first, that you're employed; and second, that you'll save your tax-charmed fund for retirement.

Which is tailor-made for Step Three of the Four Step program. Step Three calls for your fund to be sheltered from taxes throughout its life. To recap what we said in Chapter Two under Step Three: In the early years, when your fund is small and earning little income, the tax shelter may seem unimportant to you. So what if you have to pay income tax on your $5,000 account? If it's earning 10 percent a year ($500), and you are taxed at 15 percent, your tax bill is hiked only $75. Even at 28 percent, you may feel

$140 per year on your $500 earnings is quite affordable. It may seem a reasonable price to pay for liquidity, that is, the ability to tap your fund for emergencies without having to pay the Internal Revenue Service a substantial penalty for early withdrawal of your retirement fund. But, in fact, the price is enormous.

As your unprotected taxable fund mounts, the taxes on it would become at least onerous. At $100,000, the taxes on your 10 percent earnings would be in the low thousands; at $500,000, thousands more. If you pay the taxes out of the fund itself, you'll be bleeding the life out of the god of compounding, which demands regular feedings to work its miracles. Periodic withdrawals destroy its power.

Aha!, you think. I'll beat the system by paying the taxes out of current income, leaving my fund to compound intact. But that makes no sense at all. You'll be paying more for taxes than you'll be paying into your Four Step fund; in effect, you will be doubling and tripling the cost of your program. And that's not smart.

You're going to have to bite the bullet here, and lock it away until you're sixty-seven. You'll be able to get at your funds penalty free as early as age 59 1/2 under all of Uncle Sam's giveaway programs, but since our Four Step plans call for compounding to age 67, you'll want to keep your fund compounding tax-deferred until then. You'll have other, taxable funds, and they'll be discussed in Chapter Ten. Those will be for your short-term goals, and for them you'll have to give thirsty Sam a little blood.

**First, a little history:** Before about a hundred years ago, old folks were pretty scarce. Life expectancies were short by today's standards, so people just stayed on the job until they dropped. Pensions, as a job benefit, were nearly unknown, and Social Security didn't exist. The lucky retiree was given a gold watch and was expected to have saved for his old age. If he died married, his widow was thrown on the mercy of her family—or charity. Funds for widows and orphans were serious business; many unfortunates starved to death without them, because survivor's benefits (either public or private) were rare.

Social Security, a mandatory system where workers and employers pay into an insurance-retirement fund, came to America in the mid-1930s, but was never meant to carry the retirement burden alone.

An adequately funded retirement is likened to a three-legged stool: Social Security, pension, and investment income. Social Security coverage is nearly universal now (some teachers and older civil servants being the major exception, and yes, Social Security will be there for you; see Chapter Twelve). Pensions are strong in most government jobs, but have never covered more than half the workers in the private sector. Investment income, the third leg, was meant to pick up the slack left by the short first (Social Security) leg and the weak second (pension) leg. Unfortunately, as lifetimes lengthened, people vastly underestimated the amount of funds needed to cover fifteen or twenty years of retirement. Old folks in droves were either swelling the welfare roles or, too deeply humiliated to apply for aid, were seen buying cat food, but not for any pets. A photo essay in a popular magazine depicting old men and women furtively buying and shoplifting pet food for their one daily meal woke up a shocked nation.

**Enter Uncle Sugar Daddy:** Congress, mostly in the 1970s, created a variety of tax-deferral programs to encourage people to save for the investment leg of their stool. Some are payroll deduction plans, some allow for employer contributions, all have annual participation limits, and—except for some IRAs—all lessen your tax bite two ways: by lowering current taxes by reducing annual income, and by deferring taxes on the fund's earnings until withdrawn.

All retirement savings programs feature tax deferral; some IRAs (discussed later) don't lower current taxes. Over time, the tax deferral is *much* more important than the other, since the money you would otherwise be paying Uncle Sam every April on the earnings from your fund stays in your account to compound happily for decades and decades. Because of compounding, the taxes deferred until later are not a one-for-one trade-off. In other words, it's not a matter of paying your dollar now or paying it later. It's much, much better than that.

Earlier I said the price for keeping your fund liquid (that is, taxable) is enormous. I said someone paying 28 percent would owe $140 tax on the $500 earned by a $5,000 taxable account, and that doesn't seem like an awful lot. But defer paying that $140 until retirement in forty years, and it will grow to $7,518. If you withdraw that $7,518 when you're sixty-seven, you will owe income tax on all of it, according to your tax bracket at that time. If that's 28 percent, your tax will be $2,105. Pay the tax man his due, and you'll still have $5,413 to spend on yourself! That's just the first $140. Think of the hundreds and thousands of tax dollars down the line, breeding more dollars for you to safari through Africa in luxury in your retirement. Uncle Sugar Daddy—no kidding.

**The Golden IRA:** An individual retirement account, or IRA, like all of these tax-deferred retirement savings plans, is just Glenda's blessing that shields your account from current taxes. An IRA is not a *type* of investment; it's more like a shield that wraps around your investment, deflecting the tax attacks. Your IRA can be in mutual funds (including international funds), individual stock or bond offerings, bank accounts, certain insurance products—most investments, in fact, except hard assets such as collectibles, art, and antiques. When you open an account as an IRA, you are simply instructing the financial institution to report the account's earnings to the IRS in a certain way—a way that shields those earnings from being reported on your income tax return.

Anyone with employment or self-employment income, and/or alimony, can contribute $2,000 annually to an IRA, or 100 percent of earnings/alimony, whichever is lower. Spouses who both work *each* have the $2,000 limit; if only one works, $2,250 is the limit for the couple. These things change; check current rules.

The institution that holds your IRA (called a custodian, or trustee, for IRA purposes) is required to let the IRS know if you try to sneak some of your IRA out early (generally, absent an IRS-defined hardship, before age 59 1/2). Premature withdrawals are *very* expensive. The amount withdrawn is added to your current income for tax purposes, plus an additional 10 percent of the withdrawal is assessed as a penalty. Your $10,000 withdrawal from your IRA at age thirty-five, for example, to buy a house, will be added to your $33,000 income from your job, raising your taxable income to $43,000, for a horrid additional tax of $2,800 (at 28 percent), plus a $1,000 penalty (10 percent of the amount withdrawn). You've lost 38 percent of your withdrawal to Uncle Sam—and that's before your state takes its whack. A 40 percent loss is no way to make your fortune. After state taxes, you'll be lucky to walk away with $6,000 of your original $10,000.

Uncle Sugar won't let you borrow from your IRA; nor can you use it as collateral for a loan. It's best to consider your IRA to be what it's intended for: retirement money.

From time to time Congress considers bills that would permit penalty-free withdrawal of IRA funds for such things as first-home down payment, medical emergency, or college tuition. By the time it matters to you, a variation of these may be law. Always double-check the current status of any law, policy, or regulation discussed in these pages. Things are forever changing, especially in the wonderful world of Taxonia.

At this writing, all IRAs qualify for the immensely valuable second feature of these federal tax-deferral programs: The money earned in the account compounds tax free until withdrawn. Some also qualify for the first feature, meaning the taxpayer can deduct the amount contributed to the IRA from current income, thus lowering the annual tax bill. If your taxable income, for example, is $23,000, at 15 percent your taxes would be $3,450. If you qualify to deduct your $2,000 IRA contribution, your income falls to $21,000, and your taxes to $3,150, a tax subsidy of $300. In other words, $300 of your tax dollars goes into your own account rather than Uncle Sam's deep pockets, to compound happily for decades.

Rich and Jennifer were both aspiring millionaires. Both invested $2,000 in a stock-index mutual fund, earning an annual average of 10 percent. But Rich "wrapped" his account in an IRA and Jennifer

## Chart G

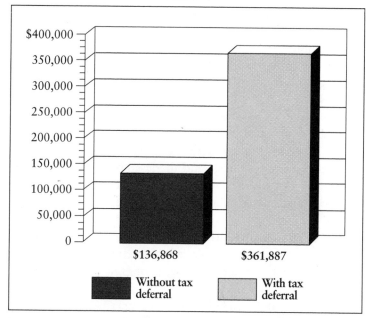

*$2,000 invested annually for 30 years at 10% in an IRA rewards the investor with over $225,000 more than the same investment in a taxable account (31% taxes are assumed).*

did not. Since both were in the 36 percent tax bracket, Jennifer's $2,000 contribution shrank to $1,280, after taxes—and the $128 it earned was also chopped by 36 percent, so her actual return was only $82, or 4.1 percent—not enough to get to that million. Rich reaped the entire 10 percent.

Whether or not your IRA will be tax-deductible depends on whether you are a participant in a qualified retirement program. Generally, this means a pension. If neither you nor your spouse is a member of such a program (your W-2, distributed to you by your employer in January, will tell you whether you are), under current (1995) tax regulations your IRA will be tax-deductible, no matter how high your income. If you or your spouse is in a qualified retirement program, then your IRA is fully deductible only if your income falls below a certain level, currently around $40,000 (joint) and $25,000 (single). Up to $50,000 (joint) and $35,000 (single), your IRA will be partially deductible, under 1995 law.

At withdrawal, only those portions of your IRA that you deducted from your taxes will be taxed, along with all accumulated earnings. If, because of pension coverage, you made IRA contributions that were not deductible from your annual income, you will not have to pay taxes on them at withdrawal. *Your nondeductible contributions will be tax free.*

Don't forget, though, that deductibility is only one of two tax benefits conferred by IRAs, and the less important one at that. Open your IRA whether or not its deductible, and let those tax-deferred dollars make your Four Step fund glitter.

**401(k)s, TSAs, and 403(b)s:** Sections 401(k) and 403(b) of the Internal Revenue Code defer federal income taxes, including those on capital gains, on voluntary savings plans offered by employers that qualify under these sections of the tax code. Like IRAs, funds withdrawn from these accounts before age 59 1/2 (with IRS-defined hardship exceptions) carry a 10 percent penalty. Withdrawals are added to current income, and taxed at whatever is the taxpayer's rate. Employers are not required to offer these plans, and if yours doesn't, you can't set one up for yourself. Most employers match employees' contributions at a certain rate, but some don't.

Unlike some IRAs, all of these plans reduce your taxable income as well as defer taxes on the earnings. You get the double whammy, which does good things for your bottom line now, and fabulous things for it after compounding.

Generally, 401(k)s are offered by private employers; 403(b)s and tax-sheltered annuities (TSAs, a variety of 403(b)) are offered by school districts, churches, and nonprofit organizations. None are available to the self-employed (but see SEPs and Keoghs, following). There are technical differences between the plans, including maximum annual contributions, but the basics are the same. In all types, your contribution is made by payroll deduction, and the investment you choose must be "offered" by your benefits department. Sometimes that means your employer's offerings are woeful, because he or she has been sold a bill of goods by some salesperson, and has stuck you with a choice of three or four highly loaded losers, like the Super-Testosteroney fund, perhaps. If this is your situation, it's very much worth your while to pressure your employer to broaden the selection. You don't want your Four Step fund burdened by performance problems and ongoing, loads. All the major mutual fund families will be eager to cooperate with your payroll department in order to qualify.

If you're stuck with lousy 401(k) choices that don't have a prayer of meeting your Four Step objectives of net 10 or 12 percent average annual return, then use your IRA for your Four Step fund, at least up to the current annual $2,000 limit. Then use your second-rate 401(k) plan for the remainder, and hope to talk your boss into better choices before too many years pass. When you leave your job, you can roll your 401(k) or 403(b) funds into a "roll-over" IRA, in a fund of your choosing.

**SEP-IRAs and Keoghs:** The Simplified Employee Pension (SEP) and the Keogh plan are tax-deferred retirement saving plans for small employers, including the self-employed. Both allow contributions to grow tax-deferred, and both lower taxable income in the year the contribution is made. If you're self-employed and setting one up for yourself, your investment options are very broad. Most fund families, banks, and brokerages will be thrilled to send you the forms and make it as easy for you as possible. Certain Keoghs permit you to put away as much as 25 percent of your income; SEPs (also known as SEP-IRAs) top out at about 15 percent. For the self-employed person, or the employee in a small company offering such a plan, these are great ways to accumulate a tax-deferred Four Step fund.

If you work in a small company that doesn't offer 401(k)s or their like, talk your employer into offering SEPs or Keoghs. A SEP does not require employer contributions, so there really is no reason for an employer to refuse to offer this valuable benefit. There need be no setup hassle or expense, since no-load mutual funds will happily do the paperwork and administer the SEP, charging only a low custodial fee of perhaps $10 per year. Your payroll department need only send the fund your money.

**Government employees:** Most state and all federal employees can contribute to similar tax-deferred savings programs. Uncle Sam's version is the Thrift Savings Plan, or TSP. A healthy 73 percent of federal workers in the Federal Employees Retirement System (FERS) contribute to a TSP by payroll deduction. It is estimated that the nonparticipants will have only one-third to one-half of the retirement income as their thrifty counterparts. If you're a federal employee, here's the place for your Four Step plan. You want the C plan (stocks). The F plan is bonds, and the G fund is government bonds.

**Uncle Sam's money-making machine:** Your tax-deferred savings plan is a miracle maker if all its features are exploited. Shirley invested in Generic Common Fund (GCF), a fictional mutual fund earning an average of 9 percent annually. Since GCF is a no-load fund, Shirley called the company and then mailed in her contributions monthly. She did not protect her fund from taxes. John bought the very same fund through his 401(k); his employer matched his contributions fifty cents on the dollar. Shirley's 9 percent shriveled to 6.48 percent after the 28 percent tax bite, but John got a whopping 63.5 percent return by investing in the very same fund, after taking tax benefits and his employer's 50 percent match into consideration. With the employer's match, John starts off with a 50 percent return, even if the GCF fund earns nothing! Add to that the two ways 401(k)s reduce taxes, and just watch John's fund smoke! Since our Four Step funds are looking for 10 and 12 percent, those future millionaires who have access to employer-matched plans should exploit them to the limit. An employer match of only ten cents on the dollar starts you off with 10 percent, before the horses are out of the gate. It's a huge leg up on Step Two of your plan, and since taxes

## Chart H

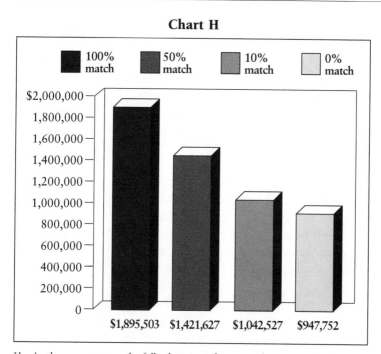

| 100% match | 50% match | 10% match | 0% match |
| --- | --- | --- | --- |
| $1,895,503 | $1,421,627 | $1,042,527 | $947,752 |

*Here's why you want to take full advantage of your employer's 401(k) match: A 401(k) with a dollar for dollar (100%) employer's match will be worth $947,751 more when a 24-year-old reaches age 67, than one with no employer's match, assuming a base of $100 per month, invested at 10%.*

are deferred, it takes care of Step Three as well. From a risk-strategy point of view, an employer's match of even 10 percent means you can afford to increase your potential returns by climbing the risk curve. A 50 percent match argues for (prudent) aggressive investing on your part, at least while in your twenties and thirties, since even if the market cratered by one-third, you'd still be above water.

A twenty-four-year-old Modest Millionaire needs to invest $106 per month at 10 percent annual average to meet our goal. Let's say that's Art, and he is looking over nearly identical job offers, with two differences: Job A requires a half-hour commute and offers a 401(k) plan with a 50 percent employer's match.

Job B has a ten-minute commute and a 401(k) with a 10 percent match. Assuming all else is equal, Art should take the commute, because when Art retires at sixty-seven, Job A's 401(k) will be $401,847 richer than Job B's, thanks to Employer A's higher contribution. More free money for Art.

Nearly one-third of employees eligible to participate in tax-deferred savings plans do not do so. Future millionaires, of course, are not among them.

**Investment options:** Your tax-deferred plan's options may be wide and wonderful, or narrow and horrible. All should offer at least one stock mutual fund, and that is where you want your Four Step money. It's been established that 401(k) investors (or those with similar savings plans) are far too conservative in their choices, overwhelmingly choosing guaranteed investment contracts (GICs), the insurance industry's answer to bank CDs (without the government insurance) and money-market funds.

The fact that you're stuck with your employer's offerings does not relieve you of the obligation of researching your options. If the stock fund is truly awful—as compared against funds with similar objectives, not those with a more aggressive focus—max out your IRA in the fund of your choice with your Four Step payments, leaving the 401(k) to pick up the remainder. Of course, if your employer contributes to your plan, you'll want to take full advantage of that free money. A dollar-for-dollar match starts you out with a 100 percent gain, before the fund even earns one cent. The fund would have to lose half your money before it eroded your out-of-pocket funds. People have lost half their capital in a handful of hapless mutual funds, so don't discount the possibility when looking over your 401(k) fund's history. If your employer offers an S&P 500 index stock fund, and many do, that's probably the best place to start. At least until you've tracked the competing funds for a couple of years or so and compared costs.

**Don't hitch your wagon to one star:** Large, publicly traded companies often include their own stock as one 401(k) investment option. Sometimes the employer contribution is tied to that selection. All companies carry single-company risk, as explained in the chapter on risk, including the one you work for. It's a poor idea to stake more than 10 percent of your holdings on any one company.

Your IRA, 401(k), and all the others can be spread among many different investments. If you want, you can spread the, say, $4,000 IRA in your account among four or more funds, but the custodial fees add up. A $10 annual charge on the $4,000 can become $40 on four accounts, so it's better, at least until your account gets to $15,000 or so, to keep it in one or two accounts, at most.

**Regulation 404(c):** Section 404(c) of the Internal Revenue Code sets standards for employers offering 401(k)s. They aren't mandatory, but are meant to protect employers who comply with them from liability for poorly managed voluntary savings programs. Under the 404(c) standards, an employer should:

- Offer at least three investment options, at different levels of risk.
- Inform employees about the options, and educate them on the appropriateness of each.
- Permit employees to switch between their options at least quarterly.
- Reeducate employees when options change.
- Make available the options' prospectuses.

You can sue your employer for mismanagement of your plan. That obviously includes malfeasance, such as embezzlement or receiving kickbacks from the benefits salesperson; negligence, such as selecting highly loaded, historically lousy performers on the word of a high-pressure salespitch; and poor plan performance related to the employer's failure to observe one of the 404(c) standards.

**Borrowing from yourself:** More than half of 401(k)s permit their owner to borrow up to half the funds, at a reasonable interest rate of prime plus 1 percent (the prime rate is the interest rate banks charge their best [biggest] clients). Some 403(b)s also permit borrowing, but generally not those held in mutual funds. Keoghs, IRAs, and SEPs do not. Of course, compounding is stopped in its tracks for the amount borrowed, so going this route is not for your Four Step money.

**Hardship withdrawals:** You can sometimes withdraw your 401(k) and 403(b) funds prematurely, in the event of genuine hardships. Generally, these are medical emergencies, and they must fit the IRS's and your plan's narrow requirements. Such a withdrawal will interrupt your Four Step program, of course, but a true hardship should come first. Be comforted that your Four Step program, even though presumably tied up for decades, can be there for you in a disaster.

IRAs, SEPs, and Keoghs can always be withdrawn prematurely, but with a 10 percent penalty, except that in the case of death or IRS-defined disability, there is no penalty for early withdrawal.

**Beware the lump-sum trap:** If you change jobs, and your tax-deferred money becomes available to you in a lump sum, you will have a short period of time to roll it over into another 401(k) or roll-over IRA. After that, the lump sum will be treated as a premature withdrawal and taxed and penalized accordingly. Don't use the lump sum to pay off debt unless you are over your head and approaching bankruptcy, or unless you are *dead positive* you will convert the debt payments into your investment program all the way to retirement. Same goes for your IRA. Tax-deferred money in IRAs, 401(k)s, and the like is *very* expensive money to spend before age 59 1/2, and the younger you are, the more expensive it is over time. Most unfortunately, government surveys establish that the vast majority of tax-deferred money taken as a lump sum on job changes never makes it into another tax-deferred account. It is taxed and penalized as an early withdrawal.

Let's say you have $4,000 owing on your car, and $3,500 on your Visa. Your monthly payments on the two debts total $650, and you'd love to get out from under. For young people, delay in investing in order to pay down debt squanders the best chance you have to win the compounding game. Plundering your investments to pay off debt is much more costly for the young, for the same reason (unless, of course, you are up against the wall, and can't make your payments). You want that money making money.

Again, when you prematurely withdraw tax-deferred money, it is added to your annual income for tax reasons—and you pay the 10 percent penalty as well. To pay off your $7,500 debt from your IRA or 401(k), you would need $10,000 if you pay 15 percent in taxes, and more than $12,000 if you pay 28 percent including the penalty, but not including any state taxes and penalties. Left alone, that $10,000 in a thirty-two-year-old's tax-deferred account averaging 10 percent will be worth $360,563 at his or her retirement at age sixty-seven; for a twenty-seven-year-old, that's $593,238. The paid-up car? Nearly worthless after ten years. The credit card? Balance zero, nothing more. Of course, if you're sure you'll add the $650 payments to your tax-deferred savings, then you might be ahead. That same twenty-seven-year-old, if he or she puts $650 a month away at 10 percent instead of the $143 that will make $1 million, will have more than $4.5 million by age sixty-seven—the thirty-two-year-old, more than $2.5 million. At this time, you can only put $2,000 per year in an IRA, but over $9,000 in a 401(k).

**If you change your job:** If you leave your job, some employers will let you keep your funds in the plan. Others require you remove it. You can transfer it directly to your new employer's 401(k), or to a roll-over IRA to continue your fund tax-deferred. The roll-over IRA differs from a regular IRA in that the limit is waived for the rolled-over funds. Rollovers, like regular IRAs, can be placed in most common investments. Simply have the mutual fund, brokerage, or bank send you the forms, then they will have the money transferred directly from your 401(k) to the roll-over IRA.

**Warning:** If you take the money yourself, then set up the IRA—or deposit it in your new 401(k)—your employer is required to withhold 20 percent of your funds for the IRS. At tax time, you'll get it back as a refund, but here's the dilemma: Your 401(k) funds, in order to escape the taxes and penalties on premature withdrawals, have to be put into the roll-over IRA—or another 401(k)—within sixty days. But since your employer withheld 20 percent, you only have 80 percent in hand to get into a qualified account within that time period. You will have to come up with the other 20 percent yourself, or pay taxes and a penalty on it as a premature withdrawal. The fact that later you will get the 20 percent back as a tax refund is small comfort. To avoid this mess, *be sure you have your 401(k) fund transferred directly to the new 401(k) or roll-over IRA.* The receiving financial institution will happily handle the transfer for you. Just ask.

Unlike 401(k)s, you can withdraw IRA funds, take custody of them yourself, and return them to another IRA within sixty days, tax and penalty free. There will be no withholding. You must change financial institutions, and you can only do this once a year; there is no annual limit on direct transfers of IRAs between custodial institutions.

**If you don't have a 401(k):** Ninety-five percent of large and medium employers offer 401(k)s or their equivalent, which means that some Four Step participants will not have access to Uncle Sugar's magical money-making machine. But Step Three of the Four Steps requires that the fund be tax-deferred until retirement. If your Four Step payments will fit into your IRA's annual limit, you're set. The Hot Starters and Golden IRAs have no problem, because their monthly payments will come under the IRA limit; so too, the Modest Millionaires under age twenty-nine and the Roller Coasters under thirty-four. The worst-case scenario is the thirty-five-year-old Modest Millionaire, who has more to shelter annually than the amount he or she puts in the IRA. With a 401(k) or equivalent, the problem is solved. The self-employed among you can set up a SEP or Keogh to pick up the extra, and some of you will be able to talk your employer into setting up a SEP, Keogh, or 401(k).

But some of you will have no recourse other than to look elsewhere to invest your excess Four Step payments. Tax-exempt vehicles, like municipal bond funds, won't earn enough to make you a million, and tax-deferred government issues such as EE savings bonds won't do the job either. You might give some consideration to a variable annuity, which will tie up your funds until age 59 1/2 like the other plans, and will compound tax-deferred. In Chapter Eight we'll talk about EEs, variables, zeros, and other instruments.

**The downside to Uncle Sugar's generosity:** The voluntary savings plans we've been discussing were designed to supplement the pension and Social Security legs of the three-legged retirement income stool. Remember, they were supposed to supply the third leg, that of investment income. Unfortunately, since pensions aren't mandatory, the advent of the 401(k) and its kin encouraged droves of employers to eliminate their traditional pensions in favor of the voluntary savings plans. Traditional pensions are funded by the employer; voluntary savings plans are principally funded by the employee, with some contribution by the employer common but not universal. This trend shifts the burden of retirement costs from employers to employees, so it's no wonder the corporate world has climbed on board.

This is ominous news for you, since the generation most affected is yours; in fact, the young white male has the most to lose under this trend, since it was he who was most likely to qualify for a traditional pension in the first place.

The trend away from traditional pensions is just the first negative. Voluntary plans are also deeply discriminatory against the lower-paid worker (and therefore, youth, women, minorities, recent immigrants, and the disabled). Congress, through these programs, gives more to the rich than the poor. Take four Golden IRA members, each with $30,000 in their Four Step fund, and each earning $3,000 per year on the investment. The IRA shelter saves the lowest-paid worker (with taxes of 15 percent) $450 in taxes which would otherwise be owed; the 28 percenter, $840; the 31 percenter, $930; the 36 percenter, $1,080; and at 39.6 percent, the payback from Uncle Sam on a $3,000 outlay is an enticing $1,188. Congress's carrot is much sweeter at the high end—so much sweeter, in fact, that it's been widely observed that most IRA and 401(k) participants come from the higher tax brackets. The lower-paid worker not only can't afford to invest, but he or she is also less rewarded by our kindly Congress for doing so. This short-sighted policy results in the obvious: more welfare bucks for the elderly poor who can't make it on Social Security alone.

Finally, traditional pensions are guaranteed by a government insurance fund. If the company goes bankrupt, or the pension plan collapses, the federal Pension Benefit Guaranty Corporation will make good on the benefits up to a limit of around $30,000 per year. The 401(k)s et al. are not included in this program.

Your Four Step plan is designed to take advantage of these programs, but a fat pension and a nice Social Security check should be in place to help with the load. As noted earlier, one million dollars today will buy about $60,000 annual income at a responsible 6 percent rate of return. If you protect your fund from inflation by adhering to Step Four, you can expect a purchasing power of about that much when you retire. That's a comfortable income, but nothing to holler about. Add a few thousand per year of Social Security, and a few more in a pension, and your older years begin to look pretty good.

**Another way to save taxes:** Municipal bond mutual funds (tax-exempt bond funds) offer freedom from federal income taxes and, in certain funds, state income taxes as well. Anyone can invest any amount in municipal bond funds; there's no annual limit, nor do you have to be employed. There's no penalty for withdrawal at any time, and money in a tax-exempt fund avoids the tax, unlike IRAs, 401(k)s, and the like, which simply defer it until withdrawal. Why isn't this a better way to go than IRAs or 401(k)s?

You need your money to grow more, that's why. Municipals make a lot of sense for people in a high tax bracket (at least 28 percent, better if higher) who need income, not growth. Municipals pay interest below market rates, so their tax-exempt feature makes them desirable to people in high tax brackets.

Municipals are not as safe as federal government instruments, because state and local governments can't print money to pay off their obligations, unlike the United States. If Uncle Sam gets into a bind, he has an almost unlimited ability to raise taxes. State and local governments are more limited in that respect, so every now and then they default on their bonds.

Old friends Dave and Sandy, for example, were looking for tax-exempt income, because each was in the 31 percent federal tax bracket. They'd been friends for years, and enjoyed spending afternoons together at the ballpark, which was always nearly sold-out. Under threat by the baseball team to leave town unless a new stadium was built, the citizenry of Fantown voted to build a spanking new stadium, financed by a bond sale. The bonds would be repaid by a surcharge on tickets sold to every event in the stadium. Sandy, ever loyal to the team, bought $50,000 of the bonds, which had a coupon rate of 6 percent over twenty years. Dave put $50,000 into ten-year bonds, also issued by Fantown at 6 percent, to build a new public hospital. The hospital bonds would be paid off out of Fantown's general revenues, and were backed by the city itself. Alas, for Sandy, the stadium far exceeded cost estimates, ticket prices soared, attendance dropped, and the project ended up in the hole. It never generated enough to retire the bonds, so the stadium bonds defaulted.

Sandy took a bath because she'd foolishly bought a type of municipal bond known as a revenue bond. Revenue bonds, backed by the money generated by the project itself, are as good as the enterprise underlying them. They are generally *not* backed by government money beyond the project revenue. Dave, on the other hand, received his interest on time, and his principal back at maturity, even though the hospital project never made money for Fantown. The hospital bonds were general obligation bonds (known as GOs), and they were paid out of the city's general fund. So long as the city remained solvent, its GOs would be paid.

Fantown could borrow from Dave and Sandy at lower rates than the bond market offered generally, because its coupons were exempt from federal income tax. Dave also owned a $10,000 long-term Suds 'n Suds bond paying 8 percent. When he received $800 interest, he had to pay tax on it at his 31 percent rate, which reduced his $800 to $552. His income from Fantown, of course, was tax-exempt. As a result, Fantown was able to sell its bonds to high-bracket taxpayers like Dave at a lower interest rate than taxable issuers, such as Suds 'n Suds—and the U.S. government. Suds 'n Suds paid Dave 8 percent to generate that taxable $800; Fantown paid Dave 6 percent to generate $600. Since Fantown's $600 beat Suds 'n Suds after-tax $552, Dave and other tax-shy investors were willing to buy Fantown bonds.

Obviously for investors in lower tax brackets, Fantown's deal doesn't make sense. Someone paying 28 percent in taxes would get $576 from their taxable bond after taxes, close enough to Fantown's $600 to give Fantown's creditworthiness a hard look. Someone paying 15 percent would be better off buying the taxable bond, and paying taxes on it, since they'd end up with $680 after taxes.

None of the Four Step programs can get you to your goal on the rates paid by creditworthy municipals over the long term. In an IRA, 401(k), and the like, you have the freedom to select higher-paying vehicles—almost anything you'd like, even high-flying funds, assuming your employer cooperates by offering a good selection—and deferring taxes on them by wrapping them in good witch Glenda's magic IRA or 401(k) package. That's why your Four Step plan depends on tax-deferred savings plans, despite their strictures, rather than low-paying tax-exempt bonds.

Taxes are one threat to your goal, and Step Three is designed to eliminate, or at least mitigate, that threat. Inflation is the other unavoidable monster, but it is easily defeated by Step Four. In the next chapter, you'll see how.

*Self-Test*
## Chapter 6

1. Under rules in effect at least through 1995, the annual IRA contribution limit for a one-earner married couple is:
   a. $2,000
   b. $2,250
   c. $3,000
   d. $4,000

2. Under 1995 law, all IRAs lower taxes by:
   a. deferring taxes on the earnings
   b. lowering annual taxable income
   c. exempting earnings from taxes forever
   d. a, b, and c

3. 401(k)s, 403(b)s, and TSAs are:
   a. types of securities
   b. guaranteed to be safe
   c. mediocre investments
   d. tax-deferred payroll deduction plans

4. A "10¢ on the dollar" employer contribution to a 401(k) earning 5% boosts the return to:
   a. 10%
   b. 12%
   c. 15%
   d. 50%

5. One-third of employees eligible to participate in a 401(k) don't:

   ☐ True    ☐ False

6. It is usually better to max out one's 401(k) before funding an IRA because:

    **a.** often the employer contributes
    **b.** it's both tax deductible and tax deferred
    **c.** the annual limit is higher
    **d.** a, b, and c

7. Spending your 401(k) on current needs when you change jobs is:
    **a.** lunacy
    **b.** very costly
    **c.** what most people do
    **d.** a, b, and c

8. 401(k)s, 403(b)s, and TSAs favor:
    **a.** women
    **b.** the lower paid
    **c.** the higher paid
    **d.** employees of small businesses

9. All 401(k)s and IRAs are insured by a government program:

    ☐ True    ☐ False

10. A revenue bond is safer than a general obligation bond:

    ☐ True    ☐ False

*Answers on Worksheet 15 in Appendix I*

# Keeping Your Million Worth a Million

*Fighting inflation the easy way*

W hen Suds 'n Suds was riding high, it raised its prices. It was the only game in town, everyone wanted to be there, so the market, in effect, bid up the price of the Suds 'n Suds's product. The five dollars that bought Rita two beers, a slice of pizza, and one load of wash a year ago, now only covers the beers and the wash. Rita's five dollars are worth 20 percent less at Suds 'n Suds after the rise in prices. In other words, she loses purchasing power. When this happens all over the economy, we have inflation. You can be sure that, like Rita, your five dollars today will buy fewer things next year.

Inflation is far more than theoretical. It doesn't destroy the numbers of dollars (or francs, or pesos) you own. What it does is annihilate purchasing power. Your $1 million will still have six nice, fat zeros in forty years, but it won't buy what $1 million does today. Economists usually describe inflation as too many dollars chasing too few goods. Although it is difficult to overstate inflation's relentless appetite, it is all too easy to underestimate the ease with which you can defeat it. Many young would-be investors are so intimidated by inflation that they throw in the towel before Round One. There is no need for this! Inflation is an easy opponent, one you will handily defeat in the last step of your Four Step program.

And just as compounding discriminates in favor of the young, inflation discriminates in favor of age. The fewer the years between you and your goal, the weaker is inflation's bite. Step Four of our Four Step program is vital because you're young.

**Step Four of the Four Step program:** In early January of every year, call your local reference librarian and ask what the rate of inflation was for the preceding calendar year. The *Wall Street Journal* will have that information as well, and probably your local newspaper's financial editor can supply it, if you can't find it elsewhere. You may find the inflation rate described as the consumer price index, or *CPI*. I'll talk more about the CPI later; for now it's enough for you to know that if the CPI rose 4.1 percent, that's the popularly quoted measure of inflation.

If inflation in the preceding year was 3.1 percent (the average over the past seventy years), increase your monthly Four Step contribution by that amount. A twenty-five-year-old Modest Millionaire would increase his or her $117 to $121, for instance. Do this every year, and you'll have nothing to fear from inflation. Your million then will be worth a million now. A little further on I explain what to do if the upward adjustment pushes your annual contributions beyond the maximums allowed in your tax-deferred accounts. Golden IRA participants, for example, cannot adjust their monthly contribution upward, because of the maximum annual IRA limit.

The Step Four annual adjustment is not going to make your program increase in cost over time, since your income should keep up with inflation as well, since wages and salaries usually do. The $121 this year should cost you about the same as $117 did the year earlier. In fact, because you are in your career-building years, you should receive real raises over this period, making even your inflation-adjusted Four Step payments an ever-diminishing percentage of your income. Those of you whose Four Step plan is in a payroll plan that deducts a percentage of your pay will find your contribution automatically rising with your raises. But raises don't always equal inflation, so keep an eye on the figures. Table 15 in Appendix II illustrates the adjustments called for in Step Four.

Here's what your fund will be worth on your sixty-seventh birthday, assuming a 4 percent inflation rate, and assuming you do not follow Step Four:

The twenty-nine-year-old's $211,848 looks like a lot of money, and it may be tempting to forget Step Four, and let inflation take its toll. That's an option, certainly. But that $211,848 (in today's dollars) will only generate $12,710 per year income, if invested at a responsible 6 percent. That may not be enough to supplement your Social Security—chances are better than good you won't have a pension worth counting—and it certainly won't buy you the lifestyle $60,000 will (in today's good dollars) with a real million in today's money to live on.

## Modest Millionaire 10 Percent Plan

| Age | If you *do not adjust for inflation* every year, then your million will be worth this at age 67: |
|-----|--------------------------------------------------------------------------------------------------|
| 20  | $148,011 |
| 21  | $155,014 |
| 22  | $160,669 |
| 23  | $166,842 |
| 24  | $173,346 |
| 25  | $180,016 |
| 26  | $188,159 |
| 27  | $194,673 |
| 28  | $203,554 |
| 29  | $211,848 |
| 30  | $219,508 |
| 31  | $228,624 |
| 32  | $237,784 |
| 33  | $247,743 |
| 34  | $257,297 |
| 35  | $267,975 |

The thirty-five-year-old is much better off than the twenty-year-old because inflation, like compounding, feeds on time. Skipping Step Four is less hazardous for those in their thirties than it is for those in their twenties, but still too much of a threat to take lightly at any age. Even eighty-five-year-olds are well-advised to protect themselves against inflation by investing about 25 percent of their portfolio in stocks. An eighty-five-year-old woman may well have ten or more years ahead of her, over which time her purchasing power might erode by over one-third, assuming an average inflation rate of 4 percent.

You Golden IRAs have a problem here, since your contribution is designed to take full advantage of the annual IRA maximum. When you raise your monthly contribution to adjust for inflation, you will go over the limit, and will have to find another place to shelter your dollars. Until the IRA maximum annual contribution is indexed to inflation, unfortunately, it loses value every year. If

## Roller Coaster 12 Percent Plan

| Age | If you *do not adjust for inflation* every year, then your million will be worth this at age 67: |
|-----|--------------------------------------------------------------------------------------------------|
| 20  | $149,196 |
| 35  | $268,705 |

Because these values are comparable to those for the Modest Millionaire 10 Percent Plan, ages 21 through 34 should refer to that table for a ballpark estimate.

you have access to a 401(k) or the like, you can put your increased contributions there. Otherwise, consider a taxable stock index mutual fund rather than a managed-growth mutual fund. Index funds throw off little taxable income compared to growth funds. There are also mutual funds that emphasize tax planning (aside from tax-exempt municipal bond funds, of course). If you must put some of your Four Step money in a taxable account, it may be worth your while to call the large fund families to see what they've got.

The Hot Start $50 payment is such a small amount that adjusting for inflation should pose no one any grief. But if you like the $50 figure, and also want to protect your fund against inflation, you Hot Starters can add to your lump sum instead. Since your annual contributions are a mere $600, you would figure the rate of inflation using that amount (at 4 percent that's $24 for the year), and add that to your fund in a lump sum at the beginning of the year. The next year, you would figure inflation on $624 ($25), the next on $649, and so forth.

Until Congress indexes the IRA program—that is, allows the maximum contribution to rise yearly automatically with inflation, you may run into a problem deferring taxes on your whole fund.

**Consumer price index:** Economists measure inflation by tracking the prices of a metaphorical market basket of goods and

### Golden IRA 10 Percent Plan

| Age | If you *do not adjust for inflation* every year, then your IRA will be worth this at age 67: |
|---|---|
| 20 | $347,431 |
| 21 | $327,022 |
| 22 | $307,782 |
| 23 | $289,645 |
| 24 | $272,545 |
| 25 | $256,422 |
| 26 | $241,219 |
| 27 | $226,882 |
| 28 | $213,360 |
| 29 | $200,605 |
| 30 | $188,573 |
| 31 | $177,221 |
| 32 | $166,508 |
| 33 | $156,397 |
| 34 | $146,853 |
| 35 | $137,842 |

services. They select a baseline year and measure from there. If the market basket costs 5 percent more next year than this, they report a 5 percent rise in the CPI. Although inflation has averaged 3.1 percent over the past several decades, the higher rates have come in the more recent years. It's prudent, therefore, when estimating future inflation, to use at least 4 percent as your guide.

The CPI is criticized by many as giving a distorted picture of inflation, since the market basket of goods and services measured does not represent everyone's market basket. The elderly have higher medical expenses and, perhaps, lower housing costs than younger generations. Mid-lifers have mortgages and tuition to cope with, while the young, the urban, and the poor are more likely to pay rent, and so on. Other indexes have been designed to fit these special cases, but the CPI remains the generally accepted measure of inflation, and if you use it for your Step Four adjustments, you'll do fine.

## Hot Start $50 Plan

| Age | If you *do not adjust for inflation* every year, then your million will be worth this at age 67: |
|-----|-----|
| 20 | $147,086 |
| 25 | $179,587 |
| 26 | $186,901 |
| 29 | $210,696 |
| 30 | $219,281 |
| 35 | $267,723 |

If your age is not represented here, refer to the Modest Millionaire chart for comparable figures.

**Inflation can be your friend:** If you have long-term fixed debt, such as a mortgage or student loans, count inflation as your buddy. Your fixed payments of $100 per month stay at $100 throughout the life of the loan. At 4 percent inflation, after only ten years, your $100 payment is only worth $60. Because your wages have risen with inflation, your nominal $100 hurts less, and you end up paying off your loan with cheaper dollars. Inflation smiles on debtors.

Inflation also favors incompetent business managers, whose bad deals end up looking profitable on paper, after inflation's loving touch. Executive Bill, for example, bought 1,000 heavy-duty washing machines for Suds 'n Suds for $178 apiece. In fact, he overpaid by $20 per machine. But rising prices on washing machines made him look good at promotion time, when he could point to comparable machines selling for $199.

**Cost-of-living adjustments:** Just as customer Rita lost out when Suds 'n Suds raised prices, Alex the bondholder lost out on his twenty-year Suds 'n Suds bond. His 8 percent interest payment remained fixed throughout the period at $400 per year. Alex was accustomed to spending the interest on a ski weekend in the Rockies, but as the years went by, Alex's $400 only covered half the weekend. For this reason, retirees living on fixed incomes from bonds suffer terribly under inflation. Wage earners suffer too, but generally wages keep up with the CPI through cost-of-living adjustments, or COLAs. Government pensions are generally adjusted for inflation (indexed to inflation); Social Security is, too. But private pensions seldom are. Stock dividends and prices, being products of businesses, loosely rise with inflation, but bond income does not. Retirees are more likely to have large bond components in their portfolios, which add to their vulnerability to inflation.

**A worthy opponent:** Step Four is worth your attention. Inflation's average of 3.1 percent over the past decades represented a bigger risk to investors than the usual risks of investing in stocks. There was no twenty-year period in this century in which stock prices shrank even 1 percent, let alone 50 percent, yet at an annual inflation rate of 3.1 percent, your investment is halved in just twenty-three years. In this century, anyway, inflation was nearly fifty times more threatening than the usual risks of investing in stocks.

The implication? Long-term investors, such as you, can increase the investment risk in your portfolios quite a lot before you equal inflation risk.

Time works in your favor for most investing risks, such as market risk and interest-rate risk. It works against you with inflation risk. That's why Step Four makes inflation fighting easy for you young investors—because it's easily the greatest risk you face over time.

Now that you've got the information you need to complete your Four Steps, it's time for you to become at least conversant with the varieties of investment vehicles available. Millionaires need to know these things, and the next chapter will get you on your way.

*Self-Test*
**Chapter 7**

1. Because of shorter lives, inflation discriminates in favor of:
    **a.** men
    **b.** older folks
    **c.** minorities
    **d.** a, b, and c

2. The CPI is:
    **a.** the Council on Practical Investing
    **b.** the consumer price index
    **c.** a common way to measure inflation
    **d.** b and c

3. Since 1926, annual inflation has averaged about:
    **a.** 2%
    **b.** 3%
    **c.** 4%
    **d.** 5%

4. Inflation is often described as too many dollars chasing too few goods:

    ☐ True    ☐ False

5. Debtors benefit from inflation because:
    **a.** they're lazy
    **b.** they pay back in cheaper dollars
    **c.** creditors adjust their debt downward
    **d.** none of these

6. Inflation worries bondholders because:
    **a.** they lend sound dollars and are repaid cheap ones
    **b.** bankruptcies rise
    **c.** defaults rise
    **d.** stocks crash

7. The best inflation protection over time has been found in:
    **a.** cash

    **b.** corporate bonds

    **c.** stocks

    **d.** government bonds

**8.** The CPI has been criticized for overstating inflation:

    ☐ True    ☐ False

**9.** A COLA is:

    **a.** a soda-pop stock

    **b.** a measure of inflation

    **c.** a cost-of-living adjustment

    **d.** required by law on all wages

**10.** At its historical average, inflation cuts your investment value in half in:

    **a.** 23 years

    **b.** 30 years

    **c.** 15 years

    **d.** 50 years

*Answers on Worksheet 15 in Appendix I*

# The A to Z of Finance

*From annuities to zero coupons*

S tock mutual funds will be the mainstay of the early decades in your Four Step program, and you've learned how bonds work as well. That means that later you can begin allocating some of your portfolio to bonds to stabilize things as your time-horizon shortens.

But the financial universe is much larger than stocks, bonds, and mutual funds. Since you're headed for a fortune, you should know about alternative investments; decades down the line you might be interested in some of them. Even when you're just starting out, it's a good idea to be familiar with what's out there. Financial literacy is the first step to financial self-defense.

Here, then, are thumbnail sketches of the more familiar varieties of investments and trading techniques commonly available to the general public today. Most of them are pretty nifty niche products; unfortunately, they have been sold to the general public as competing on a level playing field with ordinary stocks, bonds, and the mutual funds that invest in stocks and bonds. When used for what they were designed for, most of these products do an excellent job. When sold to unsophisticated investors as ordinary investments, most are more costly, more risky, or less liquid than what's available in stocks, bonds, and mutual funds.

Sometimes a little information is a dangerous thing. The following sketches can't begin to describe the complexities of these financial matters. If something intrigues you, you must not act on the little bit given here, because surely it will lead you astray. Generally, these investments are *not* recommended for your Four Step portfolio—certainly not now, and probably not ever. But each has features that fit someone's needs, or they wouldn't be around. So here they are, from A to Z:

**American depository receipts (ADRs):** These certificates represent shares in companies located outside of the United States. This is an increasingly popular way for Americans to invest overseas, thus diversifying their portfolios. Dozens of companies are traded through ADRs, which are listed on the major stock exchanges. Examples of overseas businesses traded on U.S. stock exchanges via ADRs include Fiat, Chile Telefono, Honda Motor, KLM, Royal Bank of Scotland, and Sony. You can buy ADRs through your stockbroker.

**Annuities (fixed):** An annuity is an insurance product. Instead of paying a lump sum upon death (as with life insurance), most annuities will pay you a stream of income during your life. Some annuities pay benefits until death; others pay for a stated period of time, such as ten years. Many people buy annuities to supplement their Social Security, since the regularly paid benefits won't vary over their lifetimes, making the annuity a kind of surrogate pension.

The problems? Annuities are costly, and generally aren't very competitive when it comes to yield. The earnings on annuities are taxable when withdrawn. Since they are sold through financial planners and insurance agents, sales commissions (loads) are high. And annuities usually carry a heavy redemption fee, often as much as 8 percent of your investment, which often diminishes over time, perhaps six or eight years.

For women, annuities carry a special problem. Many annuities base their benefits on gender-biased actuarial tables, which means that a woman's (statistically) longer life causes her to receive lower benefits for the same premium a man pays. The difference can be substantial. It is also unfair, since no one knows if that particular woman will outlive the male life expectancy. Asking all women to be burdened, and all men to be favored, simply because 14 percent of women outlive most males is unjust. The U.S. Supreme Court agrees, and it has outlawed gender-biased annuity tables for annuities paid to employees (pensions). Privately sold annuities, however, are free to discriminate against their women customers in this way—and many, if not most, do.

What are annuities good for? A will, for example, may instruct the executor to pay "my beloved niece $500 every month for her lifetime." The executor doesn't want to keep the estate open for the niece's lifetime, so he pays for an annuity out of estate funds, then closes the estate. Fixed annuities are perfect for this kind of estate planning. Another kind of annuity—the variable annuity—is discussed later in this chapter.

**Bank certificates of deposit (CDs):** Banks and savings and loans (S&Ls) offer these certificates. Formally speaking, they are debt instruments, in that you loan your money to the institution for a period of time, in exchange for which the bank or S&L pays you interest. Usually, the longer you tie your funds up, the higher the interest. Unlike short-term corporate bonds—the chief competitors to CDs in the private sector—most bank and S&L CDs are insured up to $100,000 in the event the institution fails (total for all accounts under one name in one bank or S&L). In this sense, CDs are nearly risk free, which, of course, means lower returns. They suffer from opportunity risk and inflation risk, but not much more.

CDs are free of costs (loads, maintenance fees), so the stated yield should be your actual yield, less inflation and taxes. CDs differ from ordinary savings and checking accounts in that your funds are unavailable to you without penalty during the specified period.

CDs are appropriate for your emergency funds, in short-term ladders as discussed in Chapter Nine. In ordinary times, they will not net the 10 or 12 percent you'll need to make your Four Step goal.

**Collateralized mortgage obligations (CMOs):** These are complex, mortgage-based securities that are extremely sensitive to interest-rate fluctuations. They are members of a class of securities known as derivatives (discussed further on), and are not for the ordinary investor.

**Collectibles:** You've heard wonderful stories about baseball cards or early comics (or antiques or classic cars) escalating in price wondrously, and making their happy owners happier still. What we have here is pure capital gain. It's not a bad way at all to make money if you're over forty-five, but it is definitely no substitute for the silent work of earnings, compounded over and over, through the years.

Why over forty-five? Because compounding is a young person's game. It needs time. The over-the-hill-gang doesn't have the time to make it work miracles, so capital gain becomes more valuable. The mathematics of the Four Step plans rely on a steady feeding of your number into an investment yielding income and gain over time.

If your collection has a substantial track record (decades) of at least an average 10 percent gain in value every year, and if you add to your collection as faithfully as the Four Step plan dictates, then you might realize your goal by retirement. Your collectible, no matter how dear to you, is nearly worthless if an established secondary market for it doesn't exist, or if it hasn't yet stood the test of time (fifty or so years, at least). Also, consider the cost of warehousing and insuring your collection as it approaches a million dollars in value. And finally, never forget the fads and whims that punch the lights out on so many beloved collections of yore. The field is rife with fraud, forgery, and illiquidity.

Keep on collecting, if you like, as a hobby. When you do sell a piece for a gain, put the cash into your Four Step mutual fund. That's the young collector's way to make money compound into riches.

**Convertibles:** Convertible securities are hybrids. A convertible bond, or shares of preferred stock, can be converted at a predetermined price into the issuing company's common stock, so the convertible's price on the secondary market rises along with the underlying stock. These bonds provide the upside potential of the stock with lower risk, and pay a higher coupon rate than bonds of comparable credit quality. Like ordinary bonds (see below), they fall in value when interest rates rise. Convertible bonds are still bonds, so they are inappropriate for your Four Step plan, which requires stocks to realize its potential.

**Corporate bonds:** When a corporation like Suds 'n Suds needs to raise money, it can go to the bank or other institutional lender, or it can go to the public, by issuing IOUs, which are called bonds. The money you lend the company is called the principal. The interest the company pays you is called the coupon rate. Corporate bonds are not insured or guaranteed by the government, so they carry the risk that the company will go under and fail to pay the interest when due, or (gulp) even the principal at maturity. Bond-rating firms like Standard & Poor's and Moody's rate corporate bonds according to their creditworthiness. The higher the rating, the lower the interest. Bonds will be part of your portfolio when you get within twenty years or so of retirement. For now, they don't return enough to make your fortune.

**Derivatives:** A derivative, as its name suggests, is a security whose value is derived from another security or asset. Well-known derivatives include options and futures. Some companies, financial institutions, and mutual funds suffer losses when they misunderstand the behavior of newer types of derivatives when interest rates rise.

**Dividend reinvestment plans (DRIPs):** Certain stocks that permit their investors to reinvest their dividends automatically in new shares of the stock are known as DRIPs. Traditionally, companies pay their shareholders a cash dividend, which goes to the brokerage to be held in the client's cash account, or directly to the investor if he or she prefers. A growing number of listed stocks permit the DRIP option, which means that instead of a check, the stockholder will be credited with additional shares. Some companies charge for the privilege, and some brokerages charge a fee for DRIPs.

**EE savings bonds:** Uncle Sam makes it easy to buy U.S. bonds through the popular EE program. You can buy them from your friendly banker, or tell your boss to deduct them from your pay. EEs are sold for half their face value; in other words, $50 will get you a $100 bond. They pay all their interest when redeemed, rather than periodically. EE savings bonds are too conservative for young investors. They are for savers (rather than investors, who generally pursue more growth) who have no risk tolerance. You cannot reach your Four Step goal with EEs, but because they are cheap and easy to get, you might consider one as a gift for a godchild or other newborn. They will mature around college time, and are guaranteed to be there when needed. Most parents can escape income taxes on EEs they purchase if they are used to pay college tuition for the children (high-earning parents are taxed), but unless that tuition will come due in five or fewer years, you'd be better off building the college fund more aggressively.

**Futures contracts:** Laura was a Texas cattle rancher. She raised beef cattle on 10,000 acres of grazing land. Every spring she bought calves at the May auctions; every fall she shipped off 1,000 head to the meat packer. Laura needed money in the spring to buy calves, but she wouldn't have the cash to cover the purchase until the fall, when she delivered the steer to the packer. Her solution was to enter into a contract in April to sell the cattle for delivery in August. She got the cash in April, and would deliver the cattle later—in the future. Cattle are deemed a commodity, so Laura signed a commodity futures contract. Laura got the current (April) price for her cattle, say, 64¢ per pound.

Laura's deal was with a commodities dealer, Bob, who in no way intended to take delivery on 1,000 head of cattle. Bob operated through the Chicago Mercantile Exchange, one of a handful of commodities exchanges in the United States. Bob agreed to the 64¢ price because he thought cattle prices would go higher than that before August, so he'd be able to sell his contract to someone else for 68¢ per pound of beef on the hoof. Bob paid Laura when they signed the contract, so Laura was able to buy her new calves. She is obligated to deliver the 1,000 head in August, but until then she is out of the deal.

In May, the Mississippi flooded the Iowa cornfields, so corn used as fodder was scarce. When fodder prices soared, ranchers began dumping cattle on the market early, since they were too expensive to keep alive on grain. Because of this surplus, speculators guessed that by August, cattle would go for as low as 60¢ a pound.

Bob's 64¢ contract looked like a loser. Who'd buy it with cattle prices heading south? Jeannie, that's who. Jeannie worked for a nutrition watchdog agency, and learned that a report was about to be made public that established beef as the essential ingredient in a delightful sex life. Jeannie bet that cattle prices would soar, thanks to the scarcity of fall deliveries due to the earlier dumping because of corn prices. So in July, Jeannie paid Bob 67¢ a pound for the contract. The beef report was published and cattle futures soared, but only for two weeks. At that point, the Carrot Council reported that although beef was good for your sex life, you'd better enjoy it while you could, because beef eaters (as opposed to carrot eaters) died during sex one hundred times more often. Jeannie watched prices fall to 59¢ a pound. It was late July and delivery was due in August. Jeannie sold her contract for future delivery of 1,000 head of cattle to Frank, who paid 65¢ a pound, since more people chose good sex and an early death over a celibate life eating carrots. In August, Frank sold his contract to the meatpacker for 64¢ a pound, the going rate. Back in April, Laura had called it right, been paid, and been saved the grief of a summer of rising and falling beef prices, and their effects on her fortunes.

Apologies to cattle ranchers and commodities traders for the literary license taken in the technicalities of Laura's tale, but the principle holds: Futures contracts are entered into by suppliers of commodities in order to provide an element of certainty in their business. The price is settled months before the commodity is delivered, enabling the farmer (or other supplier) to get on with the business of farming free of the harrowing swings in prices as the delivery date nears. It's a hedge technique on the part of the supplier—a prudent, conservative business tactic.

Commodities traders, on the other hand, are pure speculators. They aren't involved in growing or supplying the product, nor do they intend to take delivery of the goods. They're in the middle, looking in their crystal balls to determine when to buy and sell.

Eighty percent of the time they guess wrong, but the successful traders stay in the game because their occasional spectacular gains make up for the losses and then some. Or anyway, that is their hope. Futures trading is not for beginners nor investors. It's a speculator's game, so keep your Four Step fund away from it.

**GinnieMaes:** The Government National Mortgage Association (GNMA, pronounced GinnieMae) buys mortgages from banks, packages them in $25,000 sets, and sells them to investors like you and me. GNMAs can be ordinary home mortgages, but investors are protected from the homeowner's default by the government's guarantee. GNMAs are popular among fixed-income investors, because they generally carry a higher yield than U.S. treasuries and are nearly as safe. When mortgage interest rates fall, homeowners rush to refinance, meaning the nice 9 percent GNMA you hold will be paid off five years early, leaving you with your principal back to reinvest at lower rates.

GNMA mutual funds avoid some of this problem through diversification of maturities, but they will suffer principal erosion when mortgage rates fall generally. A big advantage to a GNMA fund rather than purchasing a GNMA directly is that the initial purchase price for a fund is likely to be in the $1,000 to $3,000 range, rather than $25,000.

**Guaranteed Investment Contracts (GICs):** Insurance companies wanted to capture some of that money going into bank CDs, so they came up with GICs as their answer to the low-risk, low-yield arena. They are frequently offered as part of a 401(k) or 403(b) package, and unfortunately for the worker building a retirement fund, don't offer enough after inflation to do much of a job. Unlike CDs, GICs are not insured by the government, so they carry some risks that CDs do not—namely the risk of the insurer's failure.

**Initial Public Offerings:** Think of Suds 'n Suds: Mike, Mary, Steve, Joe, and Sue were the only owners, until they took Suds 'n

Suds public, meaning they offered shares in Suds 'n Suds to the public. Their first step was to find an underwriter who would set the offering price and manage the sale. The underwriter would guarantee the offering by promising to buy any shares not bought at the initial sale. The underwriter, an investment banker, set Suds 'n Suds price at $15, which was high enough to make money for Suds 'n Suds and its five owners, but low enough so that the underwriter wouldn't get stuck having to buy up over-priced stock. This hedging on the part of the underwriter when pricing the IPO often means it's set below market. People who buy Suds 'n Suds at $15 in the IPO expect to turn right around and sell it at $20 when it opens to the general market. Individual investors seldom get in on these deals, because promising IPOs are reserved by the underwriters for their best customers, which means institutional investors (pensions, mutual funds, insurance companies and large charitable foundations) for the most part.

So Mary and Mike, their three friends, and the favored institutional investors got Suds 'n Suds at its offering price of $15. In the next week, because of all the publicity surrounding the IPO, secondary buyers bid the price of the shares up to $28. Mary stayed on as chief executive officer and kept all her shares, riding her paper profits up to $90 per share, then finally getting the picture and selling her holdings at $10 per share before the stock became worthless in the bankruptcy.

As we know, months after the IPO, and years before Suds 'n Suds's sad demise, Mavis became one of its thousands of owners. Mavis bought her shares through her broker, who found them listed on a major stock exchange, selling for $21. It's been established that soon after the initial offering—and the feeding frenzy that follows in the next few days—most IPO stock prices fall, so the winners are the first buyers, usually institutions. Mavis, by waiting a few months, did the right thing. The poor jerk who instructs his broker to buy Suds 'n Suds as soon as it's listed on the exchange is almost always too late. Most advisers say to give a promising IPO a few months before you buy in, to let the froth blow off.

Some aggressive growth funds deal in IPOs, and that's the way for you to get a piece of the action, if you want it. You don't want individual IPOs for your Four Step fund, anyway; they bear all the risks of individual stock investing, plus some.

**Investment companies:** Mutual funds are often called investment companies in other countries. In the United States they are regulated under the Investment Company Act of 1940 (among others), but they are almost universally known as mutual funds. Investment companies are available all over the world, but U.S. residents are restricted by tax and securities regulations to those registered with the SEC. It is not impossible to buy an offshore fund, but the regulators and tax authorities make it difficult. It's best for U.S. investors who want an international play to do it through an international fund registered in the United States, which may well be managed in London, Tokyo, Hong Kong, or have representatives anywhere in the world.

**Leverage:** See Options for information on leverage.

**Life insurance:** Ordinary life insurance (that is, with a death benefit, not an annuity) is often sold as an investment that builds cash value, not just a death benefit. Don't be taken in. Life insurance is a useful product for just one thing, its death benefit. You want to get that, if you need it at all, as cheaply as possible, and that means term life insurance, not whole or universal life.

The difference in premiums for a $250,000 whole-life policy versus a $250,000 term-life policy could easily exceed a couple of thousand dollars a year. The insurance salesperson will tell you that the cash value building in the whole (or universal) life policy is a competitive investment, but it is not. Take the term policy, and invest the difference in premiums in your Four Step fund. You'll be ahead all the way—even at the same rate of interest quoted by the salesperson—because of the drag on the insurance cash value imposed by the high initial sales commissions and other expenses.

If you have no dependents, you probably don't need insurance, but if group life insurance is offered as a fringe benefit on your job for just a few dollars a month, you may as well take it. Name your favorite charity as the beneficiary if you have no one depending on you financially. This is a nice way to make a meaningful gift.

**Limited partnerships:** If Charlie, a contractor, needs $2 million to finance a mall he plans to develop, he can form a partnership with several backers, who will put up the money in return for the hope of profits when the mall gets going. Charlie, the general partner, calls all the shots. The limited partners are consigned to the sidelines; they generally can't tell Charlie what to do, they just finance him. This is why they are sometimes called silent partners. In an ordinary (general) partnership, all the partners will be personally liable if something goes very wrong with the project. For example, it was later learned a toxic waste dump lay under the mall, and 300 mall workers and 5,000 customers won $700 million in judgments for their permanent disabilities that resulted from their exposure. In a limited partnership, the silent partners are generally liable up to the limits of their investment only. In other words, they could lose everything they put into the deal, but not more. Their house, cabin at the lake, yacht, and BMW are safe. The limited refers to limited liability.

Real-estate limited partnerships have a terrible reputation of late as investments because of steep losses suffered by thousands of investors who didn't really understand the deal. The deal is, Charlie runs the show. Whether you like how he runs it is pretty much immaterial. And liquidity stinks. If you decide Charlie is a loser, most of the public will probably agree with you, so finding someone to take your piece of the partnership off your hands will not only be tough, but you'll be lucky to get twenty-five cents on the dollar. Some limited partnerships are large, publicly traded enterprises, and as such, escape the illiquidity problem of their brethren. The Boston Celtics, for example, are a limited partnership that trades on the New York Stock Exchange. You want to be an owner of a major league ball club? Here's your chance—just as close as your local stockbroker.

A limited partnership is a useful legal device for shielding financiers from personal liability, thereby easing the flow of capital to worthwhile community developments. It works best for development professionals, who know everything about the general partner, the project, the market, the cost of materials, and legal hurdles such as environmental impact reviews, water permits, and local building codes. These pros are in a position to assess the probable profitability of the project, and when that should occur. As an investing opportunity for the general public, a limited partnership is a fish out of water. It's inappropriate and unduly risky, and shame on the financial planners and brokers who sell them as ordinary investment opportunities. They are not.

**Margin loans:** Discount and full-service stockbrokers are happy to loan you money, with your securities as collateral. You can borrow on margin in order to buy more securities, or take cash and use it for most anything you like.

Here's how margin transactions work: Suds 'n Suds's early success convinced Mavis she was a profoundly talented stock picker. She called her broker and instructed him to buy 500 shares of Loves-to-Tank, a hot-tub manufacturer. Loves-to-Tank was selling for $25 per share, so Mavis needed to come up with $12,500. She could either put up the cash, or she could borrow the money from her broker, using her 600 Suds 'n Suds shares (then worth $28,800) as collateral. This is known as a margin loan, and Mavis's broker could lend her up to half the value of her marginable portfolio, which includes most stocks traded on the major exchanges. Mavis's broker was thrilled to loan her the money because he earned interest on the loan, plus he got the commissions from the margin purchase of 500 shares of Loves-to-Tank. It was Mavis's hope that Loves-to-Tank would rise to $35, whereupon she would sell her 500 shares for $17,500, repay the $12,500 she owed her broker, and pocket a nifty $5,000 profit.

But poor Mavis. Loves-to-Tank couldn't wait to tank, and her

Suds 'n Suds position went right with it. Her portfolio no longer had enough value to collateralize the loan at the 30 percent floor the broker demanded. Mavis received a margin call from her broker. She was instructed to come up with enough cash or other securities to bring her collateral up, or the broker would begin liquidating her Loves-to-Tank and Suds 'n Suds shares to reduce the loan. Since Mavis didn't have the cash, she had to sell all her Loves-to-Tank shares at $11 ($5,500) and 200 shares of Suds 'n Suds at $38 ($7,600) to cover the $12,500 loan, plus interest and round-trip (buy and sell) commissions. Mavis had hoped to use margin borrowing to score a quick $5,000, but she ended up losing all her Loves-to-Tank shares plus 200 shares of Suds 'n Suds. Even if Suds 'n Suds was still trading at $48, Mavis would have lost nearly $10,000 on the deal, because 400 shares simply isn't 600 shares, no matter how you cut it.

Buying on margin is, like so many imaginative things in the world of finance, a marvelous device for leveraging a small investment into a large one. But like so many things, when promoted to amateurs, it can lead to ruin. As you can see by Mavis's sad tale, if the trader guesses wrong on the market's direction, she can lose far more than the borrowed shares—she can lose her proverbial shirt.

**Options:** An option is the right (but not the obligation) to buy (call) or sell (put) a security at a pre-determined price at or before a later date. A buyer of a call option hopes to profit when the stock price increases. If Mavis, with her Suds 'n Suds shares had wanted to, she could have instructed her broker to sell call options on some or all of her stock. For example, when Suds 'n Suds was selling for $35, Mavis might have sold Fred (through her broker and an options clearinghouse) an option to buy 100 of her shares for $40 per share by the end of March. Fred pays Mavis an option premium of, say, $1 per share for the call option, because he is betting that Suds 'n Suds will go to $54 before the option expires. If it does, he "calls" his option, that is, he buys the shares from Mavis for $40 (who is obligated to sell them at the $40 striking price, never mind the $54 current price), and turns around and sells them on the market for $54. He pockets a nice $1,400 profit, less his option premium and the broker's round-trip commissions. If Suds 'n Suds disappoints, Fred lets his option lapse. He's out the cost of the option, and Mavis is ahead that amount. Fred can also sell his option to someone else before it expires, perhaps for $2 or $3 per share, making himself a profit on the premium. When Suds 'n Suds stock rises above the striking price, Fred's options are said to be "in the money."

Fred might be a speculator—just betting on the direction of the market. Or he might be using calls responsibly to protect an intended future purchase against a market rise. Large purchasers, such as mutual funds and pension funds, often use calls to lock in a price, thus protecting themselves against an increase in price of a security they intend to buy later. This is another example of a useful financial tool that can be used responsibly, or not.

For Mavis, her sale of calls looks like a can't-lose proposition, right? She picks up $100 extra cash on her stock ($1 option premium × 100 shares) whether or not the price rises to the strike level. If it does, she still sells her shares to Fred at a profit. But Mavis pays a hidden price. She suffers opportunity cost, because she loses out on the opportunity to sell her shares at $54. She is forced to sell to Fred at $14 under market, so by selling calls, she limits her upside opportunity.

In this example, Mavis was selling what are known as covered calls, that is, she sold options on stock she already held. She could have sold options on stock she didn't own (naked calls), thus incurring the risk that the price would soar, forcing her to buy higher than the striking price in order to produce the stock when the option buyer called it. She might have to buy Suds 'n Suds at $53 or $63, and sell it to Fred at $40, making for a very disagreeable situation indeed.

Call and put options are safer than commodities futures, because the option holder has the "option" of calling in the deal or letting it expire. If Suds 'n Suds plunges to $33, Fred does not have to buy it. But if pork belly (bacon) prices are sour when the commodities contract comes due, the holder has to buy the bacon and (figuratively) eat his losses.

Remember, the risk of stock investing is minimized by a long holding period *only because there is enough time for the upswings to dominate the downs.* Calls limit the upswings, and lower your holding period by forcing sales. This is poison for your Four Step fund.

*Puts* are the opposite of calls. A call is an option to buy, and a put is an option to sell. The seller of a put option expects the price of the underlying stock to hold above the striking price, thus enabling him or her to profit from the premium without having to buy the stock. Say Fred sold Mavis put options on 100 shares of her Suds 'n Suds, setting the striking price at $30 per share. Mavis, who paid Fred an 85¢ premium for each of the puts, has the right to require Fred to purchase Suds 'n Suds from her at the striking price. This way Mavis protects herself from a decline in value of Suds 'n Suds below $30. Fred hopes the price stays above $30 so that he can profit from the 85¢ premium without having to buy the 100 shares of Suds 'n Suds. This can be a responsible move in the case of trustees, mutual funds, and other institutional investors. In the hands of speculators, puts become bets on a falling market.

Options are favorites of speculators because of leverage. Let's say Fred has $5,000 to invest. He can buy 100 shares of Loves-to-Tank at $50 per share, or he can buy 2,500 call options at, say, $2 per share on the same stock, with a striking price of $60. If Loves-to-Tank rises to $70, Fred's $5,000 worth of common stock would rise to $7,000, yielding him a profit of $2,000. Not bad at all. But if he bought $5,000 worth of options instead, he could call his 2,500 shares at $60 ($150,000), then sell them at $70 ($175,000), and realize a profit of $25,000 (less commissions and premiums). It's the lure of making $25,000 on a $5,000 investment, rather than just $2,000, that keeps speculators playing with options. Notice, though, that if Loves-to-Tank tanks to $45 per share and never recovers before the option expiration date, Fred will let his options expire, losing all of his

$5,000 premium. With common stock, he'd still have $4,500, plus the opportunity to recover his loss in the months ahead.

You don't need this kind of game, because you're starting early enough to make big bucks without the considerable risk incurred in options speculation.

**Precious metals:** Gold, especially, and other precious metals such as silver are valued by some as hedges against inflation. The theory is that when currencies become worthless as they inflate, precious metals, especially gold, hold their value. This is why gold prices rise when inflation threatens, and fall or stay flat when inflation is stable.

In my view, gold bugs need a reality check: After adjusting for inflation, the real value of gold bullion is slightly lower than a century ago, during which time money invested in the stock market multiplied more than eleven thousand times after adjusting for inflation.

There are a number of ways to buy precious metals: bullion (bars), coins (like the Eagle, Krugerrand, and Maple Leaf), jewelry, mining stocks, and mutual funds. If you buy stock in a gold-mining company, you would hope for dividends and gains as with any other stock. But if you buy the metal directly, it has no ability to pay you interest. Your only hope is for eventual capital gains. If this takes years (as it has in recent periods), you've lost the opportunity to earn dividends during that time.

Precious metals are a bet. Some advisers feel that up to 10 percent of a diversified portfolio might be in precious metals as an inflation hedge; others think that's lunacy. In any case, stay away from precious metals for your Four Step plan. It's not designed for securities that don't yield compoundable income or gains at a steady rate throughout your long investment period.

**Price/earnings ratio (P/E):** The price/earnings ratio is a common method of measuring the market's expectations regarding the company's earnings growth and risk. It measures the price of the stock against the earnings per share. A high P/E generally denotes high expectations. It is by no means a guarantee, however, or even a terribly reliable guideline, since everyone's hopes and wishes are wrapped into the price side of the ratio. The P/E is determined by dividing the most recent twelve months' earnings per share into the market price per share. When Loves-to-Tank was selling for $25 per share, on earnings of 50¢ per share, its P/E would be expressed as 50. When the stock market average is around 15–18, a P/E of 50 indicates high expectations of future growth. Sometimes these hopes are met; sometimes not.

**Real-estate investment trusts (REITs):** A REIT is a way to participate in the real-estate market, both commercial and residential, without having to become a landlord yourself. A number of investors pool their funds, and the manager buys real estate—perhaps apartments, office buildings, or malls. REITs are available through stockbrokers and some mutual funds. As you can imagine, the skill of the manager in picking the real estate is everything here, since a promising mall development might fail to live up to expectations because of some local problem, such as poor freeway access. In addition to the specific project risk, market risk generally applies, because both commercial and residential real-estate fortunes run in cycles.

REITs are a good way to broaden your portfolio, as they add the cycles of fortune and despair of real estate to those of stocks and bonds. A well-managed REIT can do well for you, but picking the right one can be tough. If you've picked a broad-growth mutual fund for your Four Step fund, the manager may have the authority to invest in REITs. Some do, and this is where you stand the best chance of participating in REITs intelligently. I wouldn't put an individual REIT or REIT mutual fund in your Four Step portfolio until it's approaching $100,000 and you've had years of sophisticated investing.

**Selling short:** A short sale occurs when someone sells borrowed securities. It works like this: Mavis, our Suds 'n Suds shareholder, edited a fashionable women's magazine. A major article in the next issue would establish with certainty that cigarette smoking aged women's faces ten years. Mavis speculated that Nicotine Tobacco Company (NTC) stock would dive on the news, so on Monday, Mavis borrowed 100 shares of NTC from her broker, and sold them that day for $28, or $2,800 for the lot (less broker commissions). On Tuesday, her magazine hit the stands. By the end of trading on Thursday, Nicotine Tobacco hit $18. Mavis bought 100 shares for $1,800, and returned them to her broker. Mavis pockets the $1,000 difference, less the broker's round-trip commissions and fees. If Mavis guessed wrong, and NTC rose in price instead, she would have to buy 100 shares to cover her short position at whatever price the market offered. If she had to spend $3,500 to buy 100 shares to repay her broker, so be it. Often, short sellers are speculators, acting on imagined or real (illegal) inside information. But there are professional shorts, too, known for their extremely diligent investigations of the corporations they are considering shorting. This is tricky stuff, and not a dilettante's game. You have to be right twice: first, that the price of the stock will dive; and second, when. It's definitely not for your Four Step fund, or any other fund that you're counting on.

There is a safer way to sell short, called "selling against the box." Mavis, who still had 400 shares of Suds 'n Suds after the Loves-to-Tank margin loan debacle, decided to gamble once again. She borrowed 200 shares of Suds 'n Suds, backed by the 400 shares she already owned, as collateral. She hoped to recover some of the money she lost on the Loves-to-Tank deal by betting that Suds 'n Suds would continue to decline. She sold the 200 borrowed shares short for $37 per share, or $7,400. But Suds 'n Suds recovered and climbed to $43 by the time Mavis decided to cut her losses and cover her position (that is, buy stock to return to her broker what she borrowed). She would have to pay $8,600 to replace stock she sold for $7,400, for a $1,200 loss. But rather than pay the market price, Mavis replaced the borrowed shares with 200 of the Suds 'n Suds shares she already owned. She had purchased those shares for only $21, so she was still ahead. But she owed capital gains tax on the realized gain, plus commissions and fees, and now her stake in Suds 'n Suds had eroded to only 200 shares. Selling against the box is a respectable hedge technique for institutions and knowledgeable traders. Losses are limited to the price already paid for the stock on hand. Selling against the box? It means the safe deposit box, where in the old days you'd keep the certificates of the shares you already owned.

**Small-cap stocks:** A company's market capitalization is measured by multiplying the number of shares outstanding by the price per share. Small capitalization, therefore, means on the lower end of that multiple—closer to $100 million than $3 billion, although small cap is somewhat of a term of art. Small-cap investors, including those mutual funds that concentrate on the area, hope to reap lots of growth from these smaller, generally newer companies.

In recent decades, small caps have beat the S&P by about two points, so a small-cap index fund makes sense for our Roller Coaster investors. They are riskier, and more volatile, than mid- and large-cap stocks.

**U.S. treasury securities:** You've heard of the federal deficit. When an individual spends more than comes in, he or she is in trouble. When Uncle Sam does the same thing, he calls it a deficit and asks the public for a loan to balance the budget. You loan profligate Sam your money when you buy a U.S. treasury bill, note, or bond. Because powerful Sam can print money or raise taxes to pay you back, your loan is perfectly safe in Uncle Sam's hands (so long as a catastrophe doesn't wipe out the United States—*really* wipe it out).

Treasury bills are short-term loans, from three months to one year. Notes are intermediate term, from two years through ten; and bonds go out as long as thirty years (called the long bond). You can buy these safe securities for no fee by applying directly to the federal reserve bank. Call and ask for an application to set up a treasury-direct account. Your bank can give you the phone number of your nearest federal reserve bank, or you can order the tender forms by writing the Bureau of the Public Debt (see Resources in Appendix III). You can also buy treasuries from some banks and all brokers, in both cases for a fee or commission. Because U.S. treasuries are top-of-the-line credit-wise, they pay lower interest than riskier securities. For this reason, they are not candidates for your Four Step fund until after you retire.

**Variable annuities:** With an ordinary annuity, you get a fixed benefit, that is, the insurance company promises to pay a set amount (say, $300 per month) for life, or ten years, or whatever you've agreed upon. A variable annuity doesn't promise a fixed benefit. The success of your investments will determine your return. Some mutual fund families now offer variables, which, conceptually anyway, are like an insurance "wrapper" placed around mutual funds already offered by the family. Cost is a major factor here, since (usually) another layer has been added to the fund's fee schedule already in place. Some large mutual fund families offer no-load variables, with no surrender fees and no second tier of fees. But all variable annuities carry a 10 percent tax penalty for withdrawal before age 59 1/2, imposed by the IRS.

What do you get? A way to convert ordinary mutual funds into tax-deferred funds. Variable annuities are not tax deductible, but unlike IRAs and 401(k)s, there is no annual limit on contributions, and you don't have to be employed to participate. Variable annuities may be appropriate for the investor who has already maxed out his or her superior tax-favored vehicles such as IRAs, 401(k)s, Keoghs, and the like, although the higher cost of the annuity versus a comparable (taxable) mutual fund may make it a close call. Variables are also useful as a way to defer taxes on a lump sum that is too large to protect in an IRA—an inheritance, perhaps—or a handsome bonus.

A few older members of our Four Step programs who don't have access to a 401(k), 403(b), or the like may find their annual contributions exceeding the annual IRA limit. A low-cost, no-load variable annuity program offered by a mutual fund family may be the solution for those funds left over after fully funding the IRA, but only if your taxes are at least 28 percent. Persons in the lower brackets would probably do better in a taxable mutual fund, with a lower cost structure than a variable annuity featuring a comparable fund. Then when your bracket rises, shift your taxable fund into a variable annuity. See if your library carries Morningstar's monthly *Variable Annuity/Life Performance Report* to compare variables. The weekly financial newspaper, *Barron's*, also tracks variables. One problem: Under current (1995) tax law, capital gains tax is capped at 28 percent of the gain, but withdrawals from a variable annuity are taxed at your income tax bracket. Therefore, someone in a higher tax bracket would pay more on the capital gains generated by a mutual fund "wrapped" in a variable annuity, instead of 28 percent on the same fund held outside an annuity.

**Zero-coupon bonds:** In the old days, before everything was done electronically, bonds came with coupons, which the bondholder clipped and sent in when the interest payment was due. Bond interest came to be called the coupon rate, and that habit persists. A zero-coupon bond is one whose coupons have been (metaphorically) "stripped" from the bond, so that interest is not paid periodically, but rather all at once when the bond matures. Zeros are sometimes called strips for this reason. Just as with ordinary bonds, zeros are issued by corporations and governments, including the United States.

Because the interest is paid at the end, it might appear that zeros would be a nifty tax-deferral device (like EEs, where you don't pay tax on the interest until you cash in), but they are not. That's because the interest is taxed as if it were being paid currently. In other words, you pay taxes *now* for income you'll get *later*. You're paying real money now on phantom income. Bummer. You can avoid this trap by placing zeros in an IRA or other tax-deferred program.

Zeros can be purchased to mature on just about any date you'd like—on your niece's eighteenth birthday, on your fortieth birthday, on the day you expect to retire. For this reason, many people like the certainty they provide for a future event. A $10,000 zero maturing on the day you leave law school, for example, would provide you with a nice boost when you hang out your shingle. If you're lucky, your farsighted grandma bought the zero for about $6,000 when you graduated from high school (show her the Afterword at the end of this book).

Zeros, being bonds, fluctuate in value on the secondary market according to interest-rate swings. If you want to unload a long-term zero before it matures, it may fetch more or less than its face value, depending on whether prevailing interest rates have gone up or down since you bought it. Zeros tend to swing more widely than ordinary bonds with similar maturities.

Generally zeros are not for your Four Step program; their yield is too low. Even if interest rates rise to the point that you can get a zero yielding 10 percent thirty years out, you'd have inflation problems because you would not be in a position to adjust your contributions to keep up with inflation, unlike the other investments suggested for our plans.

So there you have it—A to Z. But before you get fancy with all these financial toys, you need to get a little defensive about your plain-vanilla emergency funds—and you need to pay down your debt sensibly. The next chapter will point out the differences between investing and saving, and map out an emergency savings and debt reduction plan that will keep your Four Step program on track to your goal.

 *Self-Test*
**Chapter 8**

1. Annuities are:
   **a.** an insurance product
   **b.** like a bond

    **c.** inexpensive

    **d.** especially good for women

2. Corporate bonds are:
    **a.** always very risky
    **b.** often callable
    **c.** usually called junk bonds
    **d.** none of these

3. EE bonds are:
    **a.** Sold at a discount
    **b.** highly volatile
    **c.** high yielding
    **d.** exempt from all taxes

4. GNMAs (GinnieMaes) are packages of mortgages:

    ☐ True      ☐ False

5. Guaranteed investment contracts (GICs) are:
    **a.** uninsured
    **b.** not best for Four Step funds
    **c.** common in 401(k)s
    **d.** a, b, and c

6. Anyone can easily get in on an IPO through their broker:

    ☐ True      ☐ False

7. In other countries, mutual funds are often called:
    **a.** securities
    **b.** investment companies
    **c.** bonded companies
    **d.** common funds

8. Whole (cash value) life insurance is:
    **a.** not a competitive investment
    **b.** vastly more expensive than term
    **c.** sold with a high commission
    **d.** a, b, and c

9. A *put* is an option to buy; a *call* is an option to sell:

    ☐ True      ☐ False

**10.** U.S. treasury securities are considered fully safe because:
   **a.** everyone in the world wants them
   **b.** the United States can print money to back them
   **c.** of the taxing power of the United States
   **d.** b and c

*Answers on Worksheet 15 in Appendix I*

# Starting from Zero Minus

*Debt, credit, emergencies,*
*and other good things in life*

**B**efore you get rich, get smart. You'll want to protect yourself against emergencies, and you'll want to rid yourself of debt. Both are priorities, but not to the exclusion or delay of your investment program.

In short, you'll have to break your available funds into three parts:

- **Paying down debt**
- **Building your emergency fund**
- **Investing for your future**

First let's take a look at credit and debt, and how you can tease out a little bit more for yourself even as you pay out. Then, I'll illustrate strategies to make your emergency funds work a little harder for you in ways that won't put too much of a crimp in your excellent lifestyle.

 **Debt**

Because in your student years loans are easier to come by than earned income, many young people start out head over heels in debt. It can be a panicky feeling, especially if good jobs are few and far between when you're just starting out. Perhaps you've gone too far if you:

- **Are falling behind on necessities, like rent or utilities.**
- **Borrow from one source to pay off another.**
- **Owe more than you own, unless you just graduated.**
- **Are an impulse spender.**
- **Don't know the total of your monthly payments.**
- **Use your credit card like cash.**
- **Discover 20 percent of your net pay goes to debts (not a mortgage).**
- **Make only minimum card payments for four months in a row.**
- **Have several loans that will last more than a year.**

It's fair to say that if you don't have a job (not counting student-type sustenance jobs), you should avoid all debt except unavoidable student loans.

**Pay your debt and build your investments:** That said, you should evaluate carefully any advice to pay off your debt *before* you begin any savings or investment program. The reasoning is sound, for older folks, that is, without all that lovely time ahead to make money make money for them.

Paying down debt works like this: If you have a $1,000 credit card balance costing you 15 percent interest per year, then paying it off is the same thing as investing your money at 15 percent with perfect safety—otherwise impossible in modern financial markets. Sounds pretty nifty, right?

But things aren't that cut and dried for you because you're young. You simply can't afford to "spend" your early years stalling your investment program in favor of other priorities. If you commit all your available funds to paying down debt, you'll lose two, three, or more years on the compounding charts. And time is money. To take full advantage of youth and compounding, you need your numbers to be as low on our age charts as possible.

To find the real cost of paying off debt to the exclusion of building your investments, figure out how long it would take you to pay off your debt, then look up what your age will be at that point on the various charts provided for the Four Step programs. For example, $42 a month lies between the twenty-five-year-old and the twenty-eight-year-old on the Modest Millionaire 10 Percent Plan ($117 versus $159). Both payments will reach the same goal—about $1 million by age sixty-seven—but the twenty-eight-year-old has to pay out-of-pocket nearly $20,000 more than the twenty-five-year-old just to get to the same place. Stalling your investment program in order to accelerate your student loan payments from ten years to three will probably not save you $20,000 in interest, so it's worth it to keep your commitment to your investment program at the same time you repay your obligations and build a sensible emergency fund.

**Credit**

Whenever you buy on credit, apply for a credit card, buy a car on time, get a student loan, mortgage your house, and so on, it's more than likely your lender (creditor) makes a report to a credit-reporting agency, such as one of the "big three": TRW, Trans Union, and Equifax. Your repayment record is then tracked for the life of the loan. When you apply for credit, your records are checked, and depending on your credit history and other measures such as net worth and current income, the loan is granted or denied.

An excellent credit record means real money to you. Not only will your record determine loan grants or denials, but in many cases it will determine how much interest you will pay—in the case of a mortgage, perhaps for decades. The difference can mount to many thousands of dollars over the life of the loan. Poor credit risks pay interest at the legal limit—the real dollar cost of sloppy repayments from an earlier life. The credit bureaus track both whether you ultimately pay off the loan when due, and how timely your interim payments are made. Problems here brand you as a "slow pay," something that can haunt you in years to come.

A major problem in recent years has been erroneous credit reports. Imagine your delight at learning you were denied the loan on your dream house because the bureau mixed you up with a two-time felon. You are entitled by law to correct your record. You can get a copy for free or a low charge by contacting the bureau. (It's always free if a bad report resulted in credit denial.) Look under Resources in Appendix III for the addresses of the big three agencies, and write them for their procedures.

**Building your good credit:** You really do want a good credit record. It's money in your pocket in a whole lot of ways. For many folks, entry into the wonderful world of credit comes in the mail during their first year at college, when a kindly bank offers a student Visa or MasterCard, just to get you hooked. They will be cautious at first, perhaps by requiring a parental cosigner, an account with the bank securing the card, or by giving you a very low credit limit.

If you are having trouble getting credit, some banks will start you out with a secured card. You would establish a savings account with the bank for, say, $750, and the bank would issue you a card with a credit limit of the same amount, or in some cases, even more. You usually can't withdraw from your savings so long as there is a balance on your card, because the bank is testing you. If you fail to perform according to their terms (make timely payments, and stay within your credit limit), they will take the money from your savings account to repay your outstanding balance. Many banks, after a year or so of good performance on your part, will automatically convert your card to a regular card. With others, you'll have to ask. At this point, you have accomplished your goal, and established good credit. Make it a priority to protect it.

To establish a good record, you must *use* credit. Ironically, the person with a pristine record because he or she has always paid cash does *not* have a good credit record. In fact, he or she has *no* credit record, and there is no way for potential creditors to evaluate the individual's ability to pay regularly and on time. So the thing to do with your brand new credit card is to use it modestly for a few months, always paying the balance in full well before the due date.

Here are ways to stay in the good graces of your credit card company:

- **Pay more than the minimum whenever you can.**
- **Pay on time, rather than delay until you can pay more.**
- **Mail your payment at least one week before it's due.**
- **Never exceed your credit limit.**
- **Never use a "cash advance" for regular living expenses.**
- **Carry only two cards, with credit limits of no more than $5,000 each.**

*Timeliness* is the most important rule. If you can't make even the minimum payment on time, call the card company and see what you can work out. Just stiffing the bank will result in a blotch on your credit record that can cost you money for years to come.

Although you are playing by the rules if you only pay the minimum amount due, a consistent habit of this does not speak especially well for you when the card company reviews your record for an upgrade to a higher credit line. Neither will they love you if you never carry a balance. The card makes money on the atrocious interest they charge you, the percentage of your purchase they charge the merchant, and on the annual fee. Their ideal customer uses the card regularly, carries a nice balance, but pays well more than the minimum in advance of the due date every month. You don't want to carry a balance, because it's too expensive. You don't need to, either, in order to build a good credit record. Make your modest purchases for four or five months after getting your card, pay off the monthly balance in full ahead of the due date, then pocket your card and forget about it.

**The use and abuse of credit:** After noting your responsible beginning, your card company will send you a congratulatory letter: You no longer need a cosigner or a secured card. Your credit line jumps up. Soon, card offers are flooding your mailbox. Whoopee, you think—and it *is* good news. Your strategy to build a good credit record has paid off. But you want to be very careful here. Believe it or not, too much of a good thing can wreck your credit record—even if you've never missed a payment, or never even used your available credit lines.

Here's how it works: You apply for a $100,000 mortgage for your first home. The lender evaluates your application based on the appraised value of the house (the security), your loan repayment record as reported by the credit bureau, and your ability to repay the mortgage. This last is the sticking point, because the lender uses a formula that measures debt to earnings. In other words, if your debt (including the mortgage and all outstanding lines of credit even if unused) exceeds a certain percent of your income, say, 28 percent, then the deal's off. Here you are, with your thousands of dollars of unused credit sitting on your several credit cards, being denied a loan for having too much of a good thing.

You only need one—at most two—credit cards, with credit limits of no more than $5,000 each. When your bank bumps your line up above that, write them to decline it. You don't want to borrow large sums at such high interest, nor do you need the temptation. And as stated, thousands of dollars of unused credit can work against you when you want the big loan of your life, your mortgage.

**Credit cards the right way:** Visa and MasterCard represent networks of banks and other financial institutions that offer loans to the public through the use of credit cards. Although similar, each network has somewhat different rules. Your card will be issued by a particular financial institution, and will be labeled either Visa or MasterCard. Other institutions offer similar lines of credit, such as American Express, Diner's Club, and individual merchants such as department stores, gas companies, and national retail chains. You may think that loading up on every card you can qualify for is a good idea, but it isn't, for the reasons stated earlier.

The right thing to do is this: Carry one Visa and one Master-Card, because a very few places, especially abroad, accept only one of the cards, as do some ATMs. You don't need the others unless you have a special reason for wanting them. You want a card that features low interest and no annual fee. Don't be taken in by advertising that implies that carrying a particular card puts you among the elite. Clubs with millions of members are anything but exclusive, but they can be costly. An expensive card in your pocket does not make you special, but it can advertise your insecurity.

Both Visa and MasterCard offer standard and gold cards. The gold cards offer a schedule of benefits that can be useful, such as extending the warranty time on purchases made with the card,

lowering your rental car cost by insuring you against certain liabilities, and offering emergency assistance overseas. When you do
qualify for a gold card, look around for one offered free, at reasonable interest. They exist. Look up back copies of personal finance magazines such as *Money* or *Kiplinger's* in your library for
lists of the best credit card deals in the country. You don't need to
stick with your local bank for your card, but if it offers a competitive deal, it's useful to do business with the same folks in case you
want another loan from them in time.

Resist the blandishments of your alma mater or favorite charity
to sign up for their "affinity" cards (which pay a percentage of your
purchases to the school or charity's ever-hungry coffers). When you
read the fine print, you'll find the price is high, either in annual fees
(which may be waived at first) or in interest charged. Make your
charitable donations directly, then you may be able to deduct them
from your taxable income.

Evaluate carefully the cards that bear gifts, such as airline mileage, new car discounts, or "free" gasoline. Many such cards charge
hefty annual fees, some exceeding $100 per year. Think through
any benefit very carefully. For an airline card, you might figure it
this way: The big carriers require 25,000 miles for a free round-trip
domestic ticket—a flight of, at most, about 5,000 miles. That
means, at a mile earned per dollar spent, each actual flight mile
costs you about $5 per mile (25,000 ÷ 5,000). If the cut-rate ticket
coast-to-coast is generally under $500, then by earning a mile per
dollar spent, you will need to spend $25,000 within three years
(because in the large airline programs, mileage expires after three
years) to earn your $500 ticket, or nearly $700 per month. Assume
a card fee of $60 per year, or $180 for three years, and your "free"
$500 ticket is now worth only $320. Assume as well that you are
paying 4 percent more interest than you could be if you refused
their generous offer and carried a standard credit card instead. If
your unpaid balance averages $2,000, then even using simple in-
terest, your extra interest cost over three years is $240. Now your
free ticket is worth only $80. If you get your free ticket during a
fare war, when the cost of coast-to-coast travel falls into the $300

range, your credit card is costing you money. And of course, if you're not traveling coast to coast, your "free" ticket is very likely to be worse than worthless. An airline mileage card might make sense if you are frequently running large purchases through the card and immediately paying it off. Businesspeople on expense accounts, for example, can do well with these cards, because they charge large amounts, and pay off the balance when they are reimbursed.

If you pay off your balance each month, then the interest rate on your card is not as important as the annual fee, and the interest-free grace period allowed between the time of your purchase and your payment due date. Look for at least a twenty-three-day grace period. Remember, cash advances do not earn a grace period; interest accrues immediately, on top of a 2 percent or so transaction fee. Use your ATM card for cash, not your credit cards. If you carry a balance, then the interest rate is more important to you than the annual fee.

Card companies face stiff competition these days for customers, so many will cut their interest-rate or annual fees on the request of valued clients. Who is a valued client? One with a large balance, and a perfect track record of on-time payments. In many cases, just the threat of transferring the balance to another card is enough to trigger these perks.

**Here's one good strategy:** Carry one card with no annual fee for small purchases that you pay off monthly. Your second card should have superlow interest, for large purchases that you mean to pay for over time. Look in Resources in Appendix III for the Bankcard Holders of America and Ram Research's Cardtrak. Write them for their inexpensive services listing low-fee, low-interest credit cards.

**Stand on your rights:** Sometimes things go wrong, even in the well-planned life, and cards get lost or stolen. If this happens to you, it may be some comfort to know that state and federal laws will protect you against too painful a loss. The most you'd have to pay your credit-card company for unauthorized use would be

$50, presuming you notify them in writing within sixty days after the erroneous or fraudulent charge first appears on your statement. If you notify the card company *before* any charges have been made, you're even off the hook for the $50. The $50 maximum applies even if the unauthorized billings amount to thousands of dollars. The $50 limit is per card, not per transaction, and also includes department store credit cards and gasoline cards. You have similar protection on your ATM card, except that two business days after loss or theft, your liability climbs to $500 if you haven't notified the company, and you have unlimited liability after sixty days.

**Card security plans:** For a fee, various companies will protect you against your liability for unauthorized use. This is a waste of money, since the just-described Fair Credit Billing Act and the Electronic Funds Transfer Act already protect you. The best thing to do when you discover a loss, theft, or erroneous bill is to call the card company immediately, then follow up with a letter. Your rights are protected by the federal acts *only* when you notify the company in writing. A certified letter with return receipt is an excellent way to prove the company received your letter (of which, of course, you keep a copy).

Some card protection plans offer a "one-call notifies all" feature. You send them all your card numbers, then, when they're lost or stolen, you call the security company and hope they contact all the others. Legally, of course, you're still on the hook. If the security company messes up the notification, *you* pay. You shouldn't be carrying so many cards that this "one-call" feature makes sense; nor should you feel good about sending in a handy list of all your card numbers to strangers.

A card protection plan, therefore, will save you, at most, $50 for fraudulent use of your credit card, so long as you are vigilant about the sixty-day reporting period. If it covers ATM cards, it could save you $500 if you miss the two-business-days' reporting period.

**Having your way with SallieMae:** Here's one way to manage your student debt, and find a little hidden money to commit to your

Four Step program to boot. If you are making your payments to SallieMae (the Student Loan Marketing Association, the largest administrator of student loans), you can earn a 0.25 percent break in your interest rate if you instruct your bank to make your payments automatically to SallieMae from your account. If you make your payments on time over four years, you will get an additional (and hefty) 2 percent break. If your payback schedule is ten years, and you owe $23,000, you would save more than $1,500 in interest.

**When they're after your butt:** If you really screw up your loan repayments, more than likely you'll get a call from a friendly (or not-so-friendly) collection agency. A collection agency works for the lender to collect your debt. The federal Fair Debt Collection Practices Act protects you from overbearing harassment on the part of the collector. They are not supposed to:

- **Call you before 8 A.M. or after 9 P.M.**
- **Use abusive language.**
- **Tell others about your debt, such as family or employer.**
- **Collect more than you owe.**

Collection agencies usually keep a percentage of what they collect, so if you owe $500, and finally settle with the agency for $400, they'll probably collect up to $200.

If you feel abused, you can complain to the Better Business Bureau in your area (but don't expect too much action from this overrated agency, especially if the collection agency is a member of the bureau). Serious stuff should be reported to the Federal Trade Commission in Washington, DC, which goes after agencies with class action lawsuits.

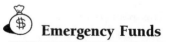 **Emergency Funds**

There's a big difference between "savings" and "investments." Savings are for emergencies, and investments are for growth or income. You want your emergency savings to be available right now—cash-in-hand today, if need be—and you want all your emergency money to be there when you want it. You don't want surprises, so you don't want stocks or bonds for your emergency funds. In other words, you want your emergency fund to have two qualities: ready accessibility (liquidity) and safety. Don't think of your emergency fund as investment money, because its paltry interest will barely keep up with inflation. These are savings, pure and simple.

**Your humble bank account:** Your local bank or savings and loan will be happy to oblige you on both counts. Banks offer a variety of products that will meet your needs, and your account should be insured by the federal government up to $100,000 (This covers all accounts under one name, per bank rather than branch. These things change, however, so always check.) The federal deposit insurance (FDIC) takes care of safety. Access is immediate with checking accounts or ordinary savings accounts (demand accounts), but be sure to double-check with the bank on savings accounts, because there are so many different kinds.

The usual advice is to put six month's living expenses (or salary) into an ordinary bank or savings and loan savings account. You can get right at it—today, if need be. The downside is you'll be tying up quite a bit of money without putting it to work for you. If half of your salary is $15,000, for example, you could be earning $600 per year invested at 4 percent, instead of $300 invested at 2 percent. That extra 2 percent per year, when compounded out over forty years (when a twenty-seven-year-old will retire at sixty-seven) is worth more than $40,000 down the road. Even a 1 percent advantage puts you $16,366 ahead. You want that money.

Your youth will help you get it. This book is for the young investor, because the advantage of time and compounding are emphasized throughout. My purpose is to make you rich with the minimum input on your part (consistent with good sense), so I'll always be looking for that little bit extra to put to work for you. If you can have $20,000 or $30,000 more by intelligently deploying your emergency fund, why not? Let's see how you can protect your emergency funds, and pull in a percentage or two more interest to keep you in cruises in your golden years.

First, you should sign up for one of those bank or S&L linked savings and checking accounts (hereafter, when I say bank, I mean both banks and S&Ls). Find a bank where your savings account balance will count toward your minimum balance for free or low-cost checking services. If the bank will also use your savings account to cover your checks if you accidentally over-draw your checking account (overdraft protection), so much the better, but since these are emergency funds, don't overdraw on purpose. It's just too hard to put the money back in there, and the bank fees for the service can be high. Then keep one month's living expenses in that account, or the minimum required for free services, whichever is more.

Let's assume that you earn $30,000 per year (take-home pay), so your emergency fund goal is $15,000. One month's salary is $2,500, so you establish your savings account with that amount. What you're looking for is the differential between your low-paying ordinary savings, and other accounts that offer safety and acceptable accessibility. The difference in interest between the lowest-paying account and slightly higher-paying alternatives will remain more or less the same (a percentage point or so) whether the low account is paying 2 percent or 6 percent.

**A little help from CDs:** The trick, then, is to find a little more interest for your emergency fund, once you've set aside one month's salary in an ordinary savings account. Since this account will give you instant access to enough funds to last a month (should you suddenly lose your job, for instance), you can afford to tie up some of the remaining five months' worth of your emergency money for slightly longer periods, which should nudge your interest return up a little.

Bank certificates of deposit are in a good position to help. With a CD, in return for a little more interest, you agree not to withdraw your funds for a period of time, generally ranging from one month to five years. If you must get at your money, you can do it by paying a penalty, one that's usually not too draconian. By using six-month CDs, you can divide your fund into six parts, with one-sixth becoming available without penalty every month. This way you will have covered your living expenses for six months, should you lose your job.

Here's one way a $15,000 fund, divided into six parts of $2,500 each, might be handled:

- **$2,500 in an ordinary bank or S&L savings account**
- **$2,500 in a six-month CD maturing in, say, January**
- **$2,500 in a six-month CD maturing in February**
- **$2,500 in a six-month CD maturing in March**
- **$2,500 in a six-month CD maturing in April**
- **$2,500 in a six-month CD maturing in May**

This way, one CD is maturing every month. This may seem like a hassle, but it's a one-time-only chore. Instruct the bank to reinvest them automatically (roll them over) as they become due. This way you'll always have one month's salary available to you immediately (the ordinary savings account), and monthly payments for six months, as each CD matures. You will also pick up a little extra interest to feed the angel of compounding—with perfect safety—since your bank CDs are insured, along with your other accounts at the same bank, up to $100,000 total by the feds. If you were to need more than $2,500 at once (catastrophic medical bills, for example), you can liquidate your CDs immediately by paying the bank a penalty, which is usually not too harsh. As your income (and, inevitably, your expenses) grows, be sure your emergency fund keeps up. One way to do this is to reinvest the interest paid as you roll over the CDs.

A traditional safe harbor for short-term money is U.S. treasury bills. They are issued in three-month (90-day), six-month (180-day), and one-year (52-week) increments, generally pay more than CDs, and are completely safe. Unfortunately, you need at least $10,000 to buy one, making them inappropriate for your emergency fund as we've outlined it.

**Money-market funds:** You can also get higher interest in a money-market mutual fund. Since they pose little risk to your savings, they are worth considering for your emergency account. Your bank probably offers an insured money-market account that may pay close to what a money-market mutual fund pays, but since we're looking for small increments of interest here, don't go with the bank's money-market account if the differential exceeds one-half of 1 percent.

You don't want their tax-exempt money-market funds, because you are probably not in a high enough tax bracket to make that matter, and also, they are not thought to be as safe as ordinary money-market funds, which historically have been remarkably safe, albeit uninsured.

**Savings are not investments:** Your emergency savings cannot help you get rich, because the interest is turned into a negative through taxes and inflation. Let's say you have $3,000 in a CD paying 4 percent. Assume annual inflation is 3.5 percent, so you are left with a 0.5 percent real gain after one year, or $15 ($3,000 × .005). The IRS taxes you on the nominal gain (.04 × $3,000), however, which amounts to $120. So if you are taxed at a low rate, say, 15 percent, you'll owe Uncle Sammy $18 on the interest, leaving you in the hole by $3! This is why so-called risk-free accounts are in fact *sure losers*. They purport to protect your principal in exchange for low interest, but they are faithless lovers, and cost you dearly over time. And the younger you are, the more they will break your heart—or at least your potential net worth.

Your emergency fund doesn't have to cover every paranoid contingency. Some emergencies may be taken care of by insurance programs on your job. Health insurance, for example, will mitigate some costs of accident or illness; sick leave and vacation will cover your wages for short illnesses; Social Security disability may pick up some slack for long-term disabilities; and your state unemployment and short-term disability programs can be helpful as well. Worker's compensation should assist for a job-related disability, either long or short term. But ask anyone who's been there: these programs are not perfect. They can be slow in paying, difficult to qualify for, and low in benefits. A healthy emergency fund is a must, but don't think of it as an investment—and don't let any hungry salesperson talk you into putting it into anything flashy. It has a humble job to do, and it has to do it in a humble way.

**Build your savings and investments together:** Most advisers will tell you to build your emergency fund first, then begin your investment program. *Don't do it.* This is a terrific way to lose your youthful edge in the compounding sweepstakes. Every year that you postpone your Four Step program makes it much more expensive—an expense you'll live with month in and month out for decades. You have to keep your Four Step payments going at the *same time* that you build your emergency fund. If you have $200 per month available for investment, and your Step One number is $87, then put $113 in your emergency fund, as well as any windfalls that come your way, such as tax refunds, birthday money, or bonuses. Keep slogging away on your Four Step account, but put everything else into your emergency fund until you reach your goal. In a catastrophic emergency, you can break into your Four Step money, but because of early withdrawal penalties and taxes it will be costly.

Of course, emergency funds—and Four Step money, too—are boring. They aren't there for the fun things you want—your dream house, an expensive (and well-deserved) toy, an exotic vacation—or for educating your kids. In the next chapter, you will be put on track for the good things in life, made possible chiefly because you had the foresight to fund your retirement on the cheap, by letting compounding make you a fortune for peanuts.

**Self-Test**
**Chapter 9**

1. Young people should not abandon their investment program in favor of paying down debt because of:
   a. compounding
   b. the need to build good habits
   c. the need to build a credit record
   d. debt is never a problem

2. Which of these is *not* the way to please your credit card company?
   a. timely payments
   b. staying within the credit limit
   c. always paying only the minimum
   d. none of these

3. An airline mileage card is a great way to get free travel:

   ☐ True    ☐ False

4. If you report your lost or stolen credit card within 60 days, the most you'll have to pay for unauthorized use is:
   a. $25
   b. $60
   c. $100
   d. $50

5. A collection agency cannot:
   a. swear at you
   b. threaten physical harm
   c. call you at midnight
   d. a, b, and c

6. Which should *not* be a feature of your emergency fund?
   a. liquidity
   b. volatility
   c. safety
   d. adequacy

7. Your Four Step fund should not double as your emergency fund because it will be too volatile:

   ☐ True     ☐ False

8. You cannot negotiate your debt with most collection agencies:

   ☐ True     ☐ False

9. Bank CDs are appropriate for your:
   a. Four Step fund
   b. college fund
   c. emergency fund
   d. none of these

10. You can never have too many credit cards:

   ☐ True     ☐ False

*Answers on Worksheet 15 in Appendix I*

# And the Rich Get Richer

*Buying the house, schooling the kids,
stockpiling the toys*

Think of yourself in your middle years, cruising home in your hot car, looking forward to your hot tub bubbling next to the pool in your spiffy backyard. You have these good things because when you were younger, you did the right things: You stashed away your emergency fund, and you took care of your retirement with your Four Step program. From here on out it's play time, big time. Because you started early and can fund your retirement with low-level bucks, you have hundreds more dollars every month to spend on all sorts of things that your laggard friends who are beginning their retirement savings now in their forties can never have.

Lucky you. Of course, as you well know, luck had nothing to do with it. You had the foresight to think of these things while still in your twenties or early thirties, and then you had the gumption to stick with the program year after year. You used sound judgment in your Four Step investing, carefully choosing funds that would perform well over the long term, in tax-deferred accounts, adjusted annually for inflation.

But investing is not a one-size-fits-all affair. None of the long term strategies talked about so far is appropriate for your short-term goals. Investing for the short term is fundamentally different from investing for the long term. Every one of the Four Steps is wrong for the short term:

- **Time and compounding will be weaker allies.**
- **Stocks and stock funds may well be inappropriate.**
- **Your short-term funds will probably be taxable.**
- **Inflation will be a lesser consideration.**

Since you'll want to get at your funds long before you reach 59 1/2, they cannot be in tax-deferred accounts such as IRAs or 401(k)s. Nor can you rely on decades of soothing time to calm the swings in the financial markets. Remember, statistically anyway, an investment in the stock market (measured by the S&P 500) will incur a net loss one year out of three. For this compelling reason, short-term money should never be in stocks. Finally, the shorter the term, the less you can count on compounding to come up with all that lovely free money you're getting in your Four Step account. But on the other hand, you will not fear inflation's heavy toll nearly as much. So you can see, much of what you've learned about long-term investing should be put aside as you begin to reap the second harvest of your Four Step commitment—not the million or so at age 67 (although that's nice, too), but the hundreds of dollars a month you'll have free to spend on yourself when you're much younger, rather than having to save for your retirement.

Your first step is to complete Worksheet 10 in Appendix I. Here you will assign time-horizons, prices, and priorities to your various goals. As you already know, getting your time-horizon right is the first essential element of good financial planning. The time available defines the investment strategies.

**Buying the house:** Your home is a real-estate investment, of course, but you should think of it primarily as a place to live. If it appreciates in value, that's terrific. But don't count on huge jumps in equity like those in the 1970s and 1980s. The two principal drivers of the housing boom have stabilized. First, 76 million baby boomers reached home-buying age beginning in the mid-1970s, which pressured supply and created a sellers' market. Second, women entered the labor force in unprecedented numbers, also beginning in the mid-1970s, vastly increasing the numbers of two-earner families. This, in turn, enabled families to buy houses costing much more than at any other time in American history. Today, most of the boomers have bought their first homes, and women's participation in the labor force has apparently plateaued. Recent years have seen a decline in home values in most places in the country, although this may be slowly turning around. The sellers' market became a buyers' market with a vengeance. Hope that your home's value will keep up with inflation. If it does better than that, that's a bonus.

Let's see how to bring wishes into line with realities. Suppose you'd like to buy your first house in five years. Worksheet 10 might look something like this:

Goal:                house down payment
Funds needed in:     five years
Estimated cost:      $30,000
Monthly payment:     $500
Annual yield:        6%

You arrive at these figures by estimating the cost of the house at $150,000. Assuming a 20 percent down payment, $30,000 is the sum you project will get you by the fireside. Dividing $30,000 by the number of months in five years (sixty), you arrive at $500 per month in savings. Because five years is not very long term, you realistically set your hoped-for yield on your house savings account at 6 percent, which is usually available in bonds or bond funds, even CDs, depending on the current market.

Since your budget can't manage $500 per month, what can you do? Fiddle with the numbers, of course. You have three variables, each of which affects the bottom line: yield, cost, and time.

First, take a hard look at yield. You realize the $500 figure is off, because yield was ignored in calculating the monthly payment. Compounding is your friend, even over the short term. If your account yields 6 percent, you only need to come up with $425 per month to make your down payment in five years. You'll need a financial calculator or software (or compounding tables available in your library) to make these calculations, but as you can see, using raw numbers without considering yield seriously distorts the result.

Second, take a look at cost. Can you live with a $125,000 house and a $25,000 down payment? If so, your monthly savings slide down to $354. How about going for a 10 percent down payment? A mere $177 per month will get you there in five years, invested at 6 percent. If you can cut the down payment even further—help from family, perhaps—things look even rosier. A $10,000 goal gets you down to $142 per month.

Cutting your dollar goal is one way to get the numbers in line. Another way is to wring a little extra out of your current budget, so that the savings goal can be met. Here's where savings—or nonexpenditures—really begin to count. Instead of buying a new car, you decide that enjoying your own home in five years is worth relying on car pools and the bus for those years. You save $4,000 per year by eliminating the need for insurance, upkeep, gas, tires, license fees, interest payments, parking, and depreciation (the amount of resale value your car loses as it ages). Deduct your alternative transportation costs of $2,000 per year and bingo! You have $167 per month to put toward that house. If giving up your car is just too much to bear, find another way to wring the payment from your budget.

Finally, tinker with your time line. Delaying your purchase by only six months brings your monthly savings below $100. Your rejiggered worksheet might look like this:

| Goal: | house down payment |
| --- | --- |
| **Funds needed in:** | 5 1/2 years |
| **Estimated cost:** | $10,000 |
| **Monthly payment:** | $98 |
| **Annual yield:** | 6% |

Without too much sacrifice, and without going out on a limb yield-wise, you've brought your payments into line—and your house will be a reality. Always write out your goals this way, so that you can squeeze the juices out of all three elements: *yield, cost,* and *time.*

You may be able to raise the down payment by borrowing from yourself—by using tax-deferred funds without waiting until you are 59 1/2. If you find your dream home, and your down-payment fund is a little skinny, most employers will permit you to borrow against your 401(k). You can also borrow against some 403(b) programs. Most workplaces permit you to borrow up to

50 percent of your saving plan's value, with repayment within five years. The interest is generally lower than market rates, and better yet, you pay it into your own 401(k) or 403(b) account. Borrowing from your 401(k) or 403(b) carries a special risk: if you fail to repay it in a timely fashion, it counts as a premature withdrawal, complete with taxes and penalty. You cannot borrow from or against your IRA as of this writing.

But here's your greatest risk: *If you borrow against your Four Step fund, keep in mind that you'll decimate the compounding action*, and this will ultimately have drastic consequences for your goal. Also, check with the banker who will be giving you the mortgage before you borrow part of the down payment from Mom and Pop. Some lenders don't want to see borrowed money in the down payment, reasoning that you'll be more serious about re-payments if you have your own money in the home.

When you do get that home, complete with mortgage, take some time to calculate the cost, over time, of the interest. The result will stun you. Your modest home, after thirty years, may cost hundreds of thousands more than you thought you were paying, all because of interest. If you can manage it, even if only now and then, send extra money to the lender when you send in your payment. There should be a place on your payment stub that allows you to designate the payment as pay-down of princi-pal. If there is no way to designate that on the payment stub, write a note with the payment designating the extra money to principal. Otherwise, it will just go to interest, and that will de-feat your purpose. When you pay down the principal early, not only will you pay off your loan earlier, but you will also save thousands of dollars off the interest.

Assume a $150,000, thirty-year mortgage at 9 percent. The monthly payment will be about $1,207, $1,125 of that, at first, being interest. The interest cost of the loan will be $284,502, on top of the $150,000 principal, for a grand total of more than $434,000! If you can manage to increase your monthly payment by $315 to $1,522, you'll pay off your loan in fifteen years, sav-ing $160,650 in interest. Even if you can't increase your payments regularly, consider adding "found" money to your principal payments whenever possible. If your interest rate is 9 percent, it's the same as earning 9 percent on your investment risk free. And that's a terrific deal.

In addition, paying off your mortgage early builds equity in your home faster. Of the $1,207 monthly payment in the thirty-year mortgage discussed above, at first less than $82 a month goes to principal—and it's about twenty-two years before the portion of the payment going to principal equals the portion going to interest.

Some will argue that paying off your mortgage early causes you to lose your mortgage-interest tax deduction. And so it does. But since a tax write-off only benefits you to the extent of your tax bracket (if you are paying 15 percent in taxes, your $100 payment will cost you, in effect, $85; at 28 percent, $72; and so forth), it's better to save 100 percent of the $100 interest payment than it is to save the smaller percentage due to the deduction.

Inflation is one factor in favor of a lengthy loan. Thirty years down the line, your $1,207 payment would be worth only $364 in today's dollars, assuming an average annual inflation rate of 4 percent. For this reason, if you have a low-interest mortgage (6 or 7 percent) and are in a high tax bracket when you consider your state taxes as well, the longer payment period may favor you. To take financial advantage of that, though, you should put the extra money you would have used to pay off your loan earlier into savings. To get a customized handle on this, you need your banker and tax adviser to run the numbers for you.

**Schooling the kid:** The college fund, assuming you begin when your baby is a baby—or a toddler at the latest—will be easier going than your down-payment fund. It has a longer time-horizon, compounding will take more of the load off your back, and you can invest more aggressively, bumping up the yield portion of the equation.

| Goal: | Mills College for Joan |
|---|---|
| Funds needed in: | 17 years |

| Estimated cost: | $100,000 |
|---|---|
| Monthly payment: | $188 |
| Annual yield: | 10% |

If there's only ten years before Joannie hits Mills, you'll need to save $488 per month; if only five years, $1,291! Even though the $188 looks steep, it works out to only $38,352 out-of-pocket over the years. Compounding and time contribute more than $61,000, or about two-thirds of the cost of Joan's college education. The ten-year plan costs more than $58,000 out-of-pocket, so you can readily see that an early start means real money. Don't forget inflation. You'll have to bump up your monthly contribution annually in line with the CPI, following Step Four of our program.

Your first step to your kid's B.A. is to complete Worksheets 11 and 12 in Appendix I. When you're finished, you'll have identified the amount you'll need to contribute monthly to the college fund. The time-horizon is the first variable, and if your child is already born, the target date is pretty much known. The yield you've worked out will determine the kind of investment you need. Ten percent? A no-load, low-cost S&P 500 index fund would be the couch-potato approach. Eleven? You'll need a growth fund with a good track record of beating the S&P by at least 1 percent. Twelve? Aggressive growth, or small cap. Reread Chapter Four if you need a refresher on mutual funds.

In recent years, college costs accelerated well past the inflation rate, but this trend is leveling off, because no institution wants to price itself out of the market. Many colleges set a nominal tuition rate that is sky-high (and is paid by only the very rich), then grant aid packages to most of their students to fill the classrooms.

Bankers, financial planners, and other financial professionals that have products to sell have a vested interest in hyping the future costs of college (and retirement)—and boy, have they. When you see the scary figures they present, keep your eye on the inflator. What is the inflation rate they are using for tuition? If it's more than a point or two above the current CPI, it cannot be sustained in real life for more than a very few years, and definitely not for more than ten. Charts using high inflators for twelve, fourteen, or eighteen years are irresponsible, in that the projected costs are so shocking, many young parents throw in the towel at the start, figuring their budgets can't support a college fund.

Never forget scholarships, loans, and work-study. Costs really come down when you assume the student will live at home, and even further if you aspire to a public university.

If you plan to continue your monthly contribution after the student registers, you'll be deferring a substantial amount of the cost. Projections, including mine, that assume you'll need to contribute the full four-year cost on the first day of class overstate the cost, since it deprives the equation of up to three years' yield and compounding, at least for the portions due in the sophomore, junior, and senior years. If your child is eight, the time line for his or her first tuition is only ten years—but eleven, twelve, and thirteen for the remainder, and this brings your monthly numbers down.

Still, college is costly. If you can't swing the payments for a private school, aim for a good public university. The "public ivies"—the Universities of California, Illinois, Wisconsin, Michigan, Texas, and many more—award degrees that open as many doors as any school in the country. And don't be shy about shooting for a private ivy, if that's what your kid qualifies for, and wants. The more prestigious the college, the bigger the endowment. The financial aid packages can be extraordinarily attractive in the top institutions. Grants, loans, and scholarships abound that will ease your path when the time comes.

You can (almost) painlessly start a college fund when your baby graduates from diapers. Switch your diaper budget (perhaps $50 per month) into a stock mutual fund with a good record, and hope for an annual average of 10 percent on your investment. When your child begins school, put the $300 per month childcare (or preschool) cost into the fund as well. When your kid is eighteen, the college fund will be more than $116,000.

Some colleges offer guarantees of various sorts, designed to reduce costs. One variation is the promise that the student will graduate in four years, or the college will eat the difference in costs, assuming the college was responsible for the delay because of unavailable classes. Another is a prepayment plan, whereby current tuition is paid now, then guaranteed at that rate when the child finally matriculates. Some schools offer a fast track, so that students can finish in three years.

Finally, there's a good chance you will have been a homeowner for several years before your first child gets to college. If your college fund is short, consider taking out a home-equity loan on your house. The interest rate will probably be lower than a personal loan, and the interest is tax deductible.

Don't forget grandparents. Under current (1995) law, gifts of up to $10,000 per year per donor and per donee do not incur a gift tax. For example, if your mom and pop wanted to reduce their estate for tax purposes, a Christmas gift of $10,000 from each of them to your future student, then a New Year's gift of another $10,000 from each will add $40,000 to the college fund within one week's time, since Christmas and the New Year occur in different tax years. If they wish, they can rewrite their wills so that a substantial gift made now would be deducted from any bequest made to you or your child. This would equalize the situation with other heirs. A welcome gift of $20,000 donated at birth would grow to more than $120,000 invested at 10 percent for eighteen years. See the Afterword for more on intergenerational assists.

Tax planning is the next step. If you open a custodial account under your child's Social Security number, the taxes will be paid by the child, not you. The child's bracket may or may not be lower than yours, depending on age. You need a tax adviser here, because laws in this area keep changing. They are complex, involving calculations of the child's age, exempt amount, and your tax bracket.

Keep in mind that some advisers suggest leaving the account in the parents' names, even if it means a higher tax bite, because eligibility for student loans and grants are figured on both the student's and the parents' assets, with the latter getting a higher exemption. Again, it's pretty hard to strategize long term around government regulations such as student loans, since they are very changeable.

Another consideration is control. When you establish a custodial account, you have irrevocably given that money to the child. Upon majority (eighteen or twenty-one in most states), the child can take the money and do with it what he or she will. If that's Rio rather than Rutgers, there goes the fund.

When the child reaches age thirteen or fourteen, begin converting the college fund into shorter-term investments, such as growth and income mutual funds, or balanced funds. When the child is a high-school sophomore, move half of your fund into a short- or intermediate-term bond fund, and the other half into a money-market fund. When the SAT looms, three-quarters should be in the money fund. And when you cut your first tuition check, have it all in a money fund.

Since you are young, college for your kids is many years away. For this reason, I won't go into student-aid strategies; they are too subject to change. Just understand that student-aid planning should begin before application, and a professional experienced in the ins and outs of this complicated field will be well worth your money. The pro will help you manipulate resources, determine which fund should be tapped first, sort through the maze of aid and grant programs, and in many ways more than earn his or her fee.

Keep an eye out for IRA-type tax-deferred accounts that may become available for college tuition, first-home down payments, and medical emergencies. Congress routinely considers such bills, and one day may pass one. This would solve your tax problems for these important short-term responsibilities.

**Stockpiling the toys:** Your emergency fund is set up, your Four Step program takes care of retirement, and your home and kids' college funds are perking along. Now it's time to play. Since you wisely chose to lay your biggest financial burdens on the back of the compounding beast, unlike most of your peers, you have money to play with.

Go back to Worksheet 10 and order your priorities. Remember, when assigning yield, you shouldn't consider 10 percent feasible on time-horizons of fewer than ten years. Money you need in one or two years is best kept in a money-market fund or short-term bond mutual fund. Three to five years? Think of an intermediate-term bond fund, or U.S. treasury notes purchased directly from the federal reserve bank nearest you. Phone numbers are given in Appendix III. From five to ten years, an equity-income mutual fund might do the trick, and ten and over, growth or index stock funds.

**The true cost of credit.** With credit cards abundantly available outfitted with credit limits in the high thousands, and car financing the common way to buy a car, it's easy to go the credit route to clear out your wish list, rather than investing for a cash purchase. But future millionaires must not flinch from knowing the true cost of their financial decisions. Every time you buy something on credit, whether it be a house, a car, or gasoline, you incur two extra costs, only one of them generally recognized. The second is the most important one, and the one to which the wealthy pay attention. The obvious one that everyone recognizes is the cost added to the product by the interest charged. If you rush to a sale to charge a new jacket at 20 percent off, and then pay the store 20 percent interest on the installment charge, what have you gained?

It's the second cost of credit that is so insidious, because it is invisible—and, in theory, it costs you over your lifetime. Assume you finance your new car. Over five years, you pay a total of $4,000 interest. Of course, your car costs you $4,000 more than if you had paid cash, but you already know that and accept it as the trade-off for getting your car now rather than waiting five years. What you probably don't consider is the opportunity cost of that $4,000 interest expenditure. Had you invested $4,000 rather than spending it on interest, at an annual average 10 percent yield, that $4,000 would be worth $6,581 in five years, $10,828 in ten, and $214,803 in forty. If you assume you buy ten cars over your working years, think how the opportunity cost adds up! If you're the disciplined type, try calculating the interest saved every time you buy something for cash instead of credit. Then put that money into an aggressive stock mutual fund for the purpose of buying a major treat just for you, sometime down the road.

I'm not telling you never to buy big things on credit. I do it myself. Life is too short to be always prudent and defer all good things to the future. But it is important that you understand the true, lifetime costs of the credit decisions you do make, so that the judgment risk discussed in Chapter Five won't be your nemesis.

**Wishes and taxes**. Your Four Step money isn't available to you without penalty (or hardship) before age 59 1/2. To reward your commitment, Uncle Sam defers taxes on your retirement accounts. Alas, your uncle is not so generous when it comes to short-term money. Savings for your house, tuition, car, furniture, vacation, and so on are going to be shared with Uncle Sam, unless Congress comes through with that IRA-type savings plan for first homes, tuition, and medical emergencies.

Because the earnings on your short-term accounts will be taxable, it's important that you understand how your tax bracket affects your true yield. If your $10,000 account is earning $800 per year, $800 is added to your other income, and taxed accordingly. Here's what you'll take home under 1995 law after the IRS takes a bite from your $800:

| Tax bracket | After-tax return | Reciprocal |
|---|---|---|
| 15% | $680 | .85 |
| 28% | $576 | .72 |
| 31% | $552 | .69 |
| 36% | $512 | .64 |
| 39.6% | $483 | .604 |

Multiply the earnings ($800) by the reciprocal to get the result (the reciprocal is simply the bracket subtracted from 100). As you can easily see, as you go up the brackets, the incentive to protect your investment from taxes becomes compelling. For this reason, municipal bonds and municipal bond funds are popular among folks paying 28 percent or more in taxes, since munis' earnings are exempt from federal taxes, and sometimes state taxes as well, although any capital gains earned are taxed.

Because, as of 1995, the capital-gains tax is capped at 28 percent, many people in the higher brackets try to fund their taxable accounts with growth-stock mutual funds, since they invest for capital gains, rather than income. Capital-gains tax, and tax brackets generally, are among the more changeable things on earth. Always check for current rates before taking any action affected by taxes.

**Early out**. Our Four Step program is predicated on investing until your 67th birthday. But plenty of folks can't stomach the notion of working so long. Accordingly, Tables 11 through 13 in Appendix II show you what your Four Step plan will be worth if you loot it at age 59 1/2, when penalty-free withdrawals begin. You'll do much better by waiting until 67, but for some of you, the early out may be worth a little belt-tightening. Pensions often feature early retirement benefits beginning at age 55, and Social Security offers a (reduced) retirement benefit at age 62 (60 for widows and widowers drawing on their deceased spouse's account).

When you find your "early-out" number in the tables, multiply it by 6 percent, 7 percent, and 8 percent to get an idea of what kind of income it will generate for you. It's too early to predict what the interest environment will be when you reach 59 1/2, but it's reasonable to expect yields somewhere in that range.

If you don't like the result, you'll have to work longer, or live on less, or sell your house and add a goodly portion of its equity to the fund. Under current law, people over age 55 can take up to $125,000 equity from the sale of their residence free of capital-gains tax. At a maximum capital-gains tax rate of 28 percent, that's like a $35,000 gift from the IRS. Add $125,000 to your early-out number, multiply it by a prudent yield, and see if you can live with the result.

The only reason you can even think of funding these short-term goals is because your Four Step program is taking care of your retirement at a bargain-basement price. These goals are your reward for getting your golden years out of the way early—and cheap. It is the extra money available for other things that makes your Four Step program such a great deal.

The next chapter will describe another Four Step program, this one a free or low-cost financial education just for the asking. When you consider the cost of information today (that is, college costs, continuing education fees, seminars), reliable expertise for free is a real deal. And in the financial world, it's readily available, but only if you know where to look, and how to sort out the quick-buck artists and scams. Future millionaires need to know the ropes, and how to untie the knots.

 *Self-Test*
**Chapter 10**

1. Saving for short-term goals is fundamentally the same as saving for long-term goals:

   ☐ True    ☐ False

2. Short-term money shouldn't be in stocks or stock mutual funds because there's this much chance you'll lose money after one year:
   a. 1 in 3
   b. 2 in 4
   c. 7 in 10
   d. 9 in 10

3. A reasonable yield target for five-year money might be:
   a. 3%
   b. 8%
   c. 6%
   d. 10.3%

4. Which of these is not part of your short-term equation:
   a. time
   b. yield
   c. your age
   d. cost

5. Financial institutions and planners have an incentive to inflate the future costs of college:

   ☐ True    ☐ False

6. Under current law, you can give away this much every year, per person, without incurring a gift tax:
   a. $2,000
   b. $5,000
   c. $25,000
   d. $10,000

7. Under the Uniform Gift/Transfers to Minors acts, upon majority the child:
   a. can blow the money
   b. must use the funds for college
   c. must save the funds for retirement
   d. must obey the parents

8. Which is the most costly aspect of a credit purchase?
   a. sales tax
   b. opportunity cost
   c. interest
   d. income tax

9. In figuring the after-tax yield on investment earnings, someone paying 28% in taxes should multiply the earnings by:
   a. .28
   b. .72
   c. .604
   d. .33

**10.** Jessie sold fund shares at a profit of $1,000. As of 1995, her tax on her profit will be:

   **a.** 15%
   **b.** 31%
   **c.** 28%
   **d.** whatever her tax bracket is

   *Answers on Worksheet 15 in Appendix I*

# Have I Got a Deal for You

*Help yourself to a fortune*

L ucky you. Everyone loves a winner. You'll be rich, and everyone will want to be your friend, or at least help you make more money. For a fee. For a very comfortable fee. And sometimes, an unnecessary, costly, and counterproductive fee. And that's before we even talk scams.

Use the time while your holdings are still small to educate yourself. You can do this for free, or you can put out some money here and there and rationalize it as tuition. The only down side to your early education is the possibility you'll get hooked on this stuff, and get impatient with the slow early growth of your Four Step fund. *Resist this.* Use other money if you become a financial hobbyist, because you'll probably be chalking up many of your early forays to more than just tuition.

Your Four Steps are now in place: your million-dollar number is invested at 10 or 12 percent in a tax-deferred account, adjusted annually for inflation. You really don't need to know much more than this for the first five years or so of your program. This is because you won't have much money to manage. Remember, your fund will grow very slowly at first, until compounding starts smoking about two decades down the road. But if you diligently follow the program, long before retirement you will have hundreds of thousands of dollars to manage, and for this, you need lots more than this, or any one book, can give you.

This chapter will cover the works, from investment software to investment newsletters; from the financial pages to financial professionals. Everything and everybody that wants to make money for you—how to evaluate them, how to use them, and how to dismiss them. We'll begin with the simplest and cheapest—your newspaper's financial pages—and end with the most expensive—the various financial professionals from certified financial planners to certified public accountants.

## $ Four Steps to a Free Financial Education

To complement your Four Step investment program, here's a four-step educational program designed for future millionaires. I'll go into the details below, but here's a summary:

**Step A**: Go to your library and read the last twelve back issues of *Money* magazine and *Kiplinger's Personal Finance* magazine. When you've finished, read the back issues of *SmartMoney* magazine or *Worth* magazine for the last six months.

**Step B**: Read the financial pages in your local newspaper daily for one year, even the boring stuff—*especially* the boring stuff.

**Step C**: Compile your Fantasy Forty, and track them daily or weekly for one year.

**Step D**: Once a week, listen to (or watch) a financial program on radio or TV. Do this for at least one year.

**Step A: Personal finance magazines.** *Money* magazine (by the publishers of *Time*) and *Kiplinger's Personal Finance* magazine are the entry-level choices, designed to appeal to amateur investors. Both magazines offer mutual-fund performance charts and features touting "best funds to buy now," or "nine stocks to beat the market." Look over these charts, if you wish, and read the "top pick" articles—but *don't* pick up the phone to buy (except for your Fantasy Forty). The articles are usually too old to rely on for specific picks; magazines are prepared months in advance, and the writer researched the article even earlier than that. Also, the top 10 picks constantly change, and are unusually risky to boot.

Probably the best reason to avoid the magazines' hot tips with respect to individual stocks, anyway, is that the widely circulated "tip" causes enough buyers to come on board that the rush to buy artificially inflates the price of the stock *temporarily*. Since magazines reach their readers at widely varying times, the early birds get the worm, and you have no way of knowing if you're in that

nest. The last folks in line take the fall. This artificial price inflation applies to stocks and closed-end mutual funds (which are
traded on the stock exchanges like stocks). Open-end mutual
funds—the ones recommended to you for your Four Step program—simply increase their assets in response to a surge in buyers. Their share price (NAV) is set by the value of their portfolio
minus liabilities, not by buying or selling pressure.

Read personal finance magazines for background (they're good
at this), to think through strategies offered by the various advisers, and to familiarize yourself with the products generally. But it's
a mistake to use them to buy the latest hot tip.

Next up the ladder in sophistication is *SmartMoney*, published by the *Wall Street Journal*. Stock investors get more attention here than in the more mutual fund–oriented *Money* and
*Kiplinger's*. Finally, *Worth* is for the true aficionados. In addition
to the investment advice and tables presented in the other
magazines, *Worth* features personality profiles of the finance
superstars and articles revealing the "inside story" of this Wall
Street scandal or that humiliating fall from grace.

*Money* is widely distributed; you can no doubt find it in your
supermarket. *Kiplinger's* is a little less so, but still readily available
at larger magazine stands. *SmartMoney* and, especially, *Worth* are a
little harder to locate. Magazine stands that cater to the business
community, including airport newsstands, are a good place to
look for these more sophisticated offerings. All four magazines
are a good read, and a sensible place to begin your education.

**Step B: Newspaper financial pages.** Large newspapers carry
daily listings of the previous day's stock, bond, and mutual fund
activity. Specialized newspapers, such as the *Wall Street Journal*
(daily) or *Barron's* (weekly), carry comprehensive listings that include international stock exchanges, currency rates, commodities, interest rates, and much more. For your Four Step program,
you only need access to the mutual fund listings, and then only at
the beginning of your program when you're deciding which ones
to call for prospectuses. Still, it's a good idea for any investor, no

matter how modest, to be able to grasp at least the essentials as listed in the daily papers.

Some newspapers separate the listings of the larger stock exchanges—New York, American, and NASDAQ. Others combine them into one list, indicating which exchange the stock trades on by the use of symbols or codes. Either way, the listings are similar. Let's look at our two fictional companies, as they might appear in your daily newspaper:

| 52 Week | | | | Sales | | |
| High | Low | PE | Div | hds | Last | Chg |
| --- | --- | --- | --- | --- | --- | --- |
| 48 1/2 | 23 3/8 SdsnSds | 18 | .43 | 1521 | 47 3/8 | +2 1/2 |
| 21 1/8 | 12 3/4 LvsTnk | 4 | | 470 | 13 1/4 | −5/8 |

From this we know that yesterday Suds 'n Suds traded near its high for the year (the fifty-two-week high is listed as $48.50 per share), and Loves-to-Tank nearer to its fifty-two-week low (which was $12.75 per share). The last investor who bought Suds 'n Suds yesterday paid $47.38 (up 2 1/2—or $2.50—per share from the previous day's closing price) and Loves-to-Tank's last buyer paid $13.25, down 5/8 of a dollar, or 63¢ from the day before. Does this mean it's time to buy Loves-to-Tank because it's a bargain, and sell Suds 'n Suds to take your profits? Maybe, and maybe not. It could be that Loves-to-Tank is on its way to nowhere, and Suds 'n Suds is on its way to the sky.

The P/E, or price/earnings ratio, helps us decide if a stock is overpriced. Suds 'n Suds P/E that day is 18, which means the price of the stock is eighteen times more than the earnings per share. (Remember, earnings are not the same as dividends; a company can have good earnings and no dividend, because it's new and is ploughing its earnings back into the company for expansion, for instance.) Historically, a P/E of 18 would be acceptable for a mature, healthy American company. The P/E average is a moving bellwether, however. When the market as a whole is hot, average P/Es climb as people bid up the price of stocks. And, of course, the reverse is true in down markets.

Were a lot of people buying Suds 'n Suds yesterday? Perhaps, since 152,100 shares changed hands (listed under "sales in hundreds"), but these numbers could be just one or two mutual funds and an insurance company making trades. Only 47,000 shares of Loves-to-Tank changed hands, perhaps indicating a wait-and-see attitude toward the company, which pays no dividend as yet and boasts a P/E of only 4.

If we're income investors, we see that Suds 'n Suds will pay its owners (the shareholders) 43¢ a share in dividends for the year, assuming its most recent quarterly dividend continues. That means Mavis, with her 200 shares, can expect to receive $86 this year, divided into four quarterly payments.

The mutual fund listings are similar. The individual funds are listed below their "family name," if there is one.

Super Funds's Super-Testosteroney fund reported its NAV as $16.80 per share at the close of yesterday's trading. The "change" column represents the change from yesterday's closing price. Remember, the NAV, or net asset value, is merely the assets held by the fund divided by the number of shares outstanding (issued), less liabilities. Because Super-Testosteroney aggressively invests in stocks, its NAV will rise and fall with its investments. If Super-Test's manager invested well, the change in the NAV will "beat" its competitors, either by rising more or falling less. The amount of

|  | Sell | Buy | Chg |
|---|---|---|---|
| Super Funds |  |  |  |
|    Super-Testosteroney | 16.58 | 16.80 | +.11 |
|    MuniBnds | 7.03 | N.L. | −.02 |
|    EmMkt | 23.89 | 25 | 1.09 |
| Wholecloth Financial Group |  |  |  |
|    Idx500 | 9.34 | N.L. | +.03 |
|    USTreas | 6.51 | 6.99 | −.01 |
|    Intl Stk | 2.84 | N.L. | +.12 |

the NAV is meaningless as a yardstick; that is, you cannot assume an investment in Super-Test is more valuable than one in the Municipal Bond fund, or worth less than the more risky Emerging Market fund.

It is the change in the NAV that interests you, and Super-Test appears to have moved up somewhat from yesterday's close, but not nearly as much as the Emerging Market fund. But it would be wrong to compare the two, since they are not peers. Emerging Market's performance should be measured against other emerging market funds offered by other fund families, while Super-Test should be looked at against other aggressive growth funds. Measure them both against the S&P 500's movement for the day, since you always want to know if your investments (over time) would be better off just tracking the market in a cheap S&P 500 index fund, rather than underperforming in an expensive managed fund.

Notice the N.L. under the Municipal Bond fund's "buy" listing. This means it is a no-load fund (some newspapers just use an "n" after the fund name). Super-Test and Emerging Markets carry a sales commission, and this is indicated by the increase in the buy listing over the sell. Some fund families, like Super Funds, carry both load and no-load funds, so be sure you double-check before plunking down your dollars.

Your newspaper's financial page, then, is designed to be a quick reference tool rather than a compilation of all you need to know before committing your dollars to an investment. It delivers a lot of information cheaply and quickly, which are its principal virtues, and it is the essential component of Step B of your education program.

**Step C: Your Fantasy Forty phantom portfolio.** Leave our fictitious dynamos Suds 'n Suds, Loves-to-Tank, and Super-Testosteroney behind for a while, and "buy" forty real stocks, bonds, and mutual funds that you see listed in your newspaper's financial pages. Buy companies you recognize, or believe in, or have a hunch about. You'll find Reebok, Sizzler, and Kellogg's on the big board (New York Stock Exchange); smaller or newer companies show up on NASDAQ (but not always; giant Microsoft and many other tech companies are listed there, too) or the American Stock Exchange (AmEx). Diversify across industry sectors and company size. Don't forget the international sector. Let your imagination roam the world: British Air, Daimler-Benz, Sony; there is no need to buy American. Of course, if you were using real money, you'd never buy stocks so lightly, but the mistakes made by following hunches and sentiment will be a valuable part of your education.

Follow your phantom portfolio weekly. Don't forget, in the real world you'd have to pay commissions on purchases and sales, which will cut into your profits—perhaps more deeply than you'd think. Don't fall in love with your Fantasy Forty and commit real money to it. This is educational only, and you don't want to learn your lessons the hard way. Chart your investments on a graph, or if you have one of the financial software programs discussed below, let the computer chart them for you. Buy, sell, and hold. Watch how your portfolio behaves in general market upswings and down. See how your diversity helps you out. Do this for one year.

Keep your phantom portfolio at forty stocks, bonds, or funds—no more, no less. This will discipline you to cull your duds when you discover a hot new candidate for the Forty.

**Step D: Media investment programs.** Perhaps you're familiar with *Wall Street Week* on public television, various financial talk shows on the radio, and numerous other radio, TV, and cable financial advice shows. This is one way to educate yourself for free, so long as you sample a number of such programs, without tying yourself to one approach. Since no one really knows where the market is headed tomorrow, these commentators will (disagreeably often) profoundly differ. This can be unsettling to new investors, who naturally prefer direction to being whipsawed between competing (and contrary) advice. Don't you be upset. Just tuck these disagreements away as one more way for you to evaluate your options before exercising your independent judgment.

So long as you aren't using these programs as guides to buying and selling specific securities, you'll learn quite a lot with minimal agony. For example, researchers have surveyed the "buy" recommendations on PBS's *Wall Street Week* and learned that most of the money made from recommended stocks was made in the week *before* the program aired. Whether this is due to information leaked by the guests prior to their appearance, or whether the announcement of the guest's upcoming appearance (made by the show a week in advance) tipped prescient investors off to that guest's favored stocks, is anyone's guess. It is also worrisome that a number of lawsuits have been launched against a minority of financial talk-show hosts who touted investments on their programs irresponsibly—investments which were close to fraudulent in some cases. In any case, use media programs not as buying or selling guides, but as sources of tuition-free expert information.

After three months or so of faithful listening to a money talk show, you'll be able to answer the caller's financial question in line with the host about one-third of the time. In another month, half the time. And so on. Louis Rukeyser's *Wall Street Week* is more sophisticated. Don't despair if it doesn't grab you in the early years of your investment program. You don't need this level of expertise for your Four Step fund for decades.

Financial columnists and commentators such as Jane Bryant Quinn, Ken and Daria Dolan, and many others are user-friendly and are highly reliable sources of everyday financial advice. I recommend you get in the habit of reading them faithfully, even if their subject *du jour* isn't quite your cup of tea. Some day it may be, and you'll be ahead of the curve if you already know a little something about it.

**Ratings services:** Bond buyers need to know the creditworthiness of the issuer, people looking over stocks want to know the company's financials, and mutual fund buyers are interested in the fund's historical performance as compared to other funds of its type. Ratings services fill this obvious need, and although there are many such, including the monthly personal finance magazine's performance charts and stock analyses, certain big-time services dominate their fields. *Value Line Investment Survey* is the leading reference for stock analysis; *Standard & Poor's* and *Moody's Investor Services* rate bonds; and for mutual funds, see *Morningstar Mutual Funds, Lipper Analytical Service,* and *Value Line's* mutual fund ratings. Most large libraries will carry these references. They are much too expensive to contemplate subscribing to until your Four Step fund is well along, and you decide you want to try your hand at active investing. Until then, make them a routine piece of the public library part of your financial education curriculum.

Since the Four Step programs are designed for mutual fund investing, let's take a closer look at *Morningstar Mutual Funds*, the Chicago-based service that tracks mutual funds in depth, and the originator of the (somewhat) controversial "star" ratings. If you leaf through any of the popular personal finance magazines, you'll see ads throughout that feature four and five star funds. It's the Morningstar stars they're touting, and a five-star fund manager is nearly as excited about his or her five stars as a French chef is with his three Michelin stars.

Morningstar rates funds by comparing each fund's total returns for three-, five-, and ten-year periods with the average returns for its investment category. The total returns are adjusted for risk, and stars are awarded every fund, with five stars representing the top 10 percent of funds in that category, and one star the bottom 10 percent. Four stars and two stars are awarded the next 22.5 percent (above average and below average, respectively), with the middle 35 percent getting three stars, which represent average performance.

The controversies centered on the formulas used by Morningstar to arrive at its ratings. Some respected commentators felt risk was overweighted. One fund family pointed out that two of its funds earned four stars: an aggressive growth fund with an average annual return of over 17 percent per year, and a conservative stock fund with an average return of under 12 percent. Because the latter fund, which had average returns, had lower than average risk, it ended with the same star rating as the riskier, but significantly higher-returning fund. But an investor, seeing both stock funds with four stars, might be led to believe they are equivalent investments. They are not. One is for the aggressive, growth-oriented investor, and the other is for the more cautious, income-oriented participant. Until recently, the stars didn't give you this information, but Morningstar adjusted its system. The problem is, the stars appear in the funds' ads unaccompanied by the rest of the material, a practice that surely can mislead. It's important for you to recognize the stars as a tool, not as a filter designed to lead you to the hottest performing funds.

Others point out that the star system, necessarily, rates past performance. It is a light shining off the stern, so to speak, not the bow. A five-star fund might be rapidly descending through three-star territory to two, but the ratings won't reflect that for some time. Some feel that the categories used by Morningstar to compare "like" funds are too broad. Gold funds should be compared to other gold funds; international to international; small cap to small cap, and so forth—but this is not the case.

Morningstar's managers are the first to say their ratings are a starting place, not the final word. I agree with that, and would go further by saying the real use of the service is in its report on each fund, which includes most of the statistical and financial information you'll need to form an opinion on that fund. The reports are updated regularly in a looseleaf format, one page per fund. Get thee to thy library, and spend an afternoon with Morningstar (named, ironically, for a line in Thoreau's *Walden*—about as far from the world of late-twentieth-century finance as can be imagined).

**Investment newsletters:** There are dozens of expensive newsletters out there that purport to give you hot tips, cutting-edge analysis, or exquisite systems to time the market. It's kind of like the New Year, when all those psychics push their baloney. Every year, some reporter has the good sense to collect the crystal ball gazers' predictions at the beginning of January and then expose their pathetic records at the end of the year.

A few investment newsletters are worth their price. Many are not. Many fund families and brokerages publish free newsletters for their customers, which are as informational and useful as any out there. Investors' associations also publish useful periodicals for much less than private newsletters.

Until your Four Step fund reaches $50,000 or so, the subscription price of most newsletters makes them too expensive for you. You should deduct the cost of your subscription from your investment return. If your $5,000 Four Step fund yields $500 per year, and you spend $200 on a newsletter, your 10 percent profit, in effect, drops to 6 percent. If you like newsletters—and they are worth looking over in any self-education program—go to the library. If your public library is short on financial materials, ask your librarian to direct you to a business or large university library.

Sometimes a stock picker or market timer will develop a following, much like a guru. He or she will then put out a newsletter to the true believers, who may pay dearly for the privilege in more ways than one. Each has a complicated theory that purports to give you an edge, but they seldom prove out over time. This is confirmed by the success of some of the nuttiest things going. For instance, one of the most reliable predictors of market performance, historically, anyway, is the Super Bowl. When a team from the original NFL wins (the theory goes), the market rises. If the AFC prevails, the market tanks. This awesome indicator has outperformed gurus and Nobel laureates alike. Here's another one: Historically, the Dow rises when women's hemlines shorten. Longer skirts, lower numbers.

Which just goes to show you that in the world of crystal balls and stock predictors, there are the foolish and the stupid. If you're willing to bet your fortunes on fortune tellers like these, the Four Step programs are not for you.

Not all investment newsletters are guru driven, however. Some are handy statistical compilations of whatever asset class to which they devote themselves. There are bond newsletters, stock newsletters, and plenty of mutual fund entries as well. Some are dedicated to a particular mutual fund family, although independently published. Some only cover no-load mutual funds; others are dedicated market timers.

You don't need to subscribe to an expensive advisory. Certainly not for the first many years that your Four Step fund is getting underway in a plain-vanilla index mutual fund. Many of the larger fund families put out their own newsletters, free to their investors. These tend to be responsible and informative, and although they reflect a bias toward their sponsor's funds and approach, this is usually presented in a straightforward way, along with plenty of general information that can further your education—for free. Investors' clubs also circulate newsletters to their memberships, for the price of the dues. This is a cheaper and more objective route than the private investment newsletter.

*Barron's*, the weekly financial newspaper published by Dow Jones, runs a feature called "Market Watch," which excerpts snippets from various financial newsletters. Here's a sampling of opinions from just one week:

- "[O]ur indicators continue to be bullish . . . and sentiment readings are still positive."—*Investors Intelligence*
- "With . . . the four year cycle due to bottom in a couple of months, selectivity and caution are warranted."—*The Kon-Lin Letter*
- "The current rebound has many characteristics of the beginning of a substantial new up-leg."—*The Mercer Forecast*
- "Expect a sharp and vicious market decline of between 5% and 10% which should span a three- to four-week period.—*The Winnell Report*
- "With the correction completed, the unfolding up-leg for stocks and bonds is likely to last for some time."—*Major Trends*
- "A bearish period is ahead of us."—*The Marketarian Letter*

Take your choice. There's a bear for every bull, and so it goes week after week. *Barron's* "Market Watch" is an excellent touchstone whenever one becomes overly tempted to play follow the leader.

If you do like the idea of a newsletter, fortunately there's Mark Hulbert, who ranks the performance of investment advisory newsletters. At one point he examined market-timing newsletters, and found only one that beat the market over time—and that one, marginally. Before subscribing to any advisory, consult the *Hulbert Financial Digest* in your library (*Hulbert* is listed under Resources in Appendix III).

**Handouts from the industry:** Browse through any of the personal finance magazines, paying particular attention to the ads. Brokerages and mutual funds offer a surprisingly informational array of booklets, planning kits, and other free materials that are yours for the asking. So long as you recognize going in that the material will be biased toward the product sponsored, you can pick up quite a lot of readable information by calling the 800 numbers advertised and requesting the free material.

**Books:** Your library and bookstore offer sections devoted to money. Often everything from "how to start a business" to "how to get a mortgage" are lumped together on the business shelves. Larger places add the category of finance or personal finance. Since the categories are usually shelved next to one another, asking for the business section will usually get you to finance as well. Once there, the titles are usually arranged by author, alphabetically. Notice there are hundreds. Some are standard reference works, others are how-tos of varying quality, and still others are titillating tell-alls on Wall Street's high crimes and misdemeanors.

**Roll your own numbers:** If our Four Step programs don't fit you to a tee, you can customize your own program with a financial calculator or software program. Maybe you are outside the age range I've presented, or you want to put more (or less) away and would like to see the result. Maybe you want to retire earlier or later than sixty-seven.

No problem. Financial calculators can cost you anywhere from less than $30 to more than $100. Business functions are different from financial functions, so make sure you get the right kind. It must be able to handle compounding.

**Personal finance software:** At some point, as your wealth builds, you'll want to begin tracking your investments with more sophistication than a daily glance at the financial pages in your newspaper. For that, you're in the right century. Your computer and its modem can connect you with literally hundreds of services that offer stocks, bonds, and mutual fund prices right up to the minute, including the ability to purchase your investments on-line.

Financial software generally breaks down along these lines: personal finance, computerized bill paying, on-line securities trading, and tax preparation programs. Some are super; others are unwieldy and dull. Many offer free sample disks or money-back guarantees.

All of the major on-line services—Prodigy, CompuServe, America Online—offer investor forums and access to market information. Subscribers can set up their portfolio on-line, then each time they sign on, the service will update the portfolio to the current market price, including a profit-and-loss report for each holding. Each service has a relationship with a discount brokerage, meaning you can execute your own trades on your computer, in the comfort of your home. Some brokerages offer their own software packages to their customers, including portfolio management and on-line trading. You can call up the security's history, the company's financials, all kinds of charts. Some of these services are fully international, meaning you can call up an investment interest in Brazil or Switzerland, probe international money markets or currency rates, or whatever. This kind of thing is way beyond our simple Four Step programs, which do not rely on stock or bond trading. But it's good for you to know what's out there.

If you prefer not to go on-line, several services will send you data disks at the end of each quarter, with updated returns for thousands of mutual funds, stocks, or bonds. Leading services such as Morningstar and Value Line offer a disk update service; so do some of the larger fund families. Some investor clubs deliver data disks at a lower price than the private companies. You can screen and filter the database, compare performances, and even graph your results. Other programs tie downloaded (or disk-updated) data into your personal financial profile, including your goals and objectives. Some track your checking account, and then even pay your bills electronically or write checks automatically on your printer. Many will import and export data between other financial software, such as tax programs. At this writing, financial software can include bank, credit card, and investment tracking; net-worth calculations; securities and mutual fund tracking and updating; income tax estimation; and check printing on plain paper.

Look for a personal finance program that offers "what if" scenarios, allowing you to vary the inflation rate, the rate of return, your payment schedule, and savings goal. Good ones are available for DOS, Windows, or the Macintosh. The most popular all-around program at this writing is Quicken, which will keep you on budget, write checks, balance your statements, and keep track of your portfolio. You'll find these programs advertised in computer and personal finance magazines.

It's well to remember that out there in cyberspace some things are not all they should be. Authorities are reporting an alarming number of investment scams, including sales of phony securities and fraudulent inside tips that promote a particular stock. Some who have an interest in a company (perhaps a family member of the owner) will put out optimistic but unofficial statements, leading lots of dummies into buying the stock and thereby increasing its value. Don't buy securities on the basis of on-line tips, and you'll be okay.

Don't forget, as much fun as these programs are for the computer nut, they don't do much more than you can do yourself with a glance at your daily financial pages, and some graph paper. I am myself a big fan of financial software, but if you don't like computers, or don't have access to one, don't worry. You don't really need one to do a good job for yourself as an investor. If you don't have a computer, but don't want to rely on the market quotes in the financial pages, which at only one-day-old are too stale for many investors, there are telephone services run by many brokerages that require only a touchtone phone for up-to-the-minute price quotes.

**Investment clubs:** Investment clubs break down into two distinct types: The first is a local group formed to pool its members' money, and make investment decisions collectively through regular meetings and security analysis. Many of these groups have survived for decades, filling their members' social lives as well as making money for them. Others come and go, disbanding over poor performance or internal bickering. For information on how to form your own investment club, see Resources in Appendix III for the address of the National Association of Investors Corporation (NAIC).

The second type is not an investment pool, but rather a national membership organization that disseminates information to its members, and offers free or discounted services. The American Association of Individual Investors (AAII), for example, offers its members a monthly newsletter, a free guide to no-load mutual funds, local chapters, discounted seminars, study programs, shelves of reading materials, a free on-line bulletin-board service (BBS), and telephone access to market quotes, all for a reasonable price. The AAII covers stocks, bonds, and mutual funds and is worth its dues. See Resources for how to contact it. There are other associations, many devoted only to mutual funds as well.

You don't need a club or an association to make your fortune the easy Four Step way—at least until your holdings get up to the high five figures. But if you find yourself drawn to this stuff, these organizations are good ways to broaden your knowledge at a low cost, and they can be a lot of fun.

**Free seminars:** One way to sell you a product is through free seminars, many of which are sponsored by major financial institutions.

This sponsorship doesn't make them bad, but ultimately, all are biased in favor of their thing, be it brokerage accounts, insurance products, financial planning, mutual funds, bank products, a CPA's tax program, a lawyer's trusts, or an author's books. You can get useful information from many of these programs, so long as you keep alert to the inevitable bias, no matter how subtle. If the seminar weren't being sponsored by someone trying to interest you in a product, you'd pay $100 or more per session, so if you can sort out the sales pitch from the good stuff, many free seminars are well worth your time. Stick with the ones sponsored by large financial institutions; they have much more to lose if they act irresponsibly. Collect all the handouts to read at home, buy nothing at the seminar, sign up for no classes, and then at home and away from the pressure, sort out your options.

The better seminar sponsors—and there are many—hope to inform you about their product generally and, of course, spark your interest. They don't care to pressure you into an inappropriate investment, because their various licenses would be at risk if they did so. The ones to watch out for are the hustlers out there on the lecture circuit who are selling *themselves* in one way or another, rather than a legitimate financial product. They have books, newsletters, video and audio tapes, and lecture series to sell you— MasterCard and Visa welcome, installment payments A-okay.

**Hot tips:** You've probably heard the term *inside information* tossed around in financial circles. Maybe you didn't know that buying or selling securities on the basis of inside information is illegal for both the original tipper on the inside, and for all the tippers and tippees down the line. Inside information, under the law, is information yet to be released to the public by a publicly traded business, which would reasonably affect an investor's decision to buy or sell shares in the company.

Let's look at our old friend Suds 'n Suds for a minute, since one of its original owners, Sue, was caught up in an insider trading scandal. Here's what happened: Sue stayed on after the IPO as chief financial officer (CFO) of the corporation. Sue and her old friend Bonnie always shared everything over lunch once a month at Chez Panisse in Berkeley. Bonnie had always been very discreet, and since she was not an investor, Sue felt free to confide everything to her. On one such lunch, Sue told Bonnie that she might be looking for another job soon, since a major beer company was likely to make a takeover offer (an offer to buy Suds 'n Suds from its shareholders) within the next week or so. She told Bonnie that the beer company would be offering Suds 'n Suds shareholders $43 for their stock, which was currently selling at $30. In addition, she let Bonnie know that another company—a big fast-food outfit—was also interested, and the competing bids of the two suitors might drive the stock price up to $48 or more. Because Suds 'n Suds was publicly traded on a major stock exchange and had thousands of owners, the competing buyers would keep bidding the stock price up until enough shareholders sold their shares to the bidder to give it a controlling interest in the company, or until the price reached a level where the bidder lost interest and withdrew its offer.

What Sue didn't know was that Bonnie was deeply in debt due to her child's chronic illness, with no medical insurance. She didn't have enough money to benefit from the tip herself by buying stock, so Bonnie "sold" the tip to five friends, for 10 percent of whatever profits they made on their trades. One of those friends, Lynn, recovered his cost (Bonnie's 10 percent) by selling the tip to three more friends.

Larry was one of those friends. Larry didn't have much money, so rather than buying Suds 'n Suds stock outright, he purchased call options on 1,000 shares. The striking price was set at $35, and Larry paid a total of $1,500 for the option premiums. If the stock rose to $48 as expected, Larry was in a position to buy 1,000 shares at $35, and immediately resell them at $48, for a profit of $13,000 (less broker costs) on an outlay of only $1,500 for the option premiums. After the takeover bid was announced, the SEC noted the unusual trading activity in Suds 'n Suds stock in the two weeks before the public announcement, and sued Larry, Lynn, Bonnie, and Sue for securities violations.

Every investor dreams of the moment he or she suddenly learns something no one else knows about—something that's going to push a stock, or the market generally, in a dramatic way. Because of your hot tip, you're in there first—and make out like a bandit.

Don't bet on it. The hottest tips, of course, come from inside the company, and trading on inside information is a federal offense. If your barber or hairdresser tells you he bought a biotech stock because the chief executive officer just told him, under the hairdryer, that a hot patent was just approved, the CEO, the barber, and you (if you buy or sell the stock) are all in violation of federal securities laws. The theory is that a healthy financial market is impossible so long as some traders are privy to information other traders are not.

A listed company's board members, officers, and shareholders with 10 percent or more of the company's stock are insiders under the securities regulations, and must disclose all their trades in the company's stock in public, so that everyone has a chance to know what's going on. Often, an executive is just cashing in his or her options. True insiders are prohibited from trading within a certain period before and after an announcement is made by the company that reasonably would be expected to affect the price of stock.

Nor is the SEC just interested in the big fellows. The agency monitors the volume of trades in a particular stock for the period before an important public announcement. If they find excess activity, they'll question the traders to find out why. The SEC investigators may follow tips down three or four levels, prosecuting all the way down to $5,000 trades, or even lower. If a tip was disseminated at a party, the SEC might question everyone who was there. In recent years, a Motel 6 executive provided a tip to a sick friend, who sold the information to more friends, many of them habitués of a string of tanning salons. The SEC followed the tip through four levels, indicting six on criminal charges and suing eighteen for money damages.

The idea is to protect the market. If inside information was permitted, there would be no room for ordinary investors, and the markets would collapse.

Does insider trading happen despite the law? You betcha. Ivan Boesky and Mike Milken are just two of many recently endowed with federal felon status because of insider trading.

But this shouldn't really concern you. Insider stuff appeals to market timers, and your Four Step programs aren't set up for that kind of action. You don't need inside information to make your program work, so ignore the hot tip. If the information is worth anything at all, you'll be hearing it too late. The market will have already reacted to the news, and you'll be buying a pig in a poke.

**Financial professionals:** In the ordinary course of a lifetime, you're likely to use a variety of professionals to assist you with things financial. An enrolled agent (EA) or certified public accountant (CPA) to help you with your taxes, an attorney-at-law to distribute your grandmother's estate or sort out your property in a divorce, a real-estate agent to close escrow on your first house, an insurance agent to insure it; a banker to lend you the mortgage money, and a stockbroker to lose it for you (just kidding). When you commit your money to a mutual fund, the fund's manager should be an important part of your decision to go with that fund. These old-line, or traditional financial professionals are licensed or otherwise regulated by the government, to control against fraud or overreaching. A grievance against a lawyer can be taken to his or her state bar association, and ultimately could result in disbarment (the loss of his or her license to practice law). Similarly, the National Association of Securities Dealers receives complaints against stockbrokers, and similar trade associations and regulatory bodies govern errant insurance or real-estate agents, CPAs, and bankers.

A newer profession has been developing in recent years, that of financial planning. These practitioners generally counsel individuals (or institutions) on how best to deploy their resources, in order to meet their objectives most effectively. Since there is no national licensing body for financial planners, the field is somewhat in flux.

In many places, no credentials at all are necessary to declare oneself a financial planner. To define the profession, various courses of study, complete with qualifying exams, have been developed by private concerns.

You will not have enough money in your Four Step funds to need a financial planner for decades—if ever. Many of you will fall in love with this stuff, and become more than adept at handling your own affairs, and no one will ever have your self-interest at heart more than you will.

Some of you, however, will find you loathe money matters. As your Four Step fund climbs into the five or six digits, you may do well to seek the advice of the most qualified, objective planner you can find. Keep in mind the relatively unregulated nature of the field. Check references and affiliations religiously.

The federal Securities and Exchange Commission requires that anyone offering investment advice register as an investment adviser; many states require registration with their securities regulators as well. A registered investment adviser, then, is someone who has merely completed the paperwork and paid the filing fee for the registration. On the federal level, anyway, there is no course of study required, nor is there a qualifying examination. The registration is for the purpose of disciplinary action, as well as public disclosure of the registrant's qualifications. It is not a badge of accomplishment. Someone operating as a financial planner on the strength of their SEC registration as an investment adviser is not showing you much.

Along with the SEC registration (which all persons holding themselves out as investment advisers should hold as a minimum), you are likely to encounter a veritable alphabet soup of credentials, signaling one or another kind of qualification. None of them, however, is as rigorous as the courses of study leading to the law degree (Juris Doctor, or J.D.) or CPA.

- Probably the best known among financial planners is the *certified financial planner* (CFP), qualified by the Certified Financial Planner Board of Standards, in Denver, a private institution.

The CFP course is a one- or two-year correspondence course, available also at a few colleges. CFPs are required to undergo continuing education. Most CFPs make their money on the loads, or commissions on the products they sell their clients. Some are "fee only," meaning they charge by the hour or flat fee, rather than relying on commissions. A fee-only arrangement removes the conflict of interest inherent in commission-laden transactions. But in order to make a commensurate amount of money, the fee-only practitioner might have to load up on (pad) the hours.

- A *personal financial specialist* (PFS) is a certified public accountant with at least three years financial planning experience who has passed a qualifying examination in addition to the rigorous CPA exams. The designation is awarded by the American Institute of Certified Public Accountants.

- A *chartered financial analyst* (CFA) is trained to pick stocks. Many CFAs work for mutual funds or brokerages; many are registered stockbrokers themselves. Some are in private practice as financial planners. After one year of study, would-be CFAs take a test, which only about 60 percent pass.

- The *chartered life underwriter* (CLU) may call him or herself a financial planner or estate planner, but his or her background is insurance. No prior college experience is required for entry into the CLU program of courses, most of which are insurance-oriented. The financial advice you get from a CLU will probably be heavily weighted toward insurance products, although perhaps not exclusively. The CLU program requires two-hour exams in each of ten subjects. The American Society of CLU & ChFC maintains an ethical code, and offers continuing education to its designees, of which sixty hours every two years are required. The CLU is usually paid through commissions, which erects a natural conflict of interest between adviser and client that some may find difficult to surmount.

- The *chartered financial consultant* (ChFC) goes through a similar course of study as the CLU, although with more financial content. Like CLUs, ChFCs are graduates of the American

College in Bryn Mawr, Pennsylvania, known for its insurance emphasis. ChFCs need three years' financial experience, must pass an examination, and must engage in continuing education.

- Some planners may designate themselves as members of the National Association of Personal Financial Advisors (NAPFA). NAPFA members are planners of various backgrounds (often CFPs) who practice fee-only planning, and believe commission-based work presents an insurmountable conflict of interest. See Resources in Appendix III for this and the other organizations that represent financial planners if you want more information, or wish to lodge a complaint.

Most financial planning is done by the numbers, which makes it a natural for computer programs. The planner is capable of generating tons of material—complete with graphs, charts, and tables—with very little practical use to you. An industry study in 1993 found that planners averaged over $100,000 a year, earned on commissions (load products and annual management fees), and on fees as high as $200 per hour. With the average abbreviated financial plan costing more than $300, and a lifetime plan up to $5,000, be very sure of whom you are consulting, and what you are getting before you sign the contract. As you know, it is my opinion you can do your financial planning yourself, but if you don't care to, there's no shame in seeking help.

Initials after a name usually signal that there is a disciplinary board in the background somewhere, although in some cases this threat can be very weak. Always ask a professional where you can send a grievance, if you've a mind to. If this is too awkward, call your state securities regulator and ask what your remedies are. Radio and TV consumer hot lines can be helpful, and sometimes the Better Business Bureau can tell you where to file a grievance. Your district attorney or state attorney general can also be helpful.

If you do choose to do business with a financial adviser or planner, ask for credentials, and then check them out to be sure they are current. See and check the adviser's SEC and state registrations, and get a written statement of fees. Understand that you can live your life happily without ever consulting a financial planner (or, for that matter, a lawyer, CPA, tax preparer, stockbroker, and the like), however. It's completely up to you what professionals you consult along the way. Just know that you are entirely capable of doing it yourself, provided you're willing to commit the time. It's strictly a matter of preference.

**Doing due diligence:** Due diligence is Wall Street jargon for doing your homework. Securities professionals are required to use due diligence in researching investment opportunities; directors and officers of corporations have due diligence requirements, too. So should you. You are not ready to decide if you need professional advice until you've prepared yourself under steps A through D of the already-outlined education program. Only then will you know enough to be a good client, the kind the best of professionals appreciate most.

**Scams:** Since you're going to be rich, someone will be out to trick you, so like in scouting, be prepared. There's an idea afloat that cons only target old folks. Many do, for sure, because that's where the money is. But some cons are aimed right at the young, and you'd better know about the most common ones. Some aren't strictly illegal; they're just very bad deals that almost always work out terribly. You should know about these, too, since young people are special targets because they are presumed to be looking for good opportunities, up for a challenge, eternally optimistic, and inexperienced in recognizing schemes. Here are three opportunities to lose money that will illustrate the point.

- We've already talked about Charles Ponzi and his no-miss opportunity. In the strict sense, Ponzi's scheme is illegal today in most places, but that doesn't mean there aren't deals out there that smell very much like a pyramid scheme, yet escape the district attorney's clutches for technical reasons. These promotions usually involve a hierarchy of distributorships. The distributor has a product to sell to the public—goods or services—but he really gets ahead by signing up new distributors. He accumulates points or bonuses for bringing in the new distributors, who, like him, have to put up money or buy inventory in order to participate. He moves up the hierarchical chart by building the empire below him, and so on, until the newest distributors can't induce anyone else to sign on, and thus lose all the money they've "invested" in inventory and fees. Sometimes these schemes are referred to as network marketing. You're probably most familiar with them as those irritating chain letters.

What to look out for? Any proposition pitched by someone who's own bottom line will be directly affected by the number of those who buy in. At the very least, engage in a thorough investigation of one operation, working through independent sources. And then walk away from any enterprise that ties your own prosperity more to your ability to entice others into the fold, than your ability to move the product.

- Your mailbox may be the source of another "can't miss" opportunity for you to lose money. After you begin your Four Step program, you may find yourself getting a lot of mail from investment newsletters, software companies, and other entrepreneurs. Some of it you'll welcome, because it's legit and will prove helpful to you. Most of it will go in the round file, and some of it may even be from someone on the make.

  Take this glittering offer, for example: You are sent a sample copy of an amazing investment newsletter that each week will tell you the direction the stock market will head in the following week. You're not tempted, because you already know better than to try to time the market, but others are intrigued when the market call is correct four weeks out of four. The cost to subscribe is a mere $200 a year. Half the suckers sign up—never to see their money again or the newsletter they thought they bought.

  The promoter of the scheme is in Rio with the $500,000 he

netted with only four weeks effort. Here's how he did it: He rented 150,000 names from a direct-mail company for about $15,000. He mailed a sample newsletter to all 150,000 the first week, predicting to half the list that the market would go up the following week, and to the other half that it would fall. The market rose. The 75,000 who got the "fall" prediction never heard from him again. The others got a second newsletter, again divided into half rise predictions and half fall. The market rose again, so his next letter went only to the 37,500 who got the rise version. And so on, for four weeks. The fifth week, the 18,750 who had by then received four correct calls were invited to subscribe for $200 per year. One out of six took the bait—over 3,000 suckers who never saw their money (or the newsletter) again. The cost of the promotion? Perhaps around $125,000 for printing, postage, and mailing-list rental, leaving him around $500,000 profit. This is a fictionalized version of a real scheme. Watch out for it; no one can predict the short-term direction of the market consistently, no matter who they are or what system they say they've developed.

- The clients of one California financial planner thought they'd followed all the rules. The planner had been in business in the community twelve years, so was able to present credible local references. Then she suddenly went bad, turning her clients away from safe investments into something she described as a "pool of U.S. treasuries." It sounded safe, but the hapless investors wrote their checks to her personally, not the government. They didn't check with the Institute of Certified Financial Planners to learn her CFP had lapsed; so, too, had her registration as an investment adviser with the SEC. Because she worked alone, no one was there to see her mail come and go, access her computer, or take her calls, any of which might have uncovered her fraud before it went too far. She's a convicted felon now, but the money disappeared.

Had her clients used a large firm instead of a solo practitioner, their losses probably would have been covered, in order to protect the reputation of the firm. There are plenty of excellent solo practitioners out there, and there's no denying that the personal service you can get from a solo is unbeatable. Nor is there any reason to suppose the solos are more dishonest than big-firm account executives. But for defensive purposes, you'll have a better chance recovering your losses from the big guys, if the planner or broker goes bad.

From time to time, especially when the markets are disappointing, you may be tempted to jump into this or that gimmick just to experience the rush that comes when your investments soar. Unfortunately, especially when markets are lagging, some financial professionals, whose wherewithal, after all, depends on selling their products, oversell some risky ventures, or even worse, actively defraud their clients. There are ways to protect yourself from overreaching or downright larceny. Here are some rules, if you feel you need professional advice in the first place:

- **Never, ever invest in something you don't understand.**
- **Use established firms with at least two professionals.**
- **Never write your check to the professional personally.**
- **Always check with the issuer of the license or credential.**

If you're scammed, tell the cops. If anything related to the con came through the mail, call the postal inspectors. They are the most underrated law enforcers in America. The Better Business Bureau will take your complaints against both legal and illegal operations. You can always call your district attorney's or state attorney general's fraud department. If the scam involves investments, call your state's securities division, and the SEC in large cities and Washington, DC. These agencies want to hear from you. You're their ear to the ground.

Do you want to turn your bonus, or your accident settlement into something big? The next chapter discusses how to wring the last drop of benefit from fringe benefits, windfalls, and intangibles.

*Self-Test*
## Chapter 11

1. Which of the following is *not* part of the four-step self-education program?
   a. read financial pages
   b. read personal finance magazines
   c. buy 100 shares of stock
   d. compile a fantasy securities list

2. "Hot tips" in personal finance magazines are not so hot because they are:
   a. biased
   b. too old
   c. poorly researched
   d. always wrong

3. If Suds 'n Suds P/E is 18, it means the price per share is 18 times more than the earnings per share:

   ☐ True     ☐ False

4. Earnings per share and dividends are the same thing:

   ☐ True     ☐ False

5. The newspaper's financial pages are meant to be:
   a. exhaustive
   b. all an investor needs to know
   c. up to the minute
   d. a quick reference

6. Which of the following doesn't belong?
   a. Value Line
   b. Lipper
   c. Morningstar
   d. Federal Reserve

7. No successful investor is without an investment newsletter:

   ☐ True     ☐ False

8. Free materials from fund families are likely to be:
    a. mostly responsible
    b. heavily biased
    c. erroneous
    d. for experts only

9. Personal finance computer software is:
    a. a must
    b. helpful
    c. full of bugs
    d. unavailable for Macs

10. "Inside" information is:
    a. limited to that passed by board members
    b. always untrustworthy
    c. never available
    d. illegal

*Answers on Worksheet 15 in Appendix I*

# Ain't No Free Lunch and Other Lies

*Fringe benefits, windfalls, and intangibles*

If you've stuck with me so far, you already know—emphatically—that *yes, there is such a thing as a free lunch!* Indeed, most of you will have over $900,000 dollars of free lunch if you use the Four Step programs, thanks to time and compounding. So where did this tired old cliché get its start? In times gone by, when saloons provided their customers a "free" lunch, cynics recognized that they paid for it when they bought their drinks. And ever since, someone who thinks he or she is the smartest thing going, brings up the old bromide, and everyone wearily agrees. Everyone, that is, except you, me, and economists.

Of course, it's wise to recognize the cost lurking behind many so-called freebies. After all, we know that what often looks (and is promoted as) free, sure enough isn't. In this chapter, we'll take a look at "free" job fringe benefits (which aren't), and certain windfalls and intangibles (which may be).

## Fringe Benefits

You might want to get a head start by completing Worksheet 13 in Appendix I, a little reality check on the disheartening gap between what you earn and what you're paid.

Let's begin with the biggest social program in the United States, and your stake in it.

**Social Security:** Social Security certainly isn't free (look at the FICA bite out of your paycheck), but its value to you—right now and after retirement—is the most underestimated benefit you're likely to come across. I've noticed that people your age labor under two beliefs held so firmly and universally that they very nearly qualify as generational articles of faith.

The first is that inflation is so monstrous and inevitable that attempting to save anything more than five years before you need it is a fool's errand. Inflation is a tiger, as we've seen in Chapter Seven, but a paper tiger for those who follow Step Four of the program.

The second dearly held belief is that Social Security, despite its millions upon millions of beneficiaries, will somehow go poof!, and not be there for you when you retire. This silliness is so pervasive among young people that a survey has shown that while nearly one-half of all Americans between the ages of eighteen and thirty-four believe in extraterrestrial UFOs, only one-quarter believe that Social Security will exist when they retire. The Disappearing Social Security myth is generated by armies of financial advisers whose own well-being is enhanced if they can convince battalions of clients to overbuy their financial products on the false assumption that Social Security will collapse long before 2026, when today's thirty-five-year-olds begin to retire. The Social Security libel is particularly pernicious, since it is sexy enough to be attractive to a media ever hungry for scary news affecting millions. This sells papers and ups ratings. Boring facts do not.

Social Security will be there for you. It won't look the same in forty years when you retire, but it doesn't look the same as it did forty years ago, either, or even twenty or ten.

What does it look like now? As you know if you've ever held a legitimate job with a paycheck, more than 7 percent of virtually everyone's pay is deducted for the FICA (Social Security) and Medicare tax. Your employer matches that. FICA supports the Social Security benefits now being paid out. General revenues (mostly income taxes) do not subsidize the program.

When you've accumulated enough credits, you're entitled to much more than a retirement benefit. Social Security is an insurance program as well. When a young worker dies, his or her spouse and children may be entitled to benefits. If a worker becomes disabled, Social Security can provide a benefit to the worker and his or her family. Although the retirement program requires about ten years' work to qualify, disability benefits are earned much faster.

Upon reaching full retirement age (sixty-seven for you), a monthly benefit is paid for life. An early retirement benefit is available beginning at age sixty-two; but for those born after

1960, it will be only 70 percent of the full benefit (for life), instead of 80 percent as now. A benefit is also paid to the spouse of the worker, provided his or her own work record doesn't provide a benefit larger than the spousal benefit. Upon the retiree's death, survivor's benefits are paid for the life of the widow or widower (again, assuming he or she is not entitled to a larger benefit on his or her own work record). If there should be a divorce following at least ten years of marriage, after age sixty-two the former spouse may be entitled to benefits for life. This will not diminish the worker's benefit, nor that of the new spouse.

Social Security benefits are weighted in favor of the lower paid. That means that at the higher end, a worker will find the retirement benefit equaling about 25 percent of the Social Security wages (that is, those wages that were subject to the FICA tax), while at the lower end, the benefit may be closer to 50 percent. The benefit is calculated on the basis of thirty-five-years paid work, although approximately ten years is enough to qualify for the program (forty credits are needed for retirement benefit eligibility; up to four credits per year may be earned).

Social Security is, and always was, a dynamic program that changes with the times. When it was instituted in the mid-1930s, for example, husbands supported wives and divorce was uncommon. To reflect that, Social Security benefits were available to wives (but not husbands, unless they could prove dependency) and widows. It wasn't until recent decades that divorced spouse benefits were added, and spousal and survivor's benefits extended to men as well as women. Most recently, in order to accommodate the looming retirement of the 76 million baby boomers ahead of you, the pay-in period was lengthened, and the pay-out period shortened by upping the age at which full retirement benefits are available from sixty-five to sixty-seven for those born after 1960. This is why we use age sixty-seven as the retirement norm in this book, and this is the most recent change that primarily affects your generation.

So Social Security changes. It's a highly political animal, since it's Congress that makes the rules, and the administration that runs the program. What it will be like in thirty or forty years when you retire is anyone's bet. What it won't be is broke. The program is running at a substantial surplus now, a surplus that will run out around the time you retire. Adjustments will be made to bring things into line, and there are essentially only three ways to go about it: First, increase payroll (FICA) taxes; second, decrease benefits; and third, subsidize the program out of general revenues.

Payroll taxes could be increased outright, but they are high now, and that would prove highly unpopular. More likely would be a removal of the earnings cap. At present, FICA is only applied to income up to a certain level, around $60,000, adjusted annually for inflation. Removing the cap would bring in increased payroll taxes from the well paid, a remedy always highly regarded by the electorate.

There are a number of ways to go about a benefits decrease. Extending the retirement age—even to age seventy—is a likely one. There are two things you should know about extending the retirement age, however.

First, it's so cynical, politically speaking, that it makes me shiver. Fiddling with current Social Security benefits is next to impossible because of the armies of old folks (thankfully) minding the store. Solution? Hit the youngest workers (that's you), since they, assuming that Social Security cuts only affect the old, won't be paying attention.

Second, any rise in the age of eligibility hits young men the hardest. African-American men are hit hardest of all, since their life expectancies are the lowest. Raise the age to seventy? Sure, on the assumption that millions of men will die before they recover one cent of their hard-earned FICA dollars. Don't be the fool who pays and pays, then shrugs off Social Security benefit cuts as irrelevant to your welfare. They are aiming right at you.

There are other ways to decrease benefits that you should watch out for. For example, lower-income folks don't pay income tax on their Social Security benefits, and that exemption could be abolished. The small ($225) death benefit could be abandoned.

Often discussed by both political parties is a proposition to make Social Security means-tested. That means that benefits would not be paid to the well-to-do (although under some proposals the line would be drawn not under the wealthy, but deep within the middle-income groups). Social Security supporters oppose means testing, because it will remove the rich and powerful (and their stake in, and therefore their support) from the system and raise trivial sums. As a future millionaire, you might keep an eye on means testing. The rich recipient being tossed out of the program could be you.

Finally, there are always those who support the notion of making Social Security voluntary, chief among them money managers and financial planners who drool at the thought of taking their commissions off all that investable cash were it to be returned to private hands. In their charts and tables that purport to show how much more an investment in Suds 'n Suds, Loves-to-Tank, or Super-Testosteroney would make compared to an equal sum paid to Social Security, they forget about the program's insurance feature. Securities won't pay lifetime benefits to families of young dead or disabled workers, with only five or ten years of investing behind them, but Social Security will.

In a nutshell, that's Social Security. It will be there for you in some form, and will be worth thousands and thousands of dollars to you. How much? There's an easy way to find out. Worksheet 14 in Appendix I will get you started on estimating your future Social Security benefit, as well as your current one, should you become seriously disabled. You can always call Social Security with any questions about the program in general at (800) 772-1213.

**Pensions:** Although Social Security now covers virtually everyone, there are still some governmental employees left out, primarily older civil service workers and teachers. The idea was that they didn't need Social Security because of their pensions. Pensions (the old-fashioned kind, paid for by the employer) were never the rule in private employment in the United States. No law makes them mandatory, and they mostly exist in larger companies, often unionized. One federal law, the Employee's Retirement Income Security Act (ERISA), sets the minimum standards for all pensions in private employment, so there's a certain sameness to most plans. If you're an oilworker in Texas, a logger in Oregon, a screenwriter in Hollywood, or a dive master in Florida and you're covered by a pension, you're covered by ERISA.

Here's how the typical pension works: The employee works for the employer for a certain number of years (usually five), after which he or she is vested in the plan. Vesting means that the worker is legally entitled to a pension upon reaching retirement age, no matter how small. If a vested worker should quit the job after six years, say, he or she could draw a pension from that job years later, upon retirement. It would be very small, of course, because pension benefits are calculated using such variables as length of employment, age at retirement, and pay level. Nothing says a worker can't retire with several pensions, each vested on a different job.

Unlike 401(k)s, 403(b)s, and the like (which are savings plans, not pensions, no matter what someone calls them), most traditional pensions—called defined benefit plans in the trade—are guaranteed by an agency of the U.S. government. If the company goes bankrupt, its pensioners' benefits will be protected up to about $30,000 per year.

A good pension is worth working for. It looks like a free lunch, because (except for government pensions) the employer usually pays for all of it. But of course, the worker pays in the end by foregoing a wage increase.

As was noted in Chapter Six, retirement planners like to speak of the three-legged stool. An adequate retirement is supposed to rest on the three legs of Social Security, a pension, and investment earnings. If you work forty years under a solid pension program, your benefit may well replace 40 to 50 percent of your final wage. If you expect to retire on—in today's dollars—about $60,000 per year, a pension bringing in $24,000 per year is the same as having an investment of $300,000 invested at 8 percent. That's a

good solid leg on your stool, but still leaves plenty of room for
your Four Step investment leg.

**Health insurance:** If an employer offers one fringe benefit beyond paid vacation and sick leave, health insurance is likely to be
it. Because its benefits are readily apparent to younger workers
(retirement benefits may not be), it is the benefit most likely to
attract a worker to the job. As anyone but the comatose knows,
health insurance is in flux right now. Not only have Congress and
the administration been floating various plans for years, large employers and health insurers have gotten into the act of cost con-
tainment. What this all means is that things are changing. Still, a
good health-insurance package purchased by a single person privately is likely to cost over $2,000 per year; for a married couple,
over $4,000; for a family, over $5,000. To generate the income to
pay for these premiums, you'd need $25,000, $50,000, and
$60,000 respectively (invested at 8 percent) stashed away, and
that's a whole lot of money. If your employer offers a good health
package, get in the habit of thinking of how much you'd need to
invest to earn the premium. It's a good habit for future millionaires to get into.

**Disability insurance:** Disability insurance is often dismissed by
young workers as unimportant. Nevertheless, it can be more important than life insurance if a career-ending or damaging event
occurs. On-the-job injuries will be partially compensated for by
worker's compensation, which all employers are required to carry.
But not all disabling events happen on the job. What about a
spinal injury from skiing, an auto accident, or a dumb dive?
What if an orthodontist loses some fingers? What if you get a
disabling disease, like multiple sclerosis? You never know. Social
Security pays a benefit for long-term disabilities, and of course,
there's Supplemental Security Income (SSI—welfare) for the im-
poverished. For extra protection, buy a disability policy from
your life insurance agent, but be sure to shop around. Benefits
and premiums differ widely, and women are likely to pay twice as

much as men. Women should especially look out for reproductive disabilities. They may be excluded.

**Flexible spending accounts:** Some employers permit their employees to contribute pretax dollars to an account out of which the employee can buy his or her own child care or medical insurance. Because this income is untaxed, the true cost of the health insurance or child care is lowered by 20 to 40 percent, depending on the tax bracket. For example, $5,000 in a flexible spending account is worth $1,550 to someone taxed at 31 percent; $1,400 at 28 percent; and $750 at 15 percent. As always with tax-subsidized fringe benefits, it's the rich who get the riches. Flexible benefits are controversial in Congress, and may lose their tax exemption at any time.

**Statutory rights:** Over the years, Congress and the states have enacted numerous acts that benefit employees in one way or another. Earlier these were labor and fair employment practice laws fought for by unions. Those concerned themselves with working conditions, such as safety, wages, and hours. More recently, civil rights laws were enacted to fight discriminatory employment practices against people because of their race, sex, religion, age, and national origin (Title VII of the 1964 Civil Rights Act, and the Age Discrimination in Employment Act); more recently still, statutes have been passed that protect interests dear to women workers' hearts (Family and Medical Leave Act) and to the disabled community (Americans with Disabilities Act). These and other state and federal acts apply only to employees, usually exempting employees of small businesses. In no way do they protect the self-employed worker, the freelancer, the consultant. A middle-aged African-American lawyer hanging out her shingle has no agency to complain to if her practice suffers because of her age, sex, and/or race. These statutory protections are intangibles, and are very nearly a free lunch for employees, in that everyone pays the income taxes that support the programs and their expensive enforcement agencies, but only the employed get the protection. A job that appears to offer no traditional fringe benefits nevertheless offers these, and they should never be disregarded when evaluating a job offer. But be aware: Most protective statutes exclude small businesses, that is, those that employ anywhere from five to fifty employees, depending on the statute.

So here's the bottom line: When you're comparing job offers, never disregard the fringe-benefit package. As we saw in Chapter Six, a good 401(k) package with a healthy employer contribution is a great way to build the investment leg of your stool, but it is no substitute for a traditional plan for the pension leg of your stool. The total fringe package is likely to be worth from 20 percent to over 30 percent of your pay. An employed graphic artist earning $2,000 per month plus fringes is usually earning at least 25 percent more than the self-employed artist earning the same $2,000, but paying his or her own Social Security, Keogh or SEP, and disability and health insurance. The freelancer does not get paid vacations, sick leave, or maternity or paternity leave, nor is he or she entitled to unemployment insurance when work falls off, or worker's compensation if there's an injury on the job. Not being an employee, the freelancer or consultant has no access to the statutory rights employees take for granted. When evaluating the fringes, get in the habit of thinking of the hundreds of thousands of dollars—perhaps millions—you'd need to accumulate in order to generate the income needed to replace all the benefits. Seen in this way, a good fringe benefit package is worth big, big money.

 **Windfalls**

Getting back to that free lunch. Economists say that there really is such a thing as a free lunch. Take ordinary drinking water, for example. Water, perhaps the most important commodity we humans know, is nevertheless one of the cheapest. This is no accident. It reflects the recognition by society that such a life-and-death substance is too precious to be left to unbridled private enterprise. What would you pay for drinking water if you had to? Several hundred dollars per month, no doubt—all you could come up with, in fact, since water is essential to life.

And that's your free lunch. Economists describe a free lunch as the difference between what you would be willing to pay for something, and what in fact you do pay. In other words, you are receiving value for nothing. So from now on, you can be the irritating person who pipes up with this bit of arcania whenever anyone within earshot trots out the "no free lunch" thing.

But there's a larger lesson to be learned here than just one more way to annoy your friends. As a millionaire-in-training, you should accustom yourself to recognizing hidden value (and costs), and converting them into financial terms. You are going to have a lot of money one day, and that money will be tied up in investments, which is fundamentally different from having a large salary. You will be managing hundreds of thousands of dollars, and to do so effectively, you need to recognize instinctively the true cost (and value) of various judgments you will make over time. This section, then, is about handling the windfalls that drop into most lives, such as bonuses, settlements, winnings, or inheritances. I'll also talk about generating your own windfalls, by uncovering hidden places where the easy money lies.

A windfall occurs when the wind blows the ripe fruit out of the tree, saving the farmer the cost of hiring pickers. Into every life a few windfalls blow, and how you handle yours will spell the difference between riches and want. The temptation to blow it all at once will likely be overwhelming, so rule number one when you get a windfall is:

- Blow some of it. Life isn't all about super-responsible behavior, so go ahead and spend up to 25 percent (or $1,000 maximum) of your windfall (bonus, inheritance, settlement) on something neat. If you don't have a better idea, consider visiting another country, even one close at hand, like Canada or Mexico. Although some feel travel is money wasted, since the trip is over in a week or so, anyone who travels knows differently. The experience enriches you for a lifetime, and the younger you start, the longer you'll enjoy the benefit. Future millionaires do well to learn about currency exchange rates, and the state of the economies of international destinations. However you spend it, blowing a little of your windfall will make it easier to commit the remainder to one or more of the plans below.

- Pay down debt. Select your highest-cost debt, and throw money at it. If you are paying 16 percent on your credit card balance, paying it off is like earning 16 percent risk free in the financial markets, which is something you know by now is impossible.

- Update your emergency funds. Finish funding your account if you haven't yet, and bring it up to your current needs if you have. Reevaluate it once a year or so to make sure it keeps up with your increasing wealth, then forget about it.

- Max out your 401(k) and IRA. Let's say you receive a $10,000 inheritance. You spend $1,000 on a new toy for yourself, and decide to commit $9,000 to tax-deferred accounts. Your IRA can absorb $2,000, leaving $7,000 to go. Put it in a money-market fund with check-writing privileges. Then, authorize your payroll clerk to increase your 401(k) contribution by $1,000 per month. Your paycheck will drop by $1,000 per month, but you can replace that by drawing down the $7,000 in the money-market fund at a rate of $1,000 per month to live on. Be sure you don't exceed the annual 401(k) or 403(b) maximum; have the payroll department or your 401(k) administrator work the numbers for you. This way you convert a taxable windfall into tax-deferred money, and get the benefits of dollar-cost averaging as well!

- Catch up on your Four Step program, if you've been naughty. You can buy back your youthful number with a lump sum, but to keep it tax deferred, follow the plan described immediately above. Even if you've faithfully followed the program, you can buy yourself a lower number by throwing in a lump sum.

- Accelerate your short-term goals by beefing up those accounts. To get the most out of compounding, it makes the most financial sense to augment the longer-term goals first; in other words, add the windfall to the college account that has fourteen years to go, rather than to the house account that will ripen in only three years. Still, financial considerations aren't the only things in life, nor are they even the most important things. If getting into that house a year earlier makes "quality-of-life" sense, then that's the best decision for you.

Whichever plan appeals to you, consider dollar-cost averaging the windfall into the selected account over a period of around twelve months. As was shown in Chapter Five, this is a great way to mitigate risk, and to take advantage of the mathematical principle of the harmonic mean. Dollar-cost averaging provides a free lunch.

 ## Intangibles

The free lunch is not the only example of real, although invisible value. Other dollar benefits lurk in our everyday lives that we future millionaires should learn to recognize.

The most valuable intangible in your early years may be your education. Studies repeatedly show that each year of education is worth thousands of dollars down the line. A college graduate should expect to earn hundreds of thousands of dollars more than a high-school graduate over a lifetime. This isn't a free lunch; it's an intangible return on investment of both dollars and effort.

Take a look at these other intangibles in your daily life:

- Goodwill is an intangible well-known to businesses. It's the difference between what the buyer pays for the business and what the business would be worth if all its assets were sold. Take Suds 'n Suds. If all its barware, washing machines, leases, liquor licenses, and so on were parted out and sold, they'd be worth perhaps $200 million. But if the business was sold as a going concern, a buyer might pay $500 million. That extra

$300 million is an intangible asset known as goodwill. It includes the customer base, the reputation of the company, its good credit history, the value of the trademark, the location and length of the leases, the strength of the competition, and so forth.

Even if you don't own a business, you own the intangible asset of goodwill. It may not be worth $300 million, but it's worth something—probably more than you think. You've built a good credit record that will pay you real dollars over your lifetime. Your reputation as a hard worker precedes you when you look for a job. Friends and former employers are pleased to vouch for you, and this earns you better positions. Your job history is sound, your arrest record is clean, you pay your bills on time, and you recognize your obligations. This personal goodwill will translate into real money over time. If you've slipped up a bit here and there, you're still plenty young enough to begin the repair job. Goodwill, although intangible, is not a free lunch *because it is earned.*

- Benjamin Franklin had it wrong. A penny saved is not a penny earned; in fact, under today's tax structure, it is worth much more. Not spending is a great way to accumulate wealth. Just ask any penny-pinching millionaire. If you pay combined federal and state income taxes of about 20 percent, you must earn about $1.24 in pretax dollars to buy something worth $1.00. You can put $25 in a 5 percent savings account to earn the $1.24, or you can choose not to spend the dollar. Either works out the same for you financially. So your $1.00 not spent in effect saves you $25! Think of it this way: You get a 24 percent return when you save that dollar, a totally risk-free deal that would be impossible to match in the financial markets. If you can save 10 percent per week on a food budget of $100 by using coupons, it's the same as having $10,000 invested at 5 1/4 percent—and that's before taxes. A $10,000 windfall courtesy of your daily newspaper.

Your credit card is a great convenience, but a costly one. If you apply the lesson from above, it's even more expensive than you think. At 18 percent, a $2,000 card balance costs $360 per year. No big deal, perhaps. But to earn that $360, you would need to invest $8,000 at 4.5 percent, or more if the account is taxable. Eight thousand dollars is a lot of money to tie up just for the privilege of paying the bank. In addition, think of how $360 per year invested at 10 percent will look in thirty years when you're fifty-five and yearning to retire early. Paying cash and putting the annual interest savings in your growth mutual fund will earn you nearly $60,000 more.

Learn to think of costs in this way. It's good training for a future millionaire to evaluate expenditures in terms of their true costs. It disciplines the mind.

- It is said that the true value of a college education is the art of critical thinking. Whether it's chemistry or sociology, the student learns to look at evidence objectively, putting aside prejudices in favor of fact. Long after the information learned in college physics or economics becomes obsolete, the habit of critical thinking abides. Credulous people (Ph.D.'s among them) are sitting ducks for scam artists of all kinds. Not just the out-and-out larcenous, but quick-buck artists, once-in-a-lifetime deals, crummy goods, lousy financing—all the zillions of ways out there to lose your money. The critical thinker is a better evaluator, and therein lies the lifetime value of your education. If you missed out on this valuable commodity, you can catch up for little or no cost at your local community college. You'll be dollars ahead in earnings, probably; but over your lifetime you'll reap the benefits of your education in intangible forms too numerous to count. You'll pay a price in cost and effort, so it's no free lunch. But the intangible returns are the next best thing.

- Do you have things left over from your childhood that are worth a few bucks (it doesn't have to be hundreds) to a collector? Baseball cards, Barbies, comics? Sell them now, and put all the proceeds into an aggressive growth fund, and see what compounding gets you down the road. Compounding is the free lunch here.

- When you go to your public library—or the museum, a park, or a cathedral—consider what it would cost you to maintain such a resource privately. Even if you pay taxes, fees, or donations to support the endeavor, your contribution is next to meaningless when compared to what you'd have to pay to enjoy the entity without the benefit of collective ownership. The person who makes full use of public wealth garners to him or herself intangible benefits worth billions of dollars. When you camp in a national park, cruise a country road, cross a great bridge, consider what you would pay if you had to. If the bridge toll is $2, consider how much you would be willing to pay to avoid the swim. Then enjoy your free lunch.

- We live in the information age, and information can be darned expensive. Investment newsletters can be hundreds of dollars a year, tuition is tens of thousands of dollars. When you can get good information for free or next to it, that's dollars in your pocket. Use your modem to tap into the vast databases and special interest groups available to virtually everyone with a computer. Health insurers and providers put out free medical information; use it. Your daily newspaper, for less than a dollar, is packed with information. Your library is a resource so filled with information that it's mind-boggling. Become an information junkie, and watch your life—and your fortune—improve. If you successfully follow the Four Step plan, you'll make more than $999,980 off this book. The free lunch comes in as the difference between what this information is worth to you, and what you pay for it.

- If you have a costly habit (smoking comes to mind), give it up. Use half the savings on yourself every year, and invest the rest. Do this every year. A cigarette habit costs nearly $1,000 per year for the average smoker. Quit (you can—I did), then take an extra weekend at the beach every year, invest the rest aggressively, and watch it grow! Five hundred dollars a year, invested at an annual average of 10 percent, grows to $263,524 in forty years.

Just as it's valuable to recognize the hidden benefits in your life (because it helps you take advantage of them), it's wise to understand that some intangibles work against us. The costs of discrimination and prejudice weigh all of us down, since a society whose members are all well-off can afford collectively to build sumptuous cities, fabulous parks, and pollution-free energy sources. The next chapter talks about young women investors, and how they must strategize a little differently than men, for a variety of reasons, just to get to the same place.

 *Self-Test*
**Chapter 12**

1. Social Security is:
   a. always changing
   b. broke
   c. only for the poor
   d. only for the aged

2. The Social Security divorce benefit requires a marriage of:
   a. one year
   b. two years
   c. five years
   d. ten years

3. Social Security law is made by the:
   a. president
   b. secretary of Health and Human Services
   c. Congress
   d. Social Security Administration

4. Which of the following is *not* part of the benefit calculation for the typical pension?
   a. length of employment
   b. age at retirement

    c. tax bracket
    d. wage history

5. Which is *not* a leg of the three-legged retirement stool?
    a. Social Security
    b. inheritance
    c. pension
    d. investments

6. A good pension might replace this amount of your final wages:
    a. 20–30%
    b. 40–50%
    c. 60–70%
    d. 80–90%

7. Under federal law, it is illegal for an employer to discriminate against someone because of their:
    a. youth
    b. age
    c. race
    d. b and c

8. When you get a windfall, you should:
    a. spend some on yourself
    b. pay off debt
    c. build your Four Step fund
    d. a, b, and c

9. The true value of a college education is said to be:
    a. bragging rights
    b. the ability to think critically
    c. a way to avoid the army
    d. a shot at the big time

10. Deciding to not spend $1, in effect saves you:
    a. $25
    b. $2
    c. $1
    d. nothing

*Answers on Worksheet 15 in Appendix I*

# A Word to Women

*Your gender and your money*

For women, the money picture isn't pretty. We all know that women (as a group) earn lower wages than men. Even in Moses' time, a woman's wage was only 60 percent of a man's (check it out in Lev. 27:1–4), and things haven't changed much in the thousands of years since.

Lower wages are not the only problem, however. Other things hold women back financially as well. Biology plays a role here, and so do biased laws and practices, including those affecting pensions and Social Security. These differences mean that women have to strategize dissimilarly from men because more of them:

- **Live longer**
- **Earn less**
- **Face bias in economic laws**
- **Die single**
- **Face bias in the financial community**
- **Lack confidence in their investing skills**

Given these realities, women need to come to the party early, and leave late—financially speaking, that is. An aggressive investment program is the number one strategy for leveling the playing field, but unfortunately, too many women just aren't getting the message. It's been demonstrated that today's women are saving only about half as much as men, and are beginning their savings programs later.

This is not good. With the right investment program, however, the informed woman can work around every one of these challenges. Let's take a look at them one by one.

**Women live longer:** Women live longer than men in every industrialized country, and those seven or eight extra years are expensive ones. It would be great if those additional years came in their twenties or thirties when women's health and strength are at their best. But no, those extra years will be in their eighties, just when life really gets costly. Medical expenses, long-term care, and inflation are the specters that haunt old folks. And the longer the life, the bigger their bite.

Inflation is a bigger problem for retired people because they no longer work. Wages usually rise with inflation, but pensions generally do not; nor does income from bonds, which are the mainstay of most retiree's investment portfolios. Because women have one-third more lifetime after age sixty-five than do men—the very years that are the most vulnerable to inflation—they have to employ different investment strategies just to stay even.

A long life, therefore, argues for a more aggressive investment strategy. The longer-lived among us need investments to grow more in order to cover the lengthier period. This means that women should include more stocks in their investment programs than men of the same age.

Take, for example, a common rule of thumb used by financial planners in estimating the proper mix of asset classes for their clients called the Rule of 100. Subtract your age from 100, the rule goes, and the remainder is the portion of your portfolio that should be devoted to stocks (or better, stock mutual funds). A 28-year-old, then, would devote 72 percent of her portfolio to equities, and 28 percent to fixed-income securities, such as bonds.

But one size does not fit all under this rule. If you divide the longevity difference of seven or eight years between men and women, the better rule of thumb would have men subtract their age from 96, and women from 104. A 23-year-old woman would devote 81 percent of her portfolio to growth (stocks and stock mutual funds), whereas 73 percent would be a better fit for a man of the same age. Put another way, a 30-year-old woman is seven years younger than a 30-year-old man. She should invest like a 23-year-old (don't you just love finance—how else can you strip seven years from your age?).

The risks of a more aggressive portfolio are smoothed out by the longer time-horizon women can expect. There is considerably more time to recover losses in the average female lifetime.

Probably the greatest risk is psychological. It has been established that when it comes to investments, women, more than men, are loathe to take chances. This barricade of their own making too often paralyzes the would-be female investor into inaction. She's far too likely to squander her 401(k) or IRA opportunities in a bank certificate of deposit, bond fund, money-market fund, or a guaranteed investment contract.

These low-yielding investments can never do the job for her that her long life dictates. One hundred dollars per month in a 401(k) earning 6 percent annually will be worth $242,251 when a twenty-five-year-old worker reaches age sixty-seven (when full Social Security benefits will begin). The same payments into a stock index mutual fund, earning the historic average of 10.3 percent for the stock market, will be worth $946,925. In both cases, the investor is a winner since she only put $51,600 of her own money into the fund. But in stocks, she is nearly four times better off. Assuming she protects her fund from inflation by increasing her monthly contributions every year to match the inflation rate, by retirement the stock investor will have $56,816 per year to enjoy, and the investor with a guaranteed investment contract only $14,535 (assuming both invest their funds at 6 percent when they retire). There is a major lifestyle difference between $56,000 and $14,000, and the overly cautious investor has only herself to blame for the shortfall.

Inflation, because its bite worsens with the years, is the woman investor's greatest risk. It is measurably far more of a risk to the long-term investor than the risk of stocks. As said earlier, there is no twenty-year period in this century when stock prices fell even 1 percent; yet at the historical average of 3.1 percent, inflation will cut your investment by 50 percent over the same time period. This makes inflation nearly fifty times more threatening than the usual risks of investing in stocks.

Dangerous though it is, especially to female investors, inflation is easy to defeat. (Reread Chapter Seven!) In January, watch the financial pages for announcements of the rise in the consumer price index for the year just past. Then simply increase your monthly savings by that amount. At a 3.1 percent CPI, a $100 monthly contribution becomes $103.10. Next year, if the CPI is 4 percent, the contribution goes to $107.22, and so on through the years. Since wages will rise at about the inflation rate, the small

## Chart I

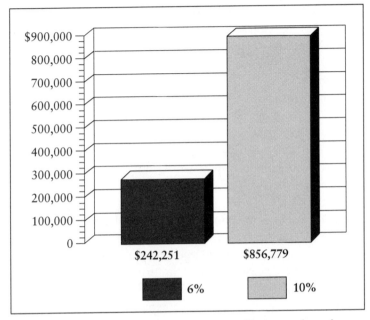

*Here's how reckless caution can do you in over time. The investor began her $100 monthly payments at age 25, and ended at 67. The 10% investment made $614,528 more than the 6% account in her 401(k) or IRA.*

annual adjustments will not represent a real increase in your investment program. Women, even more than men, must be vigorous in their defense against inflation.

**Women earn less:** Everyone knows that women in the aggregate still earn less than men. This is because of:

- **Unequal pay for equal work.**
- **Job segregation into low-paid "women's" occupations.**
- **Job mobility and time out due to family responsibilities.**

There are state and federal laws against sex discrimination in the workplace, including harassment. If a woman feels discriminated against in hiring, promotions, layoffs, on-the-job training, compensation, or treatment by an employment agency, claims can be made to the state fair employment office, or the federal Equal Employment Opportunity office. It is equally illegal to retaliate against a claimant or anyone who speaks up on her behalf with respect to her claim.

A claimant doesn't need a smoking gun for her claim to succeed. Her employer's past practices can be investigated to uncover a discriminatory pattern. After the state or federal agency rejects her claim (as usually happens in these overworked agencies), she should immediately see a lawyer skilled in employment law to advise her whether she should pursue the claim in court.

**Women face bias in economic laws:** Because pensions (if any) and Social Security are directly tied to wages, women drag their lower wage history with them into retirement. Social Security and pensions were discussed in the last chapter; here, a few ways in which Social Security conceals gender biases—some of which favor women, others that don't—are explored.

Social Security's biggest problem for most women workers is the way work is credited. The program takes into account thirty-five years of work history, including those years spent outside the paid workforce. A woman who stays home with the kids for several years will have "zero" years factored into her eventual benefit, even if her years in the workforce were spent at the highest earning level. Primarily for this reason, the average female Social Security beneficiary receives far less than the average man. Women who spend some of their years out of the workforce, or working part-time or seasonally, decimate not only their Social Security account, but their retirement benefits as well.

Even so, Social Security, in a profound way, is biased in favor of women. Any programs, such as Social Security and Medicare, that pay out for life favor the longer-lived. Also, Social Security is adjusted annually for inflation; again, a practice designed to benefit most of those who live longest. More women than men are

Social Security beneficiaries (no surprise, since women outnumber men in the older age groups).

As was pointed out in Chapter Twelve, the federal Employee's Retirement Income Security Act governs all nongovernmental pensions in the land. Enacted in 1974, ERISA was reform legislation that unfortunately had the effect of codifying the male work pattern. That is, the job pattern most rewarded by pensions happens to be that of the middle-class white male. The most successful (nongovernment) pensioner worked all his life, full time, in a well-paid position, for a large, industrial employer, probably unionized.

Women's work patterns are much more mobile than men's. Women move in and out of the labor market to assume family responsibilities, and this mobility fractures pensions. More women than men simply don't stay on the job long enough to qualify for the pension. Then, too, ERISA doesn't require an employer to offer a pension in the first place. Small employers, retailers, and service companies are the least likely to offer pensions, and women are overly represented in just those types of companies.

As a result of these biases, only about half as many women as men earn pensions, and those that do, get about half as much in benefits.

A woman's best strategy is to step up her investment program to mitigate the damage these biases will inflict on her pension and Social Security income. Just one more reason for a more aggressive investment program.

**Women die single:** Four out of five women die single; four out of five men die married. Most women today die widows, but younger generations will probably include more divorced and never-married women, which will increase the risk of dying single.

And it is a risk, financially speaking anyway. If you draw a line through the U.S. population dividing the marrieds from the singles, you'll effectively divide the rich from the poor. Marriage, for both men and women, and all ethnic groups, equates with wealth. The single life is expensive, and it has less to do with economies of scale than it does with wealth accumulation. Accumulation is the secret to wealth. This notion has been observed for hundreds of years, and various societies have sought to enhance wealth through laws and customs designed to force that accumulation. Marrieds are more likely than singles to accumulate wealth by owning homes and investments, and by seeking out jobs that include health insurance, pensions, and other valuable fringe benefits.

Divorce devastates these assets, as any alumnae of the divorce courts will readily tell you. Both men and women exit marriage the poorer, but women more so than men. A woman facing divorce will do well to invest in very competent divorce counsel. Unless the marriage was short, childless, and virtually property free, she should stay away from do-it-yourself clinics; nor should she economize by using the same attorney as her husband. Don't forget to include all the assets, including the IRAs, the 401(k)s, the pension, and the home equity. If your investment program was funded by money earned by either spouse during the term of the marriage, it is likely the divorce will divide it (perhaps not equally), no matter whose name is on it. If you come out of a divorce with a lump-sum settlement, put a good chunk of it into a growth stock mutual fund in your 401(k) or IRA, and let it compound its way to a fortune.

Whether you're widowed, divorced, or never married, ending your life single is an expensive proposition. Women should plan to finance two catastrophic illnesses and deaths, not just one. The husband is likely to go first, and all too often, the family nest egg with him. Then fifteen years later, it's the widow's turn. Only this time, no one is around to provide the free home care she gave her husband. She'll have to pay for home help or a nursing home. She'll be older and sicker; chances are she'll linger longer.

These circumstances are unavoidable, but women can strategize around them. They should invest more aggressively when they're young, not only to beat inflation, but also to cover their last, expensive single years as well.

**Women face bias in the financial community:** *Money* magazine sent test teams out to brokerages to learn if men and women investors were treated differently. The testers found pervasive discrimination against the prospective female clients. Brokers (nearly four out of five of whom were men) spent less time with the women, failed to ask enough questions to get a good idea of their financial situations, and routinely recommended low-risk, low-earning investments. Some brokers asked the women to return with their husbands; none asked men to return with their wives. After alerting the SEC, which conducted its own investigation and found the same problems, *Money* went back with its testers a year later, and found nothing changed.

The lesson for women is clear: Simply don't let it happen. Approach a financial professional (whether it be a stockbroker, CPA, tax preparer, lawyer, estate planner, financial planner, or insurance agent—male or female) with a clear eye and confident manner. Ask questions. If you don't understand, ask some more. If the professional takes the attitude that you don't need to bother your pretty little head about such things, exit the interview. Expect the pro to return your calls; don't expect him or her to be your therapist. Organize your questions, clearly state your circumstances and goals, then let him or her do the job. If you're not satisfied, take a hike. You're the boss. But there is also no question that you'll get more for your money if you take the time to inform yourself of financial (tax, estate, whatever) fundamentals. You can do this in the library.

In addition to attitude problems within the financial professions, some investment products are just a bad deal for women, insurance products chief among them. With many annuities, women pay more for the same benefit, or pay the same but get a lower benefit in the end. Insurers justify this by pointing to women's longer lives, but lots of things other than gender predict longevity. If insurers used race, for example, they would have to pay African-American males more than white males because of their shorter life expectancy. But do they use race-based life-expectancy tables? Of course not. Since only 14 percent of women outlive the male life expectancy, the U.S. Supreme Court outlawed gender-biased actuarial tables in work-related annuities, such as pensions; but as private investments, many annuities still carry substantial gender penalties.

Just as annuities carry a penalty against women because of their long lives, you would expect life insurance to reward them, since that product finds short lives costlier. And that's right, life insurance *is* cheaper for women. A three-year break is standard for women life insurance clients, but the same insurer will generally penalize her eight years when she buys an annuity. How actuarial tables can produce a mere three-year advantage for life insurance, but an eight-year penalty for annuities defies reason. And it is unreasonable, of course. It's discrimination.

Disability insurance is much more expensive for women than men—up to twice as expensive. This is a special problem for the self-employed. Such a woman might want to explore professional associations (bar associations, realtors' groups, medical societies, writers' organizations) for group disability insurance without that costly gender bias.

**Women lack confidence in their investing skills:** One-third fewer women than men report that they have confidence in their ability to handle their own financial affairs. No wonder they're babied when they come through the broker's door. And women carry other investment-unfriendly baggage around as well. Math phobia stalks the financial pages—all those fractions, decimals, tables, charts. It's well established that schoolgirls are steered away from math, a crippling practice if ever there was one when it comes to the grown-up tasks of managing one's economic life.

Fortunately, we live in the age of calculators. It's arithmetic that most women shy away from (most never get far enough to test their mettle against calculus and trigonometry), and arithmetic has been abolished by the silicon chip. Ordinary calculators will easily handle most calculations an investor will ever need; financial calculators go further by including compounding.

Math phobia notwithstanding, women's lack of financial confidence is misplaced. In surveys of single-sex investment clubs, all-female clubs out-performed the all-male clubs by a factor of about one-third. So women are one-third less confident, but one-third more competent than men when it comes to investing. Women have some psychology to overcome, it's true, whether it be math phobia, intemperate frugality, or simple intimidation. The beauty of it is that among the woman investor's greatest disadvantages—inflation exposure, lower wages, widowhood and divorce, and the confidence factor—the latter is the one that is completely within her control.

**Feminist funds:** As discussed in Chapter Four, some mutual funds cater to your conscience. The main problems with these funds are twofold: First, one person's specter may be another one's angel. Is investing in emerging countries capitalizing on slave labor, or is it encouraging democracy and free markets by infusing underdeveloped countries with sorely needed capital? And second, these funds tend not to have a spectacular track record.

Nevertheless, and it's a tribute to America's never-ending war between its puritan conscience and its love of money, these funds proliferate. It's no surprise, then, that women's concerns have found a place in many socially conscious funds. Some include women's issues in a larger laundry list, perhaps including environmental, labor, tobacco, and military concerns. At least one fund (Women's Equity Mutual Fund in San Francisco) concentrates on women's issues, and operates with a dual purpose: to help women achieve equality in the workplace by encouraging progressive corporations; and to help women gain financial independence through the fund's hoped-for strong performance. The fund refuses to invest in companies that retard women's progress by marketing sexist products, advertise in ways demeaning to women, or have weak or controversial records when it comes to the advancement of their own female employees. As with any investment, if this one interests you, investigate its performance before you plunk down your dollars.

Some economists argue that the American secret to success in the twenty-first century will be its women. Many of our major competitors have not integrated women into their workforces as effectively, so they are utilizing a lower proportion of their available talent. Women are preparing themselves for the challenge, with medical, dental, law, and business degrees going to women over one-third of the time. There are also slightly more women than men in college. It is argued that cultures that virtually exclude women from the workforce are doomed to lag behind those that include all available brainpower, no matter the sex, race, physical abilities, or immigration status.

It's a perfectly obvious proposition.

*Self-Test*
## Chapter 13

1. Women have to invest more aggressively than men because:
   **a.** more of them live longer
   **b.** four out of five die single
   **c.** they usually have lower retirement incomes
   **d.** a, b, and c

2. Inflation is a bigger problem for women because of:
   **a.** longevity
   **b.** poverty
   **c.** job discrimination
   **d.** pension bias

3. One-third fewer women than men report confidence in their investing skills:

   ☐ True     ☐ False

4. Of investment clubs, the best performers are:
   **a.** all-male clubs
   **b.** coed clubs

    **c.** all-female clubs
    **d.** teen clubs

5. Which is *not* a reason why women as a group earn less than men?
    **a.** unequal pay
    **b.** job segregation
    **c.** irresponsibility
    **d.** job mobility

6. In comparison with men, how many women receive pension income?
    **a.** 33%
    **b.** 50%
    **c.** 75%
    **d.** 90%

7. Those women who receive pension income, receive about how much of a man's?
    **a.** 20%
    **b.** 30%
    **c.** 40%
    **d.** 50%

8. ERISA governs all nongovernmental pensions in the U.S.:

    ☐ True    ☐ False

9. Congress took into account differing female work patterns when enacting ERISA:

    ☐ True    ☐ False

10. It has been established that brokers treat men and women investors the same:

    ☐ True    ☐ False

*Answers on Worksheet 15 in Appendix I*

# The Six Seductive Sirens of Stupidity

*Words of warning for future millionaires*

The program is simple; the numbers are easy. And every one of you owns the first critical factor to make it all work: *time*. The second is *persistence*, and here's where we separate the winners among you from the losers. Myths and attitudes get in the way of any kind of savings plan for too many people. Consider the Six Seductive Sirens of Stupidity:

- **Real life starts after I snag my rich spouse.**
- **Real life starts after I've sowed my wild oats.**
- **More goes out than comes in, so what's to save?**
- **I'll just lose all my money, so it's better to spend now.**
- **Live for today; the world might blow up tomorrow.**
- **When I retire, a million dollars will be worth ten cents.**

Let's slay these sirens one by one.

- **First**, there is no one out there who wouldn't be thrilled to find Mr. or Ms. Wonderful well on the way to bringing a million dollars to the table. Starting later is never as good as starting sooner on our Four Step program, and no one in the world can give you back your precious early years. Your challenge (an easy one) will be to get your program going before you meet your one-and-only, and then to keep it going all through your long marriage. Your intended will love you for it, because in your golden years he or she will be cruising right along with you. You know in your head it's stupid to bet your future on a fantasy mate. You want to be rich when you meet, and rich if you leave. Kick the bag man or lady out of your future, and get your Four Step program up and running the minute you find your magic number in Chapter Two.
- **Second**, maybe you worry that once you find Mr. or Ms. Right, the party's over. Things get serious, babies come. There is time enough then, you think, to be a grown-up. Now's the time to whoop it up. But think about this: By starting now on your Four Step program when the numbers are much smaller than they'll ever again be in your life, you'll ensure that the

party doesn't end when you settle down with your true love. Instead, it will just get better and better. Want that big-twin when you're thirty-eight? Great! You've earned it. The luxury cruise? Go! Your retirement was taken care of in your twenties. Now you've got a lifetime to indulge yourself. At the same time, your buddies have that lean-and-hungry look because they are sacrificing everything to their retirement accounts.

- **Third**, if you're spending more than your paycheck, join the party. Everyone does, even those $100,000 guys—especially those $100,000 guys, because expenses mount up faster than the pay at every level. And the $100,000 guy is forty-five years old, and just waking up to retirement planning. That means he has to put away ten times more than you do just to get the same million dollars, even though he's only twice as old as you—because he's an old guy and you've got the awesome power of youth on your side. Tomorrow you'll be closer to forty-five than you are today.

- **Fourth**, everyone worries about losing their money. And if you invest it properly, you'll lose some of yours from time to time, too. That's how you'll know you're doing it right, because the only way to avoid losing any of your money any of the time is to put it in the wrong place. You're a forty-year investor, and once again, blessed youth offers you opportunities that translate into real dollars—lots and lots of them.

- **Fifth**, the cold war's over. Besides, if a meteor destroys Europe (or the planet wilts under the greenhouse effect, or runs low on oxygen because the rain forests were destroyed), who's going to get through it most comfortably? The richies of the world, that's who. And you want to be among them. There is no better barricade between you and the world's vicissitudes than a bundle of bucks, make no doubt about it. The sibling to the "I don't need to save because the world is going to end" myth is the "I don't need to save because I'm going to die young" fantasy. No, again. Your generation is slated to live longer than any humans in the history of the world. Demographers are already terribly worried about the hundreds of thousands of you who will live past 100.

I'll let you in on a secret: Lots of young people think they'll die young, usually before 35. It's because you can't imagine yourself as older than that, so your mind denies your future. Don't let it rob you of a million.

- **Sixth**, inflation is the only real bogeyman of the six seductive sirens, but not to worry. In Step Four you built a moat around your castle that'll keep the inflation monster out.

You have the castle now by virtue of your youth. But you're only a tenant. Coming up behind you is a gang of hungry teenagers, and when they come knocking on your castle door, you'll have to give it up. It'll be their turn to own the awesome magical scepter of compounding, and there is no way in the world you can fend them off, for then they, not you, will have mighty time on their side.

Use it, or lose it. This train is leaving the station. Best of luck to you all, and enjoy your fortune.

$

# Afterword

*P.S. to parents, grandparents,*
*godparents, and other such*

It happens, from time to time, that even the most responsible young person just can't get started on a program like the Four Steps. From the perspective of years, it seems ludicrous to throw away the only opportunity to amass a fortune virtually painlessly.

But there's the rub. It's not painless to come up with $100 or so per month if your entry-level job fronts a take-home check of only $1,000, and you're so head over heels in student and credit card debt you can't see straight. Under those circumstances, it's easy to blow away those early years. Remember the Six Seductive Sirens of Stupidity in the last chapter.

But there's no need for you to wring your hands. There are several ways you can retrieve those early years for the future investor in your life. Here are some of them:

**Overcoming inertia:** Sometimes the obstacle to launching an investment program isn't so much economic as it is simple procrastination. Dealing with the unknown, such as heavy-duty financial institutions, can be sufficiently off-putting to keep the best of plans on the back burner. You can help here by setting up a mutual fund in the young person's name, and handing it over to him or her. If you can provide the minimum initial investment required by the fund (perhaps for a graduation, wedding, first job, first house, or birthday gift), then this may be all the incentive he or she will need to keep the program going. Be sure to advise your young relative or friend to switch the funds into a tax-deferred account as soon as feasible. You won't be able to set it up that way yourself without his or her signature on the original application.

**The Hot Start program:** If your beneficiary is in the upper end of the age scale, and for this reason the monthly Four Step payments seem forbiddingly steep, you might want to take another look at the Hot Start program in Chapter Two. If you could provide the start-up money, you will "lower" your relative or friend's age accordingly, thus eliminating the age penalty that may be the hurdle he or she is unable to cross.

**An early inheritance:** Perhaps you have four or five grandchildren you've written into your will for, say, $1,000 each. If you have the means to part with the money now, you can boost the ultimate value of your gift many, many times over. The same $1,000 received as a bequest at age fifty can never be as valuable as one received as a gift at age twenty. The early gift, invested at an annual average of 10 percent—and then left alone to compound merrily into the future—will be worth $119,118 on the young one's sixty-seventh birthday. The bequest at fifty? Invested at the same 10 percent, it will be worth just $6,004 at sixty-seven. The reward for foresight is worth nearly twenty times the return. Be sure that in your will you note the early gifts made in lieu of bequests, and wish your grandchildren well. If they've managed to keep their hands off the funds, they won't need your memorial gift, and will bless your wisdom and foresight.

**For the spendthrift:** Young people, no more nor less than older folks, include among themselves the impecunious. If this describes your young relative or friend, you may be loathe to provide a fund that is sure to be looted in short order. At the same time, you expect this young one to grow up in time, and would like to save him or her from squandering the valuable early years. There are several ways you can protect the fund from a spendthrift:

## Chart J

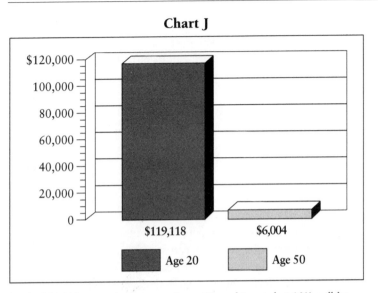

*A gift of $1,000 given when a person is age 20, and invested at 10%, will be worth $113,114 more at age 67 than a $1,000 bequest received at age 50 and invested at the same rate until the same age.*

- Launch a Four Step program in an account that is entirely your own. The tax consequences to you will not be onerous for several years, by which time maturity may have caught up with your donee and you can turn the fund over to its intended owner. Be sure to note in your will or trust for whom you intend this account.
- Set up an informal trust account, naming you as trustee and the young person as beneficiary. Any bank or fund will do this for you. Just ask for an application for a trust account. You don't need a lawyer, and you will have control of the funds until you turn the account over. The earnings will be taxed to you. The disadvantage of these informal trusts is that if you should die, the beneficiary will generally receive the funds immediately. If you want to delay receipt past your death, you'll need a formal trust as described below.

- A formal trust, usually drawn up by a lawyer, will delay deliverance of the fund to whatever date you specify. Some turn over half on, say, the twenty-eighth birthday; the remainder at thirty-five. Others use thirty and forty. Or you can have the trustee (which can be you, during your lifetime) keep the principal intact, but pay the young person the interest until a certain age, or a particular circumstance—attaining a bachelor's degree, for example.

- A joint-tenancy account, set up with you and the young person as joint tenants, would not be the best choice. It does have the advantage of survivorship, meaning that should either of you die, the other will automatically receive the entire account, free of probate. But both tenants usually have to sign for all transactions, and this can be a hassle. If one tenant is a minor, a guardian may have to be appointed before he or she can legally sign. The informal trust account is the better choice.

- U.S. treasury bonds, such as EE savings bonds or zero-coupon bonds, are popular gifts from grandparents to the very young, but there are some problems with this approach. In the case of EEs, they generally don't earn enough interest to make the numbers contemplated in our Four Step programs. But they are safe, easy to buy (at your bank), and are tax deferred in that taxes aren't due until the bond is cashed in.

Zero-coupon bonds may seem like a good idea, in that they generally pay more than EEs, and can be purchased to mature on any specific date, say, the young one's twenty-fifth birthday. But zeros have a terrible problem. As with EEs, you buy zeros at a discount and they pay you interest only when cashed in. But unlike EEs, you have to pay taxes on the interest all along as if it were being paid to you now. You pay taxes *now* on interest to be received *then*. And since inflation will reduce the value of the yet-to-be-paid interest, using today's more robust dollars to pay tax on tomorrow's weak ones doesn't make a lot of sense. Zeros can be purchased from a stockbroker, but unless you plan to shelter them in a tax-deferred account, the "taxes now—interest later" feature makes them a poor choice.

**For the very young:** A program begun at birth for a mere $3 per month will make a million by age sixty-seven using the Roller Coaster 12 Percent Plan. When the kid is old enough, he or she can take over the measly payments to complete the program. Since the teensy $3 per month invested at 12 percent through the child's twenty-second birthday (twenty-three years because you started at birth) only amounts to $4,375, you won't have to worry about setting up a tax-deferred account during the early childhood years. At most, the earnings on the account will be in the neighborhood of $500 per year, costing $155 in taxes at a 31 percent tax rate. Later, assuming the now-twenty-three-year-old child is employed, $2,000 per year can be transferred into an IRA until the amount is fully sheltered. By keeping the gift in an account in your name, you keep control over it. If you decide your young beneficiary is too young to handle the Four Step program in his or her early twenties, delay the turnover until maturity ripens. Table 14 in Appendix II supplies the numbers for a Modest Millionaire 10 Percent Plan from birth through age eighteen.

If you want to have the fund taxed to the minor, you can set the gift up in a Uniform Gift (Transfer) to Minors Act (UGMA/UTMA) account. The fund or bank will happily do this for you. You as donor can be the custodian, meaning you have control of the funds until the child reaches eighteen or twenty-one, depending on the state. At that time, the young person will gain full control of the funds, to do with as he or she pleases. If you're not comfortable with that, bite the bullet, pay the taxes, and keep the fund in your own name until you feel the time is right to turn it over, or commit it to a formal trust. If you keep the account in your own name, don't forget to designate it to your intended beneficiary in your will, or it will simply become part of your general estate.

For all of the above, include instructions on how to complete the Four Step program, or better yet, include a copy of this book (she modestly suggests). Then leave your beneficiary alone. No one wants a gift that "keeps on giving" through guilt-trip-engendering nagging. Even if he or she does nothing more than leave the lump sum leavening in its fund, you will have substantially benefited your friend or heir.

Congratulations. You will have made a substantial gift with a paltry outlay, one that in time will cushion life's shocks for your beneficiary, and provide a considerable leg up on this game of life.

# Worksheets

## Worksheet 1

### Cash-Flow Statement

**Monthly income:**
- Take-home pay                                    $_____
- Investment income                                _____
- Spousal, child support                           _____
- Other                                            _____

**TOTAL**                                          _____

**Monthly expenses:**
- Housing (include taxes, mortgage, rent)          $_____
- Electricity, water, gas                          _____
- Phone                                            _____
- Groceries                                        _____
- Restaurants, fast food                           _____
- Transportation (tolls, parking, fares, except car)  _____
- Car (include payments, repairs, gas)             _____
- Clothes                                          _____
- Cosmetics, hairdresser, etc.                     _____
- Child care                                       _____
- Savings                                          _____
- Donations, gifts                                 _____
- Child, spousal support (paid to ex-spouse)       _____
- Education                                        _____
- Medical (include health insurance)               _____
- Debt (include installment payments)              _____
- Vacations                                        _____
- Entertainment                                    _____
- Hobbies                                          _____
- Insurance                                        _____
- Income taxes                                     _____
- Miscellaneous                                    _____

**TOTAL**                                          _____

**Annual surplus available for Four Step plan:**
Difference in totals multiplied by 12              $_____

**Annual shortfall to be eliminated:**            $_____

## Worksheet 2

### Net Worth

| You own: | Worth this: |
|---|---|
| • House, condo, or co-op (equity) | $_____ |
| • Other real estate (include vacation home) | _____ |
| • IRA(s) | _____ |
| • 401(k), 403(b), TSA, Keogh, SEP | _____ |
| • Non-IRA bank accounts (checking, savings) | _____ |
| • Mutual funds (except IRAs, 401(k)s, etc.) | _____ |
| • Money-market funds (except IRAs, 401(k)s) | _____ |
| • Brokerage account (total portfolio) | _____ |
| • Art | _____ |
| • Antiques | _____ |
| • Collectibles (including classic cars) | _____ |
| • Oriental rugs | _____ |
| • Car(s) (equity) | _____ |
| • Jewelry | _____ |
| • Furniture (fair market value, used) | _____ |
| • Gold, precious metals | _____ |
| • Cash value of life insurance | _____ |
| • Vested interest in pension | _____ |
| • Other investments | _____ |
| • Miscellaneous | _____ |
| **TOTAL ASSETS** | _____ |

| You owe: | A total of this: |
|---|---|
| • Mortgage (total owed) | $_____ |
| • 2d mortgage or home equity line | _____ |
| • Credit card(s) balance | _____ |
| • Student loan(s) balance | _____ |
| • Charge account balances (retailers, gas, etc.) | _____ |
| • Car loan balance | _____ |
| • Business or professional loan | _____ |
| • Personal loans | _____ |
| • Margin loans (brokerage) | _____ |
| • Other debt | _____ |
| **TOTAL LIABILITIES** | $_____ |
| **Net worth (assets less liabilities):** | $_____ |

## Worksheet 3

### Comparing Mutual Funds
*(use with Worksheet 4)*

Call Fidelity Investments (800) 544-8888, Vanguard Group (800) 662-7447, and T. Rowe Price (800) 638-5660, and follow this script, noting their answers on Worksheet 4:

**For 10% Four Step plans:** Do you have an S&P 500 index fund?

**For 11–12% plans:** Do you have a small-cap index fund?

**If no, ask the representative to send you general information on the funds offered by the family.**

*If yes: How much, if any is the:*

- Load?
- Redemption, or exit fee?
- 12(b)-1 charge?
- IRA custodial fee?
- Annual management fee?
- Transaction fee?
- Any other fee or cost?
- Minimum initial contribution (non-IRA)?
- Minimum initial contribution (IRA)?
- Minimum additional contributions (non-IRA)?
- Minimum additional contributions (IRA)?

*Please send me the current "report to shareholders," a prospectus, and an IRA application.*

## Worksheet 4

### Index Fund Comparison Chart
*(use with Worksheet 3)*

|  | **Fidelity** | **Vanguard** | **T.R. Price** |
|---|---|---|---|
| Load | _____ | _____ | _____ |
| Redemption fee | _____ | _____ | _____ |
| 12(b)-1 fee | _____ | _____ | _____ |
| IRA custodial fee | _____ | _____ | _____ |
| Management fee | _____ | _____ | _____ |
| Transaction fee | _____ | _____ | _____ |
| Other fees/costs | _____ | _____ | _____ |
| TOTALS: | $_____ | $_____ | $_____ |
| Minimum initial contribution | _____ | _____ | _____ |
| Minimum initial IRA contribution | _____ | _____ | _____ |
| Minimum additional contributions | _____ | _____ | _____ |
| Minimum additional IRA contributions | _____ | _____ | _____ |

## Worksheet 5

### Your Four Step Plan

After you've read and digested Chapters One and Two, you're ready to start. Complete the following, and you're on your way:

**Your age** _____

**Your numbers** (include them all)
- Modest Millionaire 10%    $_____
- Roller Coaster 12%    $_____
- Roller Coaster 11% (see Table 5)    $_____
- Golden IRA    $_____
- Hot Start $50 plan (fill in lump sum)    $_____
- Hot Start $100 plan (lump sum in Table 6)    $_____

  *Pick one you can live with, and enter it under Step One, below.*

**Your fund** (name of fund from Worksheets 3, 4)    _____
- Type (index, growth, balanced, etc.)    _____
- Expected long-term yield    _____%
- Date account opened    _____
- Minimum monthly contribution    _____
- Account balance    _____

  *Enter the expected yield under Step Two, below.*

**Your tax deferral** (401(k), IRA, 403(b), SEP, Keogh, TSA)    _____

  *Enter type under Step Three, below.*

**Your inflation protection** (this year's CPI)    _____%

  *Enter current year's rate under Step Four, below.*

**Step One**:    Your monthly contribution    $_____
**Step Two**:    Target yield (10%, 11%, 12%)    _____%
**Step Three**:    Type of tax-deferred account    _____
**Step Four**:    Inflation rate for current year    _____%

# Worksheet 6

## Fantasy Forty

| Security | Shares | Price | Commission(s) | Bought | Sold | Price 8 1/4 | Gain/ (Loss) |
|---|---|---|---|---|---|---|---|
| 1. SDS 'N SDS | 100 | 15 3/8 | $95 | 2/1/94 | 3/8/96 | 8 1/4 | ($807.50) |
| 2. | | | | | | | |
| 3. | | | | | | | |
| 4. | | | | | | | |
| 5. | | | | | | | |
| 6. | | | | | | | |
| 7. | | | | | | | |
| 8. | | | | | | | |
| 9. | | | | | | | |
| 10. | | | | | | | |
| 11. | | | | | | | |
| 12. | | | | | | | |
| 13. | | | | | | | |
| 14. | | | | | | | |
| 15. | | | | | | | |
| 16. | | | | | | | |
| 17. | | | | | | | |
| 18. | | | | | | | |
| 19. | | | | | | | |
| 20. | | | | | | | |
| 21. | | | | | | | |
| 22. | | | | | | | |
| 23. | | | | | | | |
| 24. | | | | | | | |
| 25. | | | | | | | |
| 26. | | | | | | | |
| 27. | | | | | | | |
| 28. | | | | | | | |
| 29. | | | | | | | |
| 30. | | | | | | | |
| 31. | | | | | | | |
| 32. | | | | | | | |
| 33. | | | | | | | |
| 34. | | | | | | | |
| 35. | | | | | | | |
| 36. | | | | | | | |
| 37. | | | | | | | |
| 38. | | | | | | | |
| 39. | | | | | | | |
| 40. | | | | | | | |

## Worksheet 7

### Risk Comfort Level

Score each of the following according to how much you agree with the statement, using 1 through 5:

- Score of 1: That's me
- Score of 2: Agree somewhat
- Score of 3: I'm about halfway there
- Score of 4: Disagree somewhat
- Score of 5: No way

1. I can't bear the thought of losing money, even temporarily.  _____
2. At least 90% of my financial assets are in the bank.  _____
3. I have at least two dependents, not counting me.  _____
4. My emergency fund is fully funded.  _____
5. My debt payments are less than 5% of my take-home pay.  _____
6. Other than a mortgage, I have no debt.  _____
7. I am a homeowner (or condo, co-op).  _____
8. To attain a goal, I'd rather take a second job than risk funds.  _____
9. I am now employed in my career choice.  _____
10. My spouse doesn't work for pay.  _____
11. I have car, property, disability, and life insurance.  _____

**Scores:**

- 12–24: You're cautious, responsible, and prudent, and may not be comfortable with yields higher than the current prime rate.
- 25–40: You're comfortable with careful risk. Try for an investment yielding the prime rate, plus 1% or 2%.
- 41–50: A good range for Four Steppers—confident, but eyes open. Prime plus 3% should do it for you, and the Four Step program.
- 51–60: Cool it. Resist any tendency to speculate.

# Worksheet 8

## Asset Allocation

You'll need to refer to Worksheet 2 in order to complete this one. Do not distinguish tax-deferred accounts, such as IRAs and 401(k)s, from other assets. Lump them in under stocks, fixed income, etc. Complete the percentages when you get to (2), below.

1. **YOUR NET WORTH**                    $ _____
   *From Worksheet 2, combine assets into classes:*
   - Real estate equity                  $ _____ / _____ %
   - Cash
     (checking, savings, CDs, money
     market, 3-month treasury bills)      $ _____ / _____ %
   - Fixed income
     (including bond funds; corporate,
     government, and tax-exempt bonds;
     EEs)                                 $ _____ / _____ %
   - Stocks
     (including stock funds)             $ _____ / _____ %
   - Hard assets
     (including jewelry, art, antiques,
     collectibles, classic cars)         $ _____ / _____ %
   - Precious metals
     (gold, silver; metals funds; but
     excluding jewelry, silverware)      $ _____ / _____ %
   - Miscellany
     (cash value insurance, etc.)        $ _____ / _____ %
     TOTAL NET WORTH                     $ _____ / _____100%

2. Now get out your calculator and note next to each asset class what percentage it represents of the whole (divide the asset amount by your total net worth and multiply by 100, i.e., $2,000 is 4% of $50,000).

3. Is any asset class profoundly out of whack? If you've been a long-time homeowner, your equity might consume 50% or more of your net worth. As you commit your resources in the years ahead, strive to bring things into balance, so that all your eggs aren't in one financial basket.

*Now, proceed to Worksheet 9.*

# Worksheet 9

## Financial Asset Allocation

1. **YOUR FINANCIAL NET WORTH**

   *From Worksheet 8, provide the following figures:*

   - Cash
     (checking, savings, CDs, money
     market, 3-month treasury bills)          $ _____ / _____ %

   - Fixed income
     (including bond funds; corporate,
     government, and tax-exempt
     bonds; EEs)                              $ _____ / _____ %

   - Stocks
     (including stock funds)                  $ _____ / _____ %

     TOTAL                                    $ _____ / _____ 100%

2. Note next to each asset class the percentage it represents of the total. The younger you are, the more you should allocate to stocks (probably in stock mutual funds). In your twenties, a few conservative advisers would recommend a mix of 5% cash, 15% fixed income, and 80% stocks; in your thirties, perhaps 5% cash, 20% fixed, and 75% stocks. Other experts would advise 90% to 95% stocks through your twenties and thirties. The Four Step programs are hotter, recommending 100% stocks until age 45, since the programs are so very long term, and the funds won't be needed until age 67—22 years after age 45. Ultimately, this decision is up to you and your psychology.

3. Break your stock-fund assets into the following:

   - Domestic                                 $ _____ / _____ %
   - International                            $ _____ / _____ %

   Many investors aim for a stock portfolio consisting of about 30% international stocks, divided evenly among Europe, Asia, and emerging markets (which generally include Latin America).

   All of the above is FYI. You won't need to allocate your financial assets for years, if not decades. Stick with your stock index fund until you're confident of your investing skills, and have enough to put at least $5,000 in each fund.

## Worksheet 10

### Short-term Goals

Because your Four Step money is in tax-deferred accounts, and not available to you without penalty until nearly age 60 (67, if you follow the plan), money you'll need before then for big purchases, such as house down payment, tuition for the kids, a second home, and expensive toys, will need to be in taxable accounts and more conservatively invested. To get to where you want to be, you need to (1) identify each goal, (2) estimate its future cost (don't forget inflation; assume 4% per year), (3) set a time-horizon, and (4) assign a reasonable yield goal (the shorter the time-horizon, the lower the targeted yield should be).

| | |
|---|---|
| **Goal:** | College for Suzie |
| **Funds needed in:** | 14 years |
| **Estimated cost** (4% inflation): | $100,000 |
| ***Monthly payment:** | $220 |
| **Annual yield:** | 10% |

| | |
|---|---|
| **Goal:** | _____ |
| **Funds needed in:** | _____ |
| **Estimated cost** (4% inflation): | _____ |
| **Monthly payment:** | _____ |
| **Annual yield:** | _____ |

| | |
|---|---|
| **Goal:** | _____ |
| **Funds needed in:** | _____ |
| **Estimated cost** (4% inflation): | _____ |
| **Monthly payment:** | _____ |
| **Annual yield:** | _____ |

| | |
|---|---|
| **Goal:** | _____ |
| **Funds needed in:** | _____ |
| **Estimated cost** (4% inflation): | _____ |
| **Monthly payment:** | _____ |
| **Annual yield:** | _____ |

*You will need a financial calculator or compounding tables (at your public library) to calculate this figure.

# Worksheet 11

## College Savings

1.  Child's age                                                          _____

2.  Years until college (18 minus line 1)                                _____

3.  One year's tuition, room and board, books, fees
    (current year)

    • at public university                                               _____

    • at ivy league                                                      _____

    • at (your choice)                                                   _____

4.  Tuition inflator (from Table A*, Worksheet 12)                       _____

5.  Estimated cost at registration (line 3 × line 4)                     _____

6.  Four-year total (line 5 × 4 years)                                   _____

7.  Monthly investment target

    (a) factor (from Table B**, Worksheet 12)                            _____

    (b) annual savings (line 6 divided by line 7(a))                     _____

    (c) monthly savings (line 7(b) divided by 12)                        _____

8.  Reality check

    (a) What you are able to set aside (month)                           _____

    (b) Line 7(c) minus line 8(a)                                        _____

    (c) Percent of unmet cost to be met by

           • student living at home                                      _____

           • ongoing parental contribution                              _____

           • scholarships                                                _____

           • loans, grants                                               _____

           • work-study                                                  _____

*Tuition inflation is projected at 6%, the recent average for college.
**Investment average return assumed to be 8%.

## Worksheet 12

### College Cost Tables
*(to be used with Worksheet 11)*

#### Table A

| Years to college<br>(from line 2, Worksheet 11) | Tuition inflator |
|---|---|
| 1 | 1.06 |
| 2 | 1.12 |
| 3 | 1.19 |
| 4 | 1.26 |
| 5 | 1.34 |
| 6 | 1.42 |
| 7 | 1.50 |
| 8 | 1.59 |
| 9 | 1.69 |
| 10 | 1.79 |
| 11 | 1.90 |
| 12 | 2.01 |
| 13 | 2.13 |
| 14 | 2.26 |
| 15 | 2.40 |
| 16 | 2.54 |
| 17 | 2.69 |
| 18 | 2.85 |

#### Table B

| Years to college<br>(from line 2, Worksheet 11) | Monthly |
|---|---|
| 1 | 1.04 |
| 2 | 2.16 |
| 3 | 3.36 |
| 4 | 4.67 |
| 5 | 6.08 |
| 6 | 7.60 |
| 7 | 9.25 |
| 8 | 11.02 |
| 9 | 12.94 |
| 10 | 15.01 |
| 11 | 17.25 |
| 12 | 19.66 |
| 13 | 22.27 |
| 14 | 25.09 |
| 15 | 28.13 |
| 16 | 31.42 |
| 17 | 34.97 |
| 18 | 38.80 |

## Worksheet 13

### Check Your Paycheck

**INCOME**

- Regular pay                                         $_____
- Overtime pay                                        _____
- Bonus                                               _____
- Other                                               _____

TOTAL PAY                                             $_____

**DEDUCTIONS**

- Federal income tax                                  $_____
- State income tax                                    _____
- Local income tax                                    _____
- FICA (Social Security)                              _____
- Medicare                                            _____
- Health insurance                                    _____
- Dental insurance                                    _____
- Life insurance                                      _____
- Disability insurance                                _____
- Unemployment insurance                              _____
- Payroll savings plan (401(k), 403(b), TSA)          _____
- Loan repayment                                      _____
- Automatic savings deduction                         _____
- Pension contribution                                _____
- Union/employees' ass'n dues                         _____
- Savings bond                                        _____
- United Way/charitable deduction                     _____
- Other                                               _____

TOTAL DEDUCTIONS                                      $_____

## Worksheet 14

### Social Security

1. Call Social Security at (800) 772-1213 and ask for the Personal Earnings and Benefit Estimate Statement. When it comes, complete it with your best estimates and return it to Social Security.

2. When you receive the information back, complete below:

   • Number of credits earned to date          _____

   • Number of credits needed for retirement    _____

   • Full retirement age                        _____

   • Projected benefit at full retirement age   $_____

   • Projected benefit at early retirement      $_____

   • Survivor's benefit, spouse                 $_____

   • Survivor's benefit, each child             $_____

   • Survivor's benefit, family total           $_____

   • Number of credits needed for disability    _____

   • Estimated disability benefit, if paid now  $_____

   • Family disability benefit, if paid now     $_____

3. Do your records agree with Social Security's as to your work history? If not, call (800) 537-7005 and report any discrepancy right away.

4. Repeat steps 1 through 3 every two years.

## Worksheet 15

### Answer Sheet to Chapter Quizzes

Ch. 1:    1. **c.**; 2. **a.**; 3. **b.**; 4. **b.**; 5. **d.**; 6. **d.**; 7. **c.**; 8. **a.**; 9. **b.**; 10. **d.**

Ch. 2:    1. **c.**; 2. **c.**; 3. **d.**; 4. **b.**; 5. **a.**; 6. **F**; 7. **d.**; 8. **b.**; 9. **d.**; 10. **a.**

Ch. 3:    1. **b.**; 2. **a.**; 3. **c.**; 4. **d.**; 5. **b.**; 6. **c.**; 7. **b.**; 8. **a.**; 9. **T**; 10. **d.**

Ch. 4:    1. **d.**; 2. **d.**; 3. **F**; 4. **a.**; 5. **d.**; 6. **T**; 7. **F**; 8. **c.**; 9. **b.**; 10. **b.**

Ch. 5:    1. **d.**; 2. **F**; 3. **a.**; 4. **c.**; 5. **c.**; 6. **a.**; 7. **d.**; 8. **b.**; 9. **F**; 10. **d.**

Ch. 6:    1. **b.**; 2. **a.**; 3. **d.**; 4. **c.**; 5. **T**; 6. **d.**; 7. **d.**; 8. **c.**; 9. **F**; 10. **F.**

Ch. 7:    1. **d.**; 2. **d.**; 3. **b.**; 4. **T**; 5. **b.**; 6. **a.**; 7. **c.**; 8. **T**; 9. **c.**; 10. **a.**

Ch. 8:    1. **a.**; 2. **b.**; 3. **a.**; 4. **T**; 5. **d.**; 6. **F**; 7. **b.**; 8. **d.**; 9. **F**; 10. **d.**

Ch. 9:    1. **a.**; 2. **c.**; 3. **F**; 4. **d.**; 5. **d.**; 6. **b.**; 7. **T**; 8. **F**; 9. **c.**; 10. **F.**

Ch. 10:   1. **F**; 2. **a.**; 3. **c.**; 4. **c.**; 5. **T**; 6. **d.**; 7. **a.**; 8. **b.**; 9. **b.**; 10. **c.**

Ch. 11:   1. **c.**; 2. **b.**; 3. **T**; 4. **F**; 5. **d.**; 6. **d.**; 7. **F**; 8. **a.**; 9. **b.**; 10. **d.**

Ch. 12:   1. **a.**; 2. **d.**; 3. **c.**; 4. **c.**; 5. **b.**; 6. **b.**; 7. **d.**; 8. **d.**; 9. **b.**; 10. **a.**

Ch. 13:   1. **d.**; 2. **a.**; 3. **T**; 4. **c.**; 5. **c.**; 6. **b.**; 7. **d.**; 8. **T**; 9. **F**; 10. **F.**

**SCORING:** *Score 1 for each correct answer.*

| **Chapter scores:** | | **Total for book:** | |
|---|---|---|---|
| 1–2: | You're not paying attention | 1–20: | Inadequate |
| 3–4: | You're still not getting it | 21–40: | Aspiring |
| 5–6: | You're getting there | 41–69: | Competitive |
| 7–8: | You're competent | 70–85: | Capable |
| 9–10: | You love this stuff | 85–100: | Knowledgeable |

# Tables

## Table 1

### Compounding Periods for Ages 20 through 35

| | |
|---|---|
| 20 | 48 |
| 21 | 47 |
| 22 | 46 |
| 23 | 45 |
| 24 | 44 |
| 25 | 43 |
| 26 | 42 |
| 27 | 41 |
| 28 | 40 |
| 29 | 39 |
| 30 | 38 |
| 31 | 37 |
| 32 | 36 |
| 33 | 35 |
| 34 | 34 |
| 35 | 33 |

Unless otherwise noted, the annual compounding periods used throughout the book assume the first payment is made on the youngest birthday and the last payment is made on the 67th birthday.

# Table 2

## Steady-as-You-Go $50 Plan

You will have this much money if you invest $50 monthly at an average annual return of 10 percent, ending on your 67th birthday and beginning when you turn:

| | |
|---|---|
| 20 | $708,705* |
| 21 | $640,959 |
| 22 | $579,636 |
| 23 | $524,125 |
| 24 | $473,875 |
| 25 | $428,389 |
| 26 | $387,215 |
| 27 | $349,942 |
| 28 | $316,203 |

You will have this much money if you invest $50 monthly at an average annual return of 12 percent, ending on your 67th birthday and beginning when you turn:

| | |
|---|---|
| 29 | $521,469 |
| 30 | $462,214 |
| 31 | $409,629 |
| 32 | $369,962 |
| 33 | $321,547 |
| 34** | |
| 35** | |

This plan is for the person who doesn't have a lump sum to jump-start his or her Four Step program, and who wants to commit a steady $50 per month to the plan. It won't make a million, but these are good numbers anyway. Don't forget to adjust annually for inflation.

*All numbers rounded down.

**Since I do not recommend a retirement savings goal of less than $300,000, nor an investment return goal of more than 12%, this plan is inappropriate for investors age 34 and over.

## Table 3

### Steady-as-You-Go $100 Plan

*(Moderate-Risk Version)*

You will have this much money if you invest $100 monthly at an average annual return of 10 percent, ending on your 67th birthday and beginning when you turn:

| | |
|---|---|
| 20 | $1,417,410* |
| 21 | $1,281,919 |
| 22 | $1,159,272 |
| 23 | $1,048,250 |
| 24 | $947,751 |
| 25 | $856,779 |
| 26 | $774,429 |
| 27 | $699,885 |
| 28 | $632,407 |
| 29 | $571,326 |
| 30 | $516,034 |
| 31 | $465,982 |
| 32 | $420,676 |
| 33 | $379,663 |
| 34 | $342,538 |
| 35 | $308,933 |

This plan is for the person who doesn't have a lump sum to jump-start his or her Four Step program, and who wants to commit a steady $100 per month to the plan. It won't make a million if you're over age 23, but these are good numbers anyway. Don't forget to adjust annually for inflation.

*All numbers are rounded down.

## Table 4

**Steady-as-You-Go $100 Plan**

*(Aggressive Version)*

You will have this much money if you invest $100 monthly at an average annual return of 12 percent, ending on your 67th birthday and beginning when you turn:

| | |
|---|---|
| 20 | $3,073,978* |
| 21 | $2,726,874 |
| 22 | $2,418,836 |
| 23 | $2,145,469 |
| 24 | $1,902,869 |
| 25 | $1,687,574 |
| 26 | $1,496,511 |
| 27 | $1,326,952 |
| 28 | $1,176,477 |
| 29 | $1,042,938 |
| 30 | $924,429 |
| 31 | $819,258 |
| 32 | $725,924 |
| 33 | $643,095 |
| 34 | $569,589 |
| 35 | $504,356 |

This plan is for the person who doesn't have a lump sum to jump-start his or her Four Step program, and who wants to commit a steady $100 per month to the plan at an aggressive 12 percent. It won't make a million if you're over age 29, but it will make a lot more than a million if you're younger. Don't forget to adjust annually for inflation.

*All numbers are rounded down.

## Table 5

### Roller Coaster 11 Percent Plan

To make a million dollars, invest at an 11% average annual return, make your last payment on your 67th birthday, and make your first when you turn:

| | |
|---|---|
| 20 | $49* |
| 21 | $54 |
| 22 | $60 |
| 23 | $67 |
| 24 | $75 |
| 25 | $84 |
| 26 | $94 |
| 27 | $105 |
| 28 | $117 |
| 29 | $130 |
| 30 | $146 |
| 31 | $163 |
| 32 | $182 |
| 33 | $203 |
| 34 | $227 |
| 35 | $254 |

If you can come up with the payments, this plan is less risky than the 12% Roller Coaster Plan, and a surer way to aim for your million.

*All payments are rounded up.

# Table 6

## Hot Start $100 Plan

To reach a million dollars by age 67, invest $100 per month at a 10 percent average annual return, beginning with this lump sum, if you are:

| | |
|---|---|
| 24 | $654* |
| 25 | $1,979 |
| 26 | $3,442 |
| 27 | $5,059 (or $441 at 11%) |
| 28 | $6,846 (or $1,754 at 11%) |

To reach a million dollars by age 67, invest $100 per month at an 11 percent average annual return, beginning with this lump sum, if you are:

| | |
|---|---|
| 29 | $3,219 |
| 30 | $4,854 (or $809 at 12%) |
| 31 | $6,678 (or $2,180 at 12%) |

To reach a million dollars by age 67, invest $100 per month at a 12 percent average annual return, beginning with this lump sum, if you are:

| | |
|---|---|
| 32 | $3,725 |
| 33 | $5,465 |
| 34 | $7,427 |
| 35 | $9,637 |

This plan is for someone with a lump sum to jump-start their program, and a desire to spend $100 per month. Investors younger than 24 don't need the Hot Start $100 plan, because their monthly payments are smaller than $100 per month without a lump sum. Remember to adjust the payment annually for inflation.

*All numbers are rounded up.

## Table 7

### Modest Millionaire 10 Percent Plan at 10 Years into the Program

Starting age:

| Age | Amount |
|-----|--------|
| 20 | $14,544* |
| 21 | $16,183 |
| 22 | $17,822 |
| 23 | $19,665 |
| 24 | $21,714 |
| 25 | $23,967 |
| 26 | $26,630 |
| 27 | $29,293 |
| 28 | $32,570 |
| 29 | $36,053 |
| 30 | $39,740 |
| 31 | $44,042 |
| 32 | $48,753 |
| 33 | $54,079 |
| 34 | $59,815 |
| 35 | $66,370 |

If you've done your part, and the stock market has, too, then 10 years into your program, your Modest Millionaire fund will look like this. Don't be surprised if it doesn't seem like much to you. Compounding reserves its meteoric effects for the final years of your plan.

*All figures rounded off.

## Table 8

### Roller Coaster 12 Percent Plan at 10 Years into the Program

| Starting age: | |
|---|---|
| 20 | $7,591* |
| 21 | $8,511 |
| 22 | $9,662 |
| 23 | $10,812 |
| 24 | $12,192 |
| 25 | $13,802 |
| 26 | $15,413 |
| 27 | $17,483 |
| 28 | $19,553 |
| 29 | $22,084 |
| 30 | $25,074 |
| 31 | $28,295 |
| 32 | $31,745 |
| 33 | $35,886 |
| 34 | $40,487 |
| 35 | $45,778 |

If you've done your part, and the stock market has, too, then 10 years into your program, your 12% Roller Coaster fund will look like this. Don't be surprised if it doesn't seem like much to you. Compounding reserves its meteoric effects for the final years of your plan.

*All figures rounded off.

## Table 9

**Golden IRA 10 Percent Plan at
10 Years into the Program**

All ages          $34,139*

If you've done your part, and the stock market has, too, then 10 years into your program, your Golden IRA fund will look like this. Don't be surprised if it doesn't seem like much to you. Compounding reserves its meteoric effects for the final years of your plan.

*Assumes $166.66 monthly payments, the 1995 limit.

## Table 10

### Hot Start $50 Plan at
### 10 Years into the Program

#### Invested at 10%
Starting age:

| | |
|---|---|
| 20 | $16,864* |
| 21 | $19,257 |
| 22 | $21,901 |
| 23 | $24,822 |
| 24 | $28,052 |
| 25 | $31,617 |

#### Invested at 11%

| | |
|---|---|
| 26 | $24,788 |
| 27 | $28,289 |
| 28 | $32,192 |
| 29 | $36,551 |

#### Invested at 12%

| | |
|---|---|
| 30 | $30,499 |
| 31 | $35,001 |
| 32 | $40,073 |
| 33 | $45,790 |
| 34 | $52,229 |
| 35 | $59,486 |

If you've done your part, and the stock market has, too, then 10 years into your program, your Hot Start $50 fund will look like this. Don't be surprised if it doesn't seem like much to you. Compounding reserves its meteoric effects for the final years of your plan.

*All figures rounded off.

# Table 11

## Modest Millionaire Early-Out Plan

|  |  |
|---|---|
| Begin at 20 | $405,642* |
| 21 | $407,667 |
| 22 | $405,405 |
| 23 | $403,849 |
| 24 | $402,444 |
| 25 | $400,770 |
| 26 | $401,613 |
| 27 | $398,273 |
| 28 | $399,051 |
| 29 | $397,846 |
| 30 | $394,761 |
| 31 | $393,578 |
| 32 | $391,678 |
| 33 | $390,281 |
| 34 | $387,436 |
| 35 | $385,460 |

Maybe you don't want to wait until you are 67 to retire. Since the Four Step plans rely on tax-deferred savings, and since that usually means penalty-free withdrawals begin at age 59 1/2, you might want to know what your nest egg will be worth if you don't wait for it to make a million at age 67. If you follow the Modest Millionaire 10% Plan, you will have the above amounts saved by age 59. Don't forget the easy inflation adjustments, described in Step Four.

*All figures rounded off.

# Table 12

## Roller Coaster Early-Out Plan

| Begin at | | |
|---|---|---|
| Begin at 20 | $344,170* |
| 21 | $342,039 |
| 22 | $344,089 |
| 23 | $341,185 |
| 24 | $340,841 |
| 25 | $341,754 |
| 26 | $337,919 |
| 27 | $339,313 |
| 28 | $335,826 |
| 29 | $335,517 |
| 30 | $336,848 |
| 31 | $335,946 |
| 32 | $332,940 |
| 33 | $332,251 |
| 34 | $330,677 |
| 35 | $329,569 |

Maybe you don't want to wait until you are 67 to retire. Since the Four Step plans rely on tax-deferred savings, and since that usually means penalty-free withdrawals begin at age 59 1/2, you might want to know what your nest egg will be worth if you don't wait for it to make a million at age 67. If you follow the Roller Coaster 12% Plan, you will have the above amounts saved by age 59. Don't forget the easy inflation adjustments, described in Step Four.

*All figures rounded off

## Table 13

### Golden IRA Early-Out Plan

| | |
|---|---|
| **Begin at** 20 | $952,172* |
| 21 | $860,022 |
| 22 | $776,607 |
| 23 | $701,099 |
| 24 | $632,748 |
| 25 | $570,875 |
| 26 | $514,868 |
| 27 | $464,169 |
| 28 | $418,276 |
| 29 | $376,733 |
| 30 | $339,128 |
| 31 | $305,087 |
| 32** | $274,273 |
| 33** | $246,379 |
| 34** | $221,130 |
| 35** | $198,274 |

Maybe you don't want to wait until you are 67 to retire. Since the Golden IRA Four Step Plan relies on a tax-deferred IRA, and since that usually means penalty-free withdrawals begin at age 59 1/2, you might want to know what your nest egg will be worth if you don't wait for it to make a million at age 67. If you follow the Golden IRA 10% Plan, you will have the above amounts saved by age 59. Don't forget the easy inflation adjustments, described in Step Four.

*All figures rounded off.

**Ages 32 through 35 are supplied for your interest only. I do not recommend shooting for less than $300,000 (adjusted for inflation) for your retirement fund.

# Table 14

## Baby Modest Millionaire 10 Percent Plan

Make your first payment on the selected birthday, and the last on the 60th birthday, and you'll make more than $1 million on a 10% average annual return.

| Birth | $20 |
|---|---|
| 1 | 22 |
| 2 | 24 |
| 3 | 26 |
| 4 | 29 |
| 5 | 32 |
| 6 | 35 |
| 7 | 39 |
| 8 | 43 |
| 9 | 48 |
| 10 | 53 |
| 11 | 58 |
| 12 | 64 |
| 13 | 71 |
| 14 | 78 |
| 15 | 87 |
| 16 | 96 |
| 17 | 106 |
| 18 | 117 |

Because of extreme youth, the numbers are very small, so this table assumes the first payment on the selected birthday, and the last on the 60th birthday, seven years earlier than the ordinary Four Step plans. Don't forget to adjust annually for inflation, since in some cases you're going out more than half a century here.

## Table 15

**Inflation Adjusted Payments**

Year into program:

| | |
|---|---|
| 1 | $117* |
| 2 | $122 |
| 3 | $127 |
| 4 | $132 |
| 5 | $137 |
| 6 | $142 |
| 7 | $148 |
| 8 | $154 |
| 9 | $160 |
| 10 | $167 |
| 11 | $173 |
| 12 | $180 |
| 13 | $187 |
| 14 | $195 |
| 15 | $203 |
| 16 | $211 |
| 17 | $219 |
| 18 | $228 |

Note how Step Four of the program protects you from inflation. This 25-year-old Modest Millionaire's initial $117 payment nearly doubles in 18 years, assuming 4% annual inflation. However, with cost-of-living and actual raises over the years, it should be proportionately smaller than when the program began.

*All figures are rounded off.

# Resources

A.M. Best
Amherst Road
Oldwick, NJ 08858
(908) 439-2200
(*Insurance and credit-rating firm*)

American Institute of Certified Public
  Accountants
Personal Financial Planning Division
Harborside Financial Center
201 Plaza 3
Jersey City, NJ 07300
(800) 862-4272
(*Referral agency for CPAs who are financial
  planners*)

American Society of CLU & ChFCs
270 S. Bryn Mawr Avenue
Bryn Mawr, PA 19010
(800) 392-6900
(*Referral agency for insurance-oriented
  financial planners*)

American Stock Exchange
Investor Inquiries, Arbitration Department
86 Trinity Place
New York, NY 10006
(212) 306-1427

American Association of Individual
  Investors
625 North Michigan Avenue
Chicago, IL 60611
(312) 280-0170
(*Membership organization of stock, bond,
  and mutual fund investors*)

Bankcard Holders of America
560 Herndon Parkway
Herndon, VA 22070
(*Lists low-fee, low-interest credit cards*)

Barron's
Dow Jones & Company
200 Burnett Road
Chicopee, MA 01020
(800) 568-7625
(*Weekly report for experienced investors*)

Bureau of the Public Debt
Department N
United States Treasury
Washington, DC 20239

Consumer Information Center
Department 92 ₹
Pueblo, CO 81009
(*Catalog of free and low-cost consumer
  information*)

Division of Consumer and Community
  Affairs
Board of Governors of the Federal
  Reserve System
20th and C Streets N.W.
Washington, DC 20551

Equifax Information Service Center
P.O. Box 74021
Atlanta, GA 30374
(*Will provide a copy of your credit report*)

Federal Reserve Banks
- Atlanta            (404) 521-8653
- Boston             (617) 973-3800
- Chicago            (312) 322-5369
- Cleveland          (216) 579-2490
- Dallas             (214) 922-6100
- Kansas City        (816) 881-2000
- Minneapolis        (612) 340-2075
- New York           (212) 720-6619
- Philadelphia       (215) 574-6680
- Richmond           (804) 697-8375
- St. Louis          (314) 444-8703
- San Francisco      (415) 974-2330

Forbes Magazine
60 Fifth Avenue
New York, NY 10011
(800) 888-9896
(*A general-interest magazine for serious
   investors*)

Hulbert Financial Digest
316 Commerce Street
Alexandra, VA 22314
(*Rates investment newsletters*)

Individual Investor's Guide to No-Load
   Mutual Funds
American Association of Individual
   Investors
(*see above*)

Institute of Certified Financial Planners
7600 East Eastman Avenue, Suite 301
Denver, CO 80231
(800) 282-7526
(*Trains, certifies, and disciplines certified
   financial planners*)

Internal Revenue Service
   Forms:  (800) 829-3676
   Advice: (800) 829-1040

International Association for Financial
   Planning
2 Concourse Parkway, Suite 800
Atlanta, GA 30328
(800) 945-4237
(*Trade organization of financial planners*)

Kiplinger's Personal Finance Magazine
1729 H Street, N.W.
Washington, DC 20006
(800) 544-0155
(*Finance for the ordinary investor*)

Money Magazine
P.O. Box 60001
Tampa, FL 33660
(800) 541-1000
(*Finance for the ordinary investor*)

Moody's Investors Service
99 Church Street
New York, NY 10007
(212) 553-0300
(*Rates bonds and insurers*)

Morningstar
225 West Wacker Drive
Chicago, IL 60606
(800) 876-5005
(*Rating service for mutual funds*)

Mutual Fund Education Alliance
1900 Erie Street, Suite 120
Kansas City, MO 64116
(*Information about no-load mutual
   funds*)

National Association of Investors
   Corporation
P.O. Box 220
Royal Oak, MI 48068
(810) 583-6242
(*Membership organization for investment
   clubs*)

National Association of Personal Financial
   Advisors
1130 Lake Cook Road, Suite 150
Buffalo Grove, IL 60089
(800) 366-2732
(*Fee-only financial planners*)

National Association of Securities Dealers
1735 K Street, N.W.
Washington, DC 20006
(800) 289-9999
(*Trade organization for stockbrokers and
mutual-fund managers*)

National Endowment for Financial
   Education
4695 South Monaco Street
Denver, CO 80237-3403
(800) 553-5343
(*Qualifies certified financial planners*)

New York Stock Exchange
Arbitration Department
20 Broad Street, 5th floor
New York, NY 10005
(212) 656-2772

NOLO Press
950 Parker Street
Berkeley, CA 94710
(*Do-it-yourself lawbook publisher*)

North American Securities Administrators
   Association
1 Massachusetts Avenue, N.W., Suite 310
Washington, DC 20001
(202) 737-0900
(*Organization of state securities' regulators*)

Options Institute
Chicago Board Options Exchange, Inc.
400 South LaSalle Street
Chicago, IL 60605
(312) 786-7760
(*Educational material on options*)

Pension Rights Center
918 16th Street N.W., Suite 704
Washington, DC 20006
(*Information on pensions*)

Public Register's Annual Report Service
(800) 426-6825
(*Will send the latest annual report from over
   3,000 companies—free*)

Ram Research's Cardtrak
Box 1700
Frederick, MD 21702
(*Lists low-fee, low-interest credit cards*)

Securities and Exchange Commission
Office of Filings, Information and
   Consumer Services
450 5th Street, N.W., Stop 2-6
Washington, DC 20549
(800) SEC-0330 (consumer hotline)
(*Regulates the securities industry, dispenses
   free brochures*)

Securities Investor Protection Corporation
805 15th Street, N.W., Suite 800
Washington, DC 20005
(202) 371-8300
(*The federal insurer of brokerage accounts*)

Social Security
(800) 772-1213
(*All-purpose number*)

Standard & Poor's Corporation
25 Broadway
New York, NY 10004
(800) 221-7940
(*Stock, bond, insurance, and credit-rating
   firm*)

TRW Consumer Assistance
P.O. Box 2350
Chatsworth, CA 91313
(*Get your TRW credit record*)

Trans Union Consumer Relations
   Disclosure Center
760 West Sproul Road
Springfield, PA 19064
(*Get your Trans Union credit record*)

U.S. Office of Thrift Supervision
Consumer Programs
1700 G Street, N.W.
Washington, DC 20552
(*Supervises savings and loans*)

Value Line Investment Survey
220 East 42nd Street
New York, NY 10017-5891
(800) 634-3583
(*Securities and mutual funds reporting
   agency*)

Wall Street Journal
Dow Jones & Company
200 Burnett Road
Chicopee, MA 01020
(800) 568-7625
(*Daily financial newspaper*)

# Index